MANKIND'S SEARCH FOR GOD

During the
thousands of
years of man-
kind's history,
man's search for
God has led down
many pathways. The
result has been the enor-
mous diversity of religious
expression found worldwide
—from the endless variety of
Hinduism to the monotheism of
Judaism, Islām, and Christendom
and to the Oriental philosophies of
Shinto, Taoism, Buddhism, and Confucianism. In other vast regions, mankind has
turned to animism, magic, spiritism, and shamanism. Has this search for God been successful?
Through this book we invite you, regardless of your
religious background, to join in this fascinating search
for the true God.—The Publishers

Publishers
WATCHTOWER BIBLE AND TRACT SOCIETY OF NEW YORK, INC.
INTERNATIONAL BIBLE STUDENTS ASSOCIATION
Brooklyn, New York, U.S.A.

First Printing in English: 3,000,000 Copies

Symbols for translations of the Bible and for other religious books used herein:

AS	-	*American Standard Version,* American Revision Committee (1901)
AYA	-	*The Holy Qur-an,* translation by Abdullah Yusuf Ali (1934)
BG	-	*Bhagavad-gītā as It Is,* Abridged Edition, translation by A. C. Bhaktivedanta Swami Prabhupāda (1976)
Int	-	*The Kingdom Interlinear Translation of the Greek Scriptures* (1985)
JP	-	*The Holy Scriptures,* The Jewish Publication Society of America (1955)
KJ	-	*King James Version* (1611)
MMP	-	*The Glorious Qur'an,* translation by Muhammad M. Pickthall (1977)
NAB	-	*The New American Bible,* Saint Joseph Edition (1970)
NJD	-	*The Koran,* translation by N. J. Dawood (1974)
NW	-	*New World Translation of the Holy Scriptures—With References* (1984)
RS	-	*Revised Standard Version,* Catholic Edition (1966)
Ta	-	*Tanakh, The Holy Scriptures,* The New Jewish Publication Society Translation (1985)

Unless otherwise stated, Bible quotations or citations are from the *New World Translation of the Holy Scriptures.*

Bibliography of Some Major Works Consulted

■ *Abingdon Dictionary of Living Religions,* K. Crim, editor, 1981. ■ *Ancient Near Eastern Texts Relating to the Old Testament,* J. B. Pritchard, editor, 1969. ■ *Ancient Sun Kingdoms of the Americas, The,* V. W. von Hagen, 1961. ■ *Archeology of World Religions, The,* J. Finegan, 1952. ■ *Bible of the World, The,* Robert O. Ballou, editor, 1939. ■ *Buddhism,* Richard A. Gard, editor, 1961. ■ *Crucible of Christianity, The,* A. Toynbee, editor, 1975. ■ *Encyclopaedia Judaica,* 1973. ■ *Encyclopedia of Eastern Philosophy and Religion, The,* 1989. ■ *Encyclopedia of World Faiths, The,* P. Bishop and M. Darton, editors, 1988. ■ *Great Asian Religions,* C. George Fry and others, 1984. ■ *Great Voices of the Reformation,* Harry Emerson Fosdick, editor, 1952. ■ *Here I Stand,* Roland Bainton, 1950. ■ *Hinduism,* Louis Renou, 1961. ■ *Hindu Mythology,* W. J. Wilkins, 1988. ■ *History of the Arabs,* Philip K. Hitti, 1943. ■ *Insight on the Scriptures,* Watchtower Bible and Tract Society of N.Y., Inc., 1988. ■ *Islam,* John Alden Williams, editor, 1961. ■ *Judaism,* Arthur Hertzberg, 1961. ■ *Kodansha Encyclopedia of Japan,* 1983. ■ *Lao Tsu, Tao Te Ching, A New Translation,* Gia-fu Feng and J. English, 1972. ■ *Man's Religions,* John B. Noss, 1980. ■ *Manual of Buddhism, A,* Nārada Thera, 1949. ■ *Mixture of Shintoism and Buddhism, The,* Hidenori Tsuji, 1986. ■ *Mythology—An Illustrated Encyclopedia,* R. Cavendish, editor, 1980. ■ *New Encyclopædia Britannica, The,* 1987. ■ *New Larousse Encyclopedia of Mythology,* 1984. ■ *Oxford Dictionary of Popes, The,* J. N. D. Kelly, 1986. ■ *Philosophy of Confucius, The,* J. Legge, translator. ■ *Reformation of the Sixteenth Century, The,* Roland Bainton, 1965. ■ *Search for the Christian Doctrine, The,* R. P. C. Hanson, 1988. ■ *Servetus and Calvin,* R. Willis, 1877. ■ *Sources of Modern Atheism, The,* Marcel Neusch, 1982. ■ *South American Mythology,* H. Osborne, 1983. ■ *Story of Civilization, The,* W. and A. Durant, 1954-75. ■ *Story of the Reformation, The,* William Stevenson, 1959. ■ *Symbolism of Hindu Gods and Rituals, The,* A. Parthasarathy, 1985. ■ *Twelve Caesars, The,* Suetonius, translated by R. Graves, 1986. ■ *Wisdom of Confucius, The,* Lin Yutang, editor, 1938. ■ *World Religions—From Ancient History to the Present,* G. Parrinder, editor, 1983.

CONTENTS

Color Key to Maps Showing World Distribution of Religions (Inside Covers)

White areas—uninhabited

Christendom	Islām	Hinduism	Buddhism	Confucianism-Taoism-Buddhism	Shinto	Judaism	Tribal Religions

▲ Hindus revere the river Ganges —called *Ganga Ma*, or Mother Ganga

Sincere Catholics ▶ turn to Mary in their use of the rosary

▼ In some Buddhist countries, most males serve some time as saffron-robed monks

Faithful Muslim ▼ men make a pilgrimage to Mecca at least once

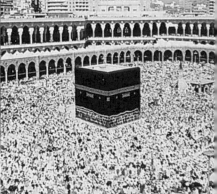

CHAPTER 1.

Why Be Interested in Other Religions?

REGARDLESS of where you live, you have no doubt seen for yourself how religion affects the lives of millions of people, maybe yours too. In countries where *Hinduism* is practiced, you will often see people doing puja—a ceremony that may include making offerings to their gods, in the form of coconut, flowers, and apples. A priest will apply a spot of red or yellow pigment, the tilak, to the foreheads of the believers. Millions also flock each year to the river Ganges to be purified by its waters.

[2] In *Catholic* countries, you will see people praying in churches and cathedrals while holding a crucifix or a rosary. The beads of the rosary are used for counting prayers offered in devotion to Mary. And it is not difficult to identify nuns and priests, distinctive in their black garb.

[3] In *Protestant* lands, chapels and churches abound, and on Sunday parishioners usually put on their best clothes and congregate to sing hymns and hear sermons. Often their clergy wear a black suit and a distinguishing clerical collar.

[4] In *Islāmic* countries, you can hear the voices of the muezzins, the Muslim criers who make the call from minarets five times a day, summoning the faithful to the

1-7. What are some manifestations of the world's various religions?

Jehovah's Witnesses, known worldwide for their preaching activity, in a Japanese city

ṣalāt, or ritual prayer. They view the Holy Qur'ān as the Islāmic book of scripture. According to Islāmic belief, it was revealed by God and was given to the prophet Muḥammad by the angel Gabriel in the seventh century C.E.

⁵ On the streets of many Buddhist lands, the monks of *Buddhism,* usually in saffron, black, or red robes, are seen as a sign of piety. Ancient temples with the serene Buddha on display are evidence of the antiquity of the Buddhist faith.

⁶ Practiced mainly in Japan, *Shinto* enters into daily life with family shrines and offerings to ancestors. The Japanese feel free to pray for the most mundane things, even success in school examinations.

⁷ Another religious activity known the world over is that of people going from house to house and standing on the streets with Bibles and Bible literature. With the

Watchtower and *Awake!* magazines in evidence, nearly everyone recognizes these people as Jehovah's Witnesses.

[8] What does this great worldwide variety of religious devotion indicate? That for thousands of years mankind has had a spiritual need and yearning. Man has lived with his trials and burdens, his doubts and questions, including the enigma of death. Religious feelings have been expressed in many different ways as people have turned to God or their gods, seeking blessings and solace. Religion also tries to address the great questions: Why are we here? How should we live? What does the future hold for mankind?

[9] On the other hand, there are millions of people who profess no religion nor any belief in a god. They are atheists. Others, agnostics, believe that God is unknown and probably unknowable. However, that obviously does not mean that they are people without principles or ethics, any more than professing a religion means that one does have them. However, if one accepts religion as being "devotion to some principle; strict fidelity or faithfulness; conscientiousness; pious affection or attachment," then most people, including atheists and agnostics, do have some form of religious devotion in their lives.—*The Shorter Oxford English Dictionary.*

[10] With so many religions in a world that gets smaller and smaller by virtue of ever faster travel and communication, the impact of various faiths is felt worldwide, whether we like it or not. The outrage that broke out in

8. What does the history of religious devotion indicate?
9. In what way do most people have some form of religious devotion in their lives?
10. Does religion make an impact on the modern world? Illustrate.

1989 over the book *The Satanic Verses*, written by what some people termed 'an apostate Muslim,' is clear evidence of how religious sentiment can manifest itself on a global scale. There were calls from Islāmic leaders for the book to be banned and even for the author to be put to death. What makes people react so vehemently in matters of religion?

[11] To answer that, we need to know something about the background of the world's religions. As Geoffrey Parrinder states in *World Religions—From Ancient History to the Present:* "To study different religions need not imply infidelity to one's own faith, but rather it may be enlarged by seeing how other people have sought for reality and have been enriched by their search." Knowledge leads to understanding, and understanding to tolerance of people with a different viewpoint.

Why Investigate?

[12] Have you ever thought or said, 'I have my own religion. It is a very personal matter. I do not discuss it with others'? True, religion is very personal—virtually from birth religious or ethical ideas are implanted in our mind by our parents and relatives. As a consequence, we usually follow the religious ideals of our parents and grandparents. Religion has become almost a matter of family tradition. What is the result of that process? That in many cases others have chosen our religion for us. It has simply been a matter of where we were born and when. Or, as historian Arnold Toynbee indicated, an individual's adherence to a certain faith is often determined by "the geographical accident of the locality of his birth-place."

11. Why is it not wrong to examine other faiths?
12. What factors usually determine a person's religion?

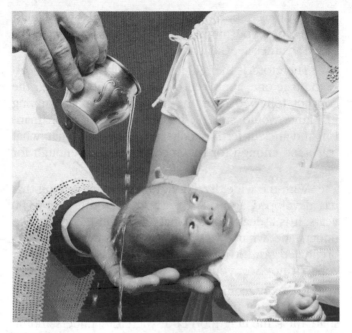

**A baby being baptized in one of Christendom's churches.
Is the religion of one's birth necessarily the true one?**

[13] Is it reasonable to assume that the religion imposed at one's birth is necessarily the whole truth? If you were born in Italy or South America, then, without any choice, you were probably raised a Catholic. If you were born in India, then likely you automatically became a Hindu or, if from the Punjab, perhaps a Sikh. If your parents were from Pakistan, then you would obviously be a Muslim.

13, 14. Why is it not reasonable to assume that the religion of one's birth is automatically approved by God?

And if you were born in a Socialist country over the last few decades, you might have had no choice but to be raised an atheist.—Galatians 1:13, 14; Acts 23:6.

14 Therefore, is the religion of one's birth automatically the true one, approved by God? If that had been the concept followed over the millenniums, many among mankind would still be practicing primitive shamanism and ancient fertility cults, on the premise that 'what was good enough for my ancestors is good enough for me.'

15 With the wide diversity of religious expression that has developed around the world over the past 6,000 years, it is at least educational and mind broadening to understand what others believe and how their beliefs originated. And it might also open up vistas of a more concrete hope for your future.

16 In many countries now, owing to immigration and population movement, people of different religions share the same neighborhood. Therefore, understanding one another's viewpoint can lead to more meaningful communication and conversation between people of different faiths. Perhaps, too, it may dissipate some of the hatred in the world that is based on religious differences. True, people may strongly disagree about their religious beliefs, but there is no basis for hating a person just because he or she holds a different viewpoint.—1 Peter 3:15; 1 John 4:20, 21; Revelation 2:6.

17 The ancient Jewish law stated: "You shall not hate

15, 16. What benefits are there in examining other religions?
17. Why should we not hate those whose religious thinking differs from ours?

your kinsfolk in your heart. Reprove your kinsman but incur no guilt because of him. You shall not take vengeance or bear a grudge against your countrymen. Love your fellow as yourself: I am the LORD [Jehovah]." (Leviticus 19:17, 18, *Ta*) The Founder of Christianity stated: "But I say to you who are listening, Continue to love your enemies, to do good to those hating you, . . . and your reward will be great, and you will be sons of the Most High, because he is kind toward the unthankful and wicked." (Luke 6:27, 35) Under the heading "She That Is To Be Examined," the Qur'ān states a similar principle (surah 60:7, *MMP*): "It may be that Allāh will bring about friendship between you and those of them whom you hold as enemies. And Allāh is Powerful; and Allāh is Forgiving, Merciful."

Aztec human sacrifice
—are all religions really "equal ways to the truth"?

[18] However, while tolerance and understanding are needed, that does not imply that it makes no difference what one believes. As historian Geoffrey Parrinder stated: "It is sometimes said that all religions have the same goal, or are equal ways to the truth, or even that all teach the same doctrines . . . Yet the ancient Aztecs, who held up the beating hearts of their victims to the sun, surely did not have as good a religion as that of the peaceful Buddha." Furthermore, when it comes to worship, is it not God himself who should determine what is and is not acceptable?—Micah 6:8.

How Should Religion Be Measured?

[19] While most religions have a body of beliefs or doctrines, these can often form a very complicated theology, beyond the understanding of the average layperson. Yet the principle of cause and effect applies in every case. The teachings of a religion should influence the personality and the daily conduct of each believer. Thus, each person's conduct will normally be a reflection, to a greater or lesser degree, of that one's religious background. What effect does your religion have on you? Does your religion produce a kinder person? More generous, honest, humble, tolerant, and compassionate? These are reasonable questions, for as one great religious teacher, Jesus Christ, stated: "Every good tree produces fine fruit, but every rotten tree produces worthless fruit; a good tree cannot bear worthless fruit, neither can a rotten tree produce fine fruit. Every tree not producing fine fruit gets cut down and thrown into the fire. Really, then, by their fruits you will recognize those men."—Matthew 7:17-20.

---

18. How does what one believes make a difference?
19. How should religion affect a person's conduct?

In the name of religion, millions have killed and been killed

²⁰ Certainly world history must give us pause and make us wonder what role religion has played in the many wars that have devastated mankind and caused untold suffering. Why have so many people killed and been killed in the name of religion? The Crusades, the Inquisition, the conflicts in the Middle East and Northern Ireland, the slaughter between Iraq and Iran (1980-88), the

20. What questions arise regarding religion and history?

Hindu-Sikh clashes in India—all these events certainly make thinking people raise questions about religious beliefs and ethics.—See box below.

[21] The realm of Christendom has been noteworthy for its hypocrisy in this field. In two world wars, Catholic has killed Catholic and Protestant has killed Protestant at the

21. What are some examples of Christendom's fruitage?

Religion, Love, and Hatred

■ "Religious wars tend to be extra furious. When people fight over territory for economic advantage, they reach the point where the battle isn't worth the cost and so compromise. When the cause is religious, compromise and conciliation seem to be evil."—Roger Shinn, professor of social ethics, Union Theological Seminary, New York.

■ "Men will wrangle for religion, write for it, fight for it, die for it; anything but live for it . . . Where true religion has prevented one crime, false religions have afforded a pretext for a thousand."—Charles Caleb Colton (1825).

■ "We have just enough religion to make us hate, but not enough to make us love one another."—Jonathan Swift (1667-1745).

■ "Men never do evil so completely and cheerfully as when they do it from religious conviction."—Blaise Pascal (1623-62).

■ "The true purpose of a higher religion is to radiate the spiritual counsels and truths that are its essence into as many souls as it can reach, in order that each of these souls may be enabled thereby to fulfil the true end of Man. Man's true end is to glorify God and to enjoy Him for ever."—Arnold Toynbee, historian.

behest of their "Christian" political leaders. Yet the Bible clearly contrasts the works of the flesh and the fruitage of the spirit. Regarding the works of the flesh, it states: "They are fornication, uncleanness, loose conduct, idolatry, practice of spiritism, enmities, strife, jealousy, fits of anger, contentions, divisions, sects, envies, drunken bouts, revelries, and things like these. As to these things I am forewarning you, the same way as I did forewarn you, that those who practice such things will not inherit God's kingdom." Yet so-called Christians have practiced these things for centuries, and their conduct has often been condoned by their clergy.—Galatians 5:19-21.

[22] In contrast, the positive fruitage of the spirit is described as: "love, joy, peace, long-suffering, kindness, goodness, faith, mildness, self-control. Against such things there is no law." All religions ought to be producing this kind of peaceable fruitage. But do they? Does yours?—Galatians 5:22, 23.

[23] Therefore, this book's examination of mankind's search for God through the world's religions should serve to answer some of our questions. But by what criteria should a religion be judged? By whose standard?

'My Religion Is Good Enough for Me'

[24] Many people dismiss religious discussion by saying, 'My religion is good enough for me. I don't do any harm to anyone else, and I help when I can.' But does that go far enough? Are our personal criteria on religion sufficient?

22, 23. In contrast, what fruitage should true religion bear?
24, 25. What challenge is presented to each person regarding his religion?

[25] If religion is "the expression of man's belief in and reverence for a superhuman power recognized as the creator and governor of the universe," as one dictionary states, then surely the question should be, Is my religion good enough for the creator and governor of the universe? Also, in that case, the Creator would have the right to establish what is acceptable conduct, worship, and doctrine and what is not. To do that, he must reveal his will to mankind, and that revelation must be easily available and accessible to all. Furthermore, his revelations, even though provided centuries apart, should always be harmonious and consistent. This presents a challenge to each person—to examine the evidence and prove for oneself what the acceptable will of God is.

All religions ought to produce peaceable fruitage. But do they?

[26] One of the most ancient books claiming inspiration by God is the Bible. It is also the most widely circulated and translated book in all history. Nearly two thousand years ago, one of its writers stated: "Quit being fashioned after this system of things, but be transformed by making your mind over, that you may prove to yourselves the good and acceptable and perfect will of God." (Romans 12:2) What would be the source of such proof? The same writer stated: "All Scripture is inspired of God and beneficial for teaching, for reproving, for setting things straight, for disciplining in righteousness, that the man of God

26. Which holy book should serve as a measuring rod for true worship? And why?

may be fully competent, completely equipped for every good work." Therefore, the inspired Bible should serve as a reliable measuring rod for true and acceptable worship. —2 Timothy 3:16, 17.

[27] The oldest portion of the Bible predates all of the world's other religious writings. The Torah, or first five books of the Bible, the Law written under inspiration by Moses, dates back to the 15th and 16th centuries B.C.E. By comparison, the Hindu writings of the *Rig-Veda* (a collection of hymns) were completed about 900 B.C.E. and do not claim divine inspiration. The Buddhist "Canon of the Three Baskets" dates back to the fifth century B.C.E. The Qur'ān, claimed to have been transmitted from God through the angel Gabriel, is a product of the seventh century C.E. The Book of Mormon, reportedly given to Joseph Smith in the United States by an angel called Moroni, is a product of the 19th century. If some of these works are divinely inspired as some assert, then what they offer in terms of religious guidance should not contradict the teachings of the Bible, which is the original inspired source. They should also answer some of mankind's most intriguing questions.

Questions That Require an Answer

[28] (1) Does the Bible teach what the majority of religions teach and what many people believe, namely, that humans have an immortal soul and that at death it moves on to another realm, the "hereafter," heaven, hell, or purgatory, or that it returns in a reincarnation?

(2) Does the Bible teach that the Sovereign Lord of the

---

27. (a) What are the holy writings of some world religions? (b) How should their teachings compare with those of the Bible?
28. What are some of the questions that require an answer?

universe is nameless? Does it teach that he is one God? or three persons in one God? or many gods?

(3) What does the Bible say was God's original purpose in creating mankind for life on earth?

(4) Does the Bible teach that the earth will be destroyed? Or does it point only to an end, or conclusion, for the corrupt world system?

(5) How can inner peace and salvation really be achieved?

²⁹ Each religion has different answers, but in our search for the "pure religion," we should eventually reach the conclusions that God wants us to reach. (James 1:27; AS; KJ) Why can we say that? Because our basic principle will be: "Let God be found true, though every man be found a liar, even as it is written: 'That you might be proved righteous in your words and might win when you are being judged.'"—Romans 3:4.*

³⁰ Now that we have a basis for examining the world's religions, let us turn to mankind's early quest for spirituality. What do we know about how religion began? What patterns of worship were established among the ancient and perhaps primitive peoples?

---

* If you are interested in an immediate Bible answer to these questions, we recommend that you check the following texts: (1) Genesis 1:26; 2:7; Ezekiel 18:4, 20; Leviticus 24:17, 18; Matthew 10:28; (2) Deuteronomy 6:4; 1 Corinthians 8:4-6; (3) Genesis 1:27, 28; Revelation 21:1-4; (4) Ecclesiastes 1:4; Matthew 24:3, 7, 8; (5) John 3:16; 17:3; Philippians 2:5-11; 4:6, 7; Hebrews 5:9.

---

29. (a) What is the basic principle that should guide our search for truth? (b) What answers does the Bible supply to our questions?
30. What are some of the questions to be considered in the next chapter?

CHAPTER 2

Religion
How Did It Begin?

THE history of religion is as old as the history of man himself. That is what archaeologists and anthropologists tell us. Even among the most "primitive," that is to say, undeveloped, civilizations, there is found evidence of worship of some form. In fact *The New Encyclopædia Britannica* says that "as far as scholars have discovered, there has never existed any people, anywhere, at any time, who were not in some sense religious."

[2] Besides its antiquity, religion also exists in great variety. The headhunters in the jungles of Borneo, the Eskimos in the frozen Arctic, the nomads in the Sahara Desert, the urban dwellers in the great metropolises of the world—every people and every nation on earth has its god or gods and its way of worship. The diversity in religion is truly staggering.

[3] Logically, questions come to mind. From where did all these religions come? Since there are marked differences as well as similarities among them, did they start independently, or could they have developed from one source? In fact we might ask: Why did religion begin at all? And how? The answers to these questions are of vital

---

1, 2. What has been observed regarding antiquity and variety in religion?
3. What questions about world religions need to be considered?

importance to all who are interested in finding the truth about religion and religious beliefs.

Question of Origin

[4] When it comes to the question of origin, people of different religions think of names such as Muḥammad, the Buddha, Confucius, and Jesus. In almost every religion, we can find a central figure to whom credit is given for establishing the 'true faith.' Some of these were iconoclastic reformers. Others were moralistic philosophers. Still others were selfless folk heroes. Many of them have left behind writings or sayings that formed the basis of a new religion. In time what they said and did was elaborated, embellished, and given a mystic aura. Some of these leaders were even deified.

[5] Even though these individuals are considered founders of the major religions that we are familiar with, it must be noted that they did not actually originate religion. In most cases, their teachings grew out of existing religious ideas, even though most of these founders claimed divine inspiration as their source. Or they changed and modified existing religious systems that had become unsatisfactory in one way or another.

[6] For example, as accurately as history can tell us, the Buddha had been a prince who was appalled by the suffering and deplorable conditions he found surrounding him in a society dominated by Hinduism. Buddhism was the result of his search for a solution to life's agonizing problems. Similarly, Muḥammad was highly disturbed by the idolatry and immorality he saw in the religious prac-

---

4. What do we know about the founders of many religions?
5, 6. How did many religions originate?

Men such as the Buddha, Confucius, and Luther changed existing religious systems; they did not originate religion

tices around him. He later claimed to have received special revelations from God, which formed the Qur'ān and became the basis of a new religious movement, Islām. Protestantism grew out of Catholicism as a result of the Reformation that began in the early 16th century, when Martin Luther protested the sale of indulgences by the Catholic church at that time.

[7] Thus, as far as the religions now in existence are concerned, there is no lack of information regarding their origin and development, their founders, their sacred writings, and so on. But what about the religions that existed before them? And the ones even before those? If we go back far enough in history, we will sooner or later be confronted with the question: How did religion begin?

7. What question regarding religion still needs to be answered?

Clearly, to find the answer to that question, we must look beyond the confines of the individual religions.

Many Theories

[8] The study of the origin and development of religion is a comparatively new field. For centuries, people more or less accepted the religious tradition into which they were born and in which they were brought up. Most of them were satisfied with the explanations handed down to them by their forefathers, feeling that their religion was the truth. There was seldom any reason to question anything, nor the need to investigate how, when, or why things got started. In fact, for centuries, with limited means of travel and communication, few people were even aware of other religious systems.

[9] During the 19th century, however, the picture began to change. The theory of evolution was sweeping through intellectual circles. That, along with the advent of scientific inquiry, caused many to question established systems, including religion. Recognizing the limitations of looking for clues within existing religion, some scholars turned to the remains of early civilizations or to the remote corners of the world where people still lived in primitive societies. They tried to apply to these the methods of psychology, sociology, anthropology, and so forth, hoping to discover a clue as to how religion began and why.

[10] What was the outcome? Suddenly, there burst upon

---

8. For centuries, what was the attitude of people toward religion?
9. Since the 19th century, what attempts have been made to discover how and why religion began?
10. What was the outcome of the investigations into the origin of religion?

the scene many theories—as many as there were investigators, it seemed—with each investigator contradicting the other, and each endeavoring to outdo the other in daring and originality. Some of these researchers arrived at important conclusions; the work of others has simply been forgotten. It is both educational and enlightening for us to get a glimpse of the results of this research. It will help us to gain a better understanding of the religious attitudes among people we meet.

[11] A theory, commonly called *animism,* was proposed by the English anthropologist Edward Tylor (1832-1917).

The advent of scientific inquiry and the theory of evolution caused many to question religion

He suggested that experiences such as dreams, visions, hallucinations, and the lifelessness of corpses caused primitive people to conclude that the body is inhabited by a soul (Latin, *anima*).

According to this theory, since they frequently dreamed about their deceased loved ones, they assumed that a soul continued living after death, that it left the body and dwelt in trees, rocks, rivers, and so on. Eventually, the dead and the objects the souls were said to inhabit came to be worshiped as gods. And thus, said Tylor, religion was born.

[12] Another English anthropologist, R. R. Marett (1866-1943), proposed a refinement of animism, which he called *animatism.* After studying the beliefs of the

---

11. Explain the theory of animism.
12. Explain the theory of animatism.

Melanesians of the Pacific islands and the natives of Africa and America, Marett concluded that instead of having the notion of a personal soul, primitive people believed there was an impersonal force or supernatural power that animated everything; that belief evoked emotions of awe and fear in man, which became the basis for his primitive religion. To Marett, religion was mainly man's emotional response to the unknown. His favorite statement was that religion was "not so much thought out as danced out."

[13] In 1890 a Scottish expert in ancient folklore, James Frazer (1854-1941), published the influential book *The Golden Bough,* in which he argued that religion grew out of magic. According to Frazer, man first tried to control his own life and his environment by imitating what he saw happening in nature. For example, he thought that he could invoke rain by sprinkling water on the ground to the accompaniment of thunderlike drumbeats or that he could cause his enemy harm by sticking pins in an effigy. This led to the use of rituals, spells, and magical objects in many areas of life. When these did not work as expected, he then turned to placating and beseeching the help of the supernatural powers, instead of trying to control them. The rituals and incantations became sacrifices and prayers, and thus religion began. In Frazer's words, religion is "a propitiation or conciliation of powers superior to man."

[14] Even the noted Austrian psychoanalyst Sigmund Freud (1856-1939), in his book *Totem and Taboo,* tried to explain the origin of religion. True to his profession,

13. What theory of religion did James Frazer propose?
14. How did Sigmund Freud explain the origin of religion?

Austrian psychoanalyst Sigmund Freud attributed religion to fear of a father figure

Freud explained that the earliest religion grew out of what he called a father-figure neurosis. He theorized that, as was true with wild horses and cattle, in primitive society the father dominated the clan. The sons, who both hated and admired the father, rebelled and killed the father. To acquire the father's power, Freud claimed, 'these cannibalistic savages ate their victim.' Later, out of remorse, they invented rites and rituals to atone for their action. In Freud's theory, the father figure became God, the rites and rituals became the earliest religion, and the eating of the slain father became the tradition of communion practiced in many religions.

[15] Numerous other theories that are attempts to explain the origin of religion could be cited. Most of them, however, have been forgotten, and none of them have really stood out as more credible or acceptable than the others. Why? Simply because there was never any historical evidence or proof that these theories were true. They were purely products of some investigator's imagination or conjecture, soon to be replaced by the next one that came along.

---

15. What has happened to most of the proposed theories on the origin of religion?

A Faulty Foundation

[16] After years of struggling with the issue, many have now come to the conclusion that it is most unlikely that there will be any breakthrough in finding the answer to the question of how religion began. First of all, this is because bones and remains of ancient peoples do not tell us how those people thought, what they feared, or why they worshiped. Any conclusions drawn from these artifacts are educated guesses at best. Second, the religious practices of today's so-called primitive people, such as the Australian Aborigines, are not necessarily a reliable gauge for measuring what people of ancient times did or thought. No one knows for sure if or how their culture changed over the centuries.

[17] Because of all the uncertainties, the book *World Religions—From Ancient History to the Present* concludes that "the modern historian of religions knows that it is impossible to reach the origins of religion." Regarding the historians' efforts, however, the book makes this observation: "In the past too many theorists were concerned not simply to describe or explain religion but to explain it away, feeling that if the early forms were shown to be based upon illusions then the later and higher religions might be undermined."

[18] In that last comment lies the clue as to why various "scientific" investigators of the origin of religion have not come up with any tenable explanations. Logic tells us that a

---

16. Why have years of investigation failed to provide the explanation of how religion began?
17. (a) What do modern historians of religions know? (b) What appears to be the main concern when analyzing religion?
18. (a) Why have the many investigators been unsuccessful in explaining the origin of religion? (b) What, apparently, were the true intentions of "scientific" investigators of religion?

The premise that the earth was the center of the universe led to erroneous conclusions about planetary movements

correct conclusion can be deduced only from a correct premise. If one starts off with a faulty premise, it is unlikely that one will reach a sound conclusion. The repeated failure of the "scientific" investigators to come up with a reasonable explanation casts serious doubts on the premise upon which they based their views. By following their preconceived notion, in their efforts to 'explain religion away' they have attempted to explain God away.

[19] The situation can be compared to the many ways

---

19. What is a basic principle behind successful scientific investigations? Please illustrate.

astronomers prior to the 16th century tried to explain the movement of the planets. There were many theories, but none of them were really satisfactory. Why? Because they were based upon the assumption that the earth was the center of the universe around which the stars and planets revolved. Real progress was not made until scientists —and the Catholic Church—were willing to accept the fact

Why Is Man Religious?

■ John B. Noss points out in his book *Man's Religions:* "All religions say in one way or another that man does not, and cannot, stand alone. He is vitally related with and even dependent on powers in Nature and Society external to himself. Dimly or clearly, he knows that he is not an independent center of force capable of standing apart from the world."

Similarly, the book *World Religions—From Ancient History to the Present* says: "The study of religion reveals that an important feature of it is a longing for value in life, a belief that life is not accidental and meaningless. The search for meaning leads to faith in a power greater than the human, and finally to a universal or superhuman mind which has the intention and will to maintain the highest values for human life."

So religion satisfies a basic human need, much as food satisfies our hunger. We know that eating indiscriminately when we are hungry may stop the pangs of hunger; in the long run, however, it will damage our health. To lead a healthy life, we need food that is wholesome and nutritious. Likewise, we need wholesome spiritual food to maintain our spiritual health. That is why the Bible tells us: "Not by bread alone does man live but by every expression of Jehovah's mouth."—Deuteronomy 8:3.

that the earth was not the center of the universe but revolved around the sun, the center of the solar system. The failure of the many theories to explain the facts led open-minded individuals, not to try to come up with new theories, but to reexamine the premise of their investigations. And that led to success.

[20] The same principle can be applied to the investigation of the origin of religion. Because of the rise of atheism and the widespread acceptance of the theory of evolution, many people have taken for granted that God does not exist. Based on this assumption, they feel that the explanation for the existence of religion is to be found in man himself—in his thought processes, his needs, his fears, his "neuroses." Voltaire stated, "If God did not exist, it would be necessary to invent him"; so they argue that man has invented God.—See box, page 28.

[21] Since the many theories have failed to provide a truly satisfying answer, is it not time now to reexamine the premise upon which these investigations were based? Instead of laboring fruitlessly in the same rut, would it not be logical to look elsewhere for the answer? If we are willing to be open-minded, we will agree that to do so is both reasonable and scientific. And we have just such an example to help us see the logic behind this course.

An Ancient Inquiry

[22] In the first century of our Common Era, Athens,

---

20. (a) What was the erroneous premise underlying the "scientific" investigation of religion's origin? (b) To what fundamental need did Voltaire refer?
21. What logical conclusion can we draw from the failure of the many theories on the origin of religion?
22. How did the Athenians' many theories about their gods affect their way of worship?

Greece, was a prominent center of learning. Among the Athenians, however, there were many different schools of thought, such as the Epicureans and the Stoics, each with its own idea about the gods. Based on these various ideas, many deities were venerated, and different ways of worship developed. As a result, the city was full of man-made idols and temples.—Acts 17:16.

[23] In about the year 50 C.E., the Christian apostle Paul visited Athens and presented to the Athenians a totally different point of view. He told them: "The God that made the world and all the things in it, being, as this One is, Lord of heaven and earth, does not dwell in hand-made temples, neither is he attended to by human hands as if he needed anything, because he himself gives to all persons life and breath and all things."—Acts 17: 24, 25.

[24] In other words, Paul was telling the Athenians that the true God, who "made the world and all the things in it," is not a fabrication of man's imagination, nor is he served by ways that man might devise. True religion is not just a one-sided effort by man to try to fill a certain psychological need or quell a certain fear. Rather, since the true God is the Creator, who gave man thinking ability and power of reason, it is only logical that He would provide a way for man to come into a satisfying relationship with Him. That, according to Paul, was exactly what God did. "He made out of one man every nation of men, to dwell upon the entire surface of the earth, . . . for them

---

23. What totally different view about God did the apostle Paul present to the Athenians?
24. In effect, what was Paul telling the Athenians about true worship?

Mankind's Search for God

to seek God, if they might grope for him and really find him, although, in fact, he is not far off from each one of us."—Acts 17:26, 27.

[25] Notice Paul's key point: God "made out of one man every nation of men." Even though today there are many nations of men, living all over the earth, scientists know that, indeed, all mankind is of the same stock. This concept is of great significance because when we speak of all mankind's being of the same stock, it means much more than their being related just biologically and genetically. They are related in other areas as well.

[26] Note, for instance, what the book *Story of the World's Worship* says about man's language. "Those who have studied the languages of the world and compared them with each other have something to say, and it is this: All languages can be grouped into families or classes of speech, and all these families are seen to have started from one common source." In other words, the languages of the world did not originate separately and independently, as evolutionists would have us believe. They theorize that cave-dwelling men in Africa, Europe, and Asia started with their grunts and growls and eventually developed their own languages. That was not the case. Evidence is that they "started from one common source."

[27] If that is true of something as personal and as

_____
25. Explain the key point of Paul's argument about mankind's origin.
26. What is known about language that supports Paul's key point?
27. Why is it logical to think that man's ideas about God and religion started from one common source?

uniquely human as language, then would it not be reasonable to think that man's ideas about God and religion should also have started from one common source? After all, religion is related to thinking, and thinking is related to man's ability to use language. It is not that all religions actually grew out of one religion, but the ideas and concepts should be traceable to some common origin or pool of religious ideas. Is there evidence to support this? And if, indeed, man's religions did originate in one single source, what might it be? How can we find out?

Different yet Similar

[28] We can get the answer in the same way that linguistic experts got their answers about the origin of language. By placing the languages side by side and noting their similarities, an etymologist can trace the various languages back to their source. Similarly, by placing the religions side by side, we can examine their doctrines, legends, rituals, ceremonies, institutions, and so on, and see if there is any underlying thread of common identity and, if so, to what that thread leads us.

[29] On the surface, the many religions in existence today seem quite different from one another. However, if we strip them of the things that are mere embellishments and later additions, or if we remove those distinctions that are the result of climate, language, peculiar conditions of their native land, and other factors, it is amazing how similar most of them turn out to be.

---

28. How can we find out if there is a common origin for the world's religions?
29. To what can many of the differences among religions be attributed?

▲ Chinese Buddhist goddess of mercy with infant

Catholic ▲ Madonna with infant Jesus

Buddhism and Roman Catholicism —why do they appear to have many things in common?

▼ Tibetan Buddhist using prayer wheel and rosary

Catholic ▼ using rosary

³⁰ For example, most people would think that there could hardly be any two religions more different from each other than the Roman Catholic Church of the West and Buddhism of the East. However, what do we see when we put aside the differences that could be attributed to language and culture? If we are objective about it, we have to admit that there is a great deal that the two have in common. Both Catholicism and Buddhism are steeped in rituals and ceremonies. These include the use of candles, incense, holy water, the rosary, images of saints, chants and prayer books, even the sign of the cross. Both religions maintain institutions of monks and nuns and are noted for celibacy of priests, special garb, holy days, special foods. This list is by no means exhaustive, but it serves to illustrate the point. The question is, Why do two religions that appear to be so different have so many things in common?

> **It is as if there was a common pool from which each religion drew its basic beliefs**

³¹ As enlightening as the comparison of these two religions turns out to be, the same can be done with other religions. When we do so, we find that certain teachings and beliefs are almost universal among them. Most of us are familiar with such doctrines as the immortality of the human soul, heavenly reward for all good people, eternal torment for the wicked in an underworld, purgatory, a triune god or a godhead of many gods, and a mother-of-

30. What similarities do you see between Roman Catholicism and Buddhism?
31. What similarities do you see among other religions?

god or queen-of-heaven goddess. Beyond these, however, there are many legends and myths that are equally commonplace. For example, there are legends about man's fall from divine grace owing to his illicit attempt to achieve immortality, the need to offer sacrifices to atone for sin, the search for a tree of life or fountain of youth, gods and demigods who lived among humans and produced superhuman offspring, and a catastrophic flood that devastated nearly all of humanity.*

32 What can we conclude from all of this? We note that those who believed in these myths and legends lived far from one another geographically. Their culture and traditions were different and distinct. Their social customs bore no relationship to one another. And yet, when it comes to their religions, they believed in such similar ideas. Although not every one of these peoples believed in all the things mentioned, all of them believed in some of them. The obvious question is, Why? It was as if there was a common pool from which each religion drew its basic beliefs, some more, some less. With the passage of time, these basic ideas were embellished and modified, and other teachings developed from them. But the basic outline is unmistakable.

33 Logically, the similarity in the basic concepts of the many religions of the world is strong evidence that they

---

* For a detailed comparison of the various flood legends found among different peoples, please see the book *Insight on the Scriptures,* published by the Watchtower Bible and Tract Society of New York, Inc., 1988, Volume 1, pages 328, 610, and 611.

32, 33. (a) What can we conclude from the remarkable similarities among the world's religions? (b) What question needs an answer?

Chinese legends speak of a golden age during the reign of Huang-Ti (Yellow Emperor) in mythical times

did not begin each in its own separate and independent way. Rather, going back far enough, their ideas must have come from a common origin. What was that origin?

An Early Golden Age

[34] Interestingly, among the legends common to many religions is one that says humankind began in a golden age in which man was guiltless, lived happily and peacefully in close communion with God, and was free from sickness and death. While details may differ, the same concept of a perfect paradise that once existed is found in the writings and legends of many religions.

[35] The Avesta, the sacred book of the ancient Persian Zoroastrian religion, tells about "the fair Yima, the good shepherd," who was the first mortal with whom Ahura Mazda (the creator) conversed. He was instructed by Ahura Mazda "to nourish, to rule, and to watch over my

34. What legend regarding man's beginning is common to many religions?
35. Describe the ancient Zoroastrians' belief about an early golden age.

Mankind's Search for God

world." To do so, he was to build "a Vara," an underground abode, for all the living creatures. In it, there "was neither overbearing nor mean-spiritedness, neither stupidity nor violence, neither poverty nor deceit, neither puniness nor deformity, neither huge teeth nor bodies beyond the usual measure. The inhabitants suffered no defilement from the evil spirit. They dwelt among odoriferous trees and golden pillars; these were the largest, best and most beautiful on earth; they were themselves a tall and beautiful race."

[36] Among the ancient Greeks, Hesiod's poem *Works and Days* speaks of the Five Ages of Man, the first of which was the "Golden Age" when men enjoyed complete happiness. He wrote:

"The immortal gods, that tread the courts of heaven,
First made a golden race of men.
Like gods they lived, with happy, careless souls,
From toil and pain exempt; nor on them crept
Wretched old age, but all their life was passed
In feasting, and their limbs no changes knew."

That legendary golden age was lost, according to Greek mythology, when Epimetheus accepted as wife the beautiful Pandora, a gift from the Olympian god Zeus. One day Pandora opened the lid of her great vase, and suddenly there escaped from it troubles, miseries, and illness from which mankind was never to recover.

[37] Ancient Chinese legends also tell of a golden age in the days of Huang-Ti (Yellow Emperor), who is said to have ruled for a hundred years in the 26th century B.C.E.

---

36. How did the Greek poet Hesiod describe a "Golden Age"?
37. Describe the ancient Chinese legendary account of a "paradise" at the beginning of history.

He was credited with inventing everything having to do with civilization—clothing and shelter, vehicles of transportation, weapons and warfare, land management, manufacturing, silk culture, music, language, mathematics, the calendar, and so on. During his reign, it is said, "there were no thieves nor fights in China, and the people lived in humility and peace. Timely rain and weather resulted in abundant harvest year after year. Most amazing was that even the wild beasts did not kill, and birds of prey did no harm. In short, the history of China began with a paradise." To this day, the Chinese still claim to be the descendants of the Yellow Emperor.

[38] Similar legendary accounts of a time of happiness and perfection at the beginning of man's history can be found in the religions of many other peoples—Egyptians, Tibetans, Peruvians, Mexicans, and others. Was it just by accident that all these peoples, who lived far from each other and who had totally different cultures, languages, and customs, entertained the same ideas about their origin? Was it just by chance or coincidence that all of them chose to explain their beginnings in the same way? Logic and experience tell us that this could hardly be so. On the contrary, interwoven in all these legends, there must be some common elements of truth about the beginning of man and his religion.

[39] Indeed, there are many common elements discernible among all the different legends about man's beginning. When we put them together, a more complete picture begins to emerge. It tells how God created the first

---

38. What conclusion can we draw from all the similar legendary accounts of man's beginning?
39. What composite picture can be assembled from the elements common to the many legends about man's beginning?

Mankind's Search for God

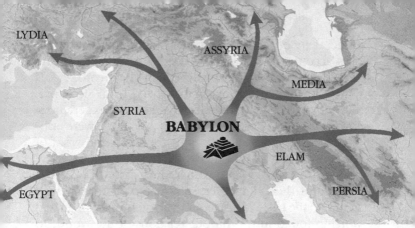

As the human race dispersed from Mesopotamia, their religious ideas and memories went with them

man and woman and placed them in a paradise. They were very content and very happy at first, but soon they became rebellious. That rebellion led to the loss of the perfect paradise, only to be replaced by labor and toil, pain and suffering. Eventually mankind became so bad that God punished them by sending a great deluge of waters that destroyed all but one family. As this family multiplied, some of the offspring banded together and started to build an immense tower in defiance of God. God thwarted their scheme by confusing their language and dispersing them to the far corners of the earth.

[40] Is this composite picture purely the result of someone's mental exercise? No. Basically, that is the picture presented in the Bible, in the first 11 chapters of the book of Genesis. While we will not go into a discussion of the

_____

40. Explain the Bible's relationship to the legends about the origin of man's religions.

authenticity of the Bible here, let it be noted that the Bible's account of man's early history is reflected in the key elements found in many legends.* The record reveals that as the human race began to disperse from Mesopotamia, they carried with them their memories, experiences, and ideas everywhere they went. In time these were elaborated and changed and became the warp and woof of religion in every part of the world. In other words, going back to the analogy used earlier, the account in Genesis constitutes the original, crystal-clear pool from which stemmed the basic ideas about the beginning of man and worship found in the various religions of the world. To these they added their particular doctrines and practices, but the link is unmistakable.

[41] In the following chapters of this book, we will discuss in greater detail how specific religions began and developed. You will find it enlightening to note not only how each religion is different from the others but also how it is similar to them. You will also be able to note how each religion fits into the time scheme of human history and the history of religion, how its sacred book or writings relate to the others, how its founder or leader was influenced by other religious ideas, and how it has influenced mankind's conduct and history. Studying mankind's long search for God with these points in mind will help you to see more clearly the truth about religion and religious teachings.

---

* For detailed information on this subject, please refer to the book *The Bible—God's Word or Man's?*, published by the Watchtower Bible and Tract Society of New York, Inc., 1989.

---

41. What should you bear in mind as you study subsequent chapters in this book?

CHAPTER 3.

Common Threads in *Mythology*

WHY consider myths? Are they not just fictions from the distant past? While it is true that many are based on fiction, others are based on fact. Take for example the myths and legends found worldwide that are based on the fact of the world Deluge, or Flood, that the Bible relates.

[2] A reason for considering myths is that they are the foundation for beliefs and rites still found in religions today. For example, belief in an immortal soul can be traced from ancient Assyro-Babylonian myths through Egyptian, Greek, and Roman mythology to Christendom, where it has become an underlying tenet in her theology. Myths are evidence that ancient man was searching for gods, as well as for a meaning in life. In this chapter we will briefly cover some of the common themes that arise in the myths of the world's major cultures. As we review these mythologies, we will note how creation, the Flood, false gods and demigods, the immortal soul, and sun worship crop up regularly as common threads in the patchwork of mythology. But why should this be the case?

[3] Very often there is a kernel of historical fact, a person, or an event that has later been exaggerated or

1-3. (a) Why should myths interest us? (b) What will we cover in this chapter?

distorted to form the myth. One of these historical facts is the Bible's record of creation.*

Fact and Fiction About Creation

⁴ Creation myths abound, but none have the simple logic of the Bible's creation record. (Genesis, chapters 1, 2) For example, the account given in Greek mythology sounds barbaric. The first Greek to put myths in writing in a systematic way was Hesiod, who wrote his *Theogony* in the eighth century B.C.E. He explains how the gods and the world began. He starts off with Gaea, or Gaia (Earth), who gives birth to Uranus (Heaven). What follows is explained by scholar Jasper Griffin in *The Oxford History of the Classical World:*

⁵ "Hesiod tells the story, known to Homer, of the succession of sky gods. First Uranus was supreme, but he

---

* For a detailed consideration of creation, see the book *Life—How Did It Get Here? By Evolution or by Creation?,* published by the Watchtower Bible and Tract Society.

4, 5. What were some of the beliefs of Greek mythology?

Mount Olympus, Greece, the supposed home of the gods

Greek and Roman Divinities

Many gods and goddesses of Greek mythology held similar positions in Roman mythology. The table below lists some of them.

Greek	Roman	Role
Aphrodite	Venus	Goddess of love
Apollo	Apollo	God of light, medicine, and poetry
Ares	Mars	God of war
Artemis	Diana	Goddess of hunting and childbirth
Asclepius	Aesculapius	God of healing
Athena	Minerva	Goddess of crafts, war, and wisdom
Cronus	Saturn	To the Greeks, ruler of the Titans and father of Zeus. In Roman mythology, also the god of agriculture
Demeter	Ceres	Goddess of growing things
Dionysus	Bacchus	God of wine, fertility, and wild behavior
Eros	Cupid	God of love
Gaea	Terra	Symbol of the earth, and mother and wife of Uranus
Hephaestus	Vulcan	Blacksmith for the gods and god of fire and metalworking
Hera	Juno	Protector of marriage and women. To the Greeks, sister and wife of Zeus; to the Romans, wife of Jupiter
Hermes	Mercury	Messenger for the gods; god of commerce and science; and protector of travelers, thieves, and vagabonds
Hestia	Vesta	Goddess of the hearth
Hypnos	Somnus	God of sleep
Pluto, Hades	Pluto	God of the underworld
Poseidon	Neptune	God of the sea. In Greek mythology, also god of earthquakes and horses
Rhea	Ops	Wife and sister of Cronus
Uranus	Uranus	Son and husband of Gaea and father of the Titans
Zeus	Jupiter	Ruler of the gods

Based on *The World Book Encyclopedia*, 1987, Volume 13.

suppressed his children, and Gaia encouraged his son Cronos to castrate him. Cronos in turn devoured his own children, until his wife Rhea gave him a stone to eat in place of Zeus; the child Zeus was brought up in Crete, compelled his father to disgorge his siblings, and with them and other aid defeated Cronos and his Titans and cast them down into Tartarus."

[6] From what source did the Greeks get this strange mythology? The same author answers: "Its ultimate origin seems to have been Sumerian. In these eastern stories we find a succession of gods, and the motifs of castration, of swallowing, and of a stone recur in ways which, though varying, show that the resemblance with Hesiod is no coincidence." We have to look to ancient Mesopotamia and Babylon as the source of many myths that permeated other cultures.

[7] The ancient mythology of Chinese folk religion is not always easy to define, since many written records were destroyed in the period 213-191 B.C.E.* Some myths have remained, however, such as the one describing how the earth was formed. A professor of Oriental art, Anthony Christie, writes: "We learn that Chaos was like a hen's egg. Neither Heaven nor Earth existed. From the

---

* The more recent mythology of China, the result of the influence of Buddhism, Taoism, and Confucianism, will be discussed in Chapters 6 and 7.

---

6. According to Jasper Griffin, what is the probable source of much Greek mythology?
7. (a) Why is it not easy to get information on ancient Chinese myths? (b) How does one Chinese myth explain the creation of the earth and man? (Compare Genesis 1:27; 2:7.)

egg P'an-ku was born, while of its heavy elements Earth was made and Sky from the light elements. P'an-ku is represented as a dwarf, clad in a bearskin or a cloak of leaves. For 18,000 years the distance between Earth and Sky grew daily by ten feet, and P'an-ku grew at the same rate so that his body filled the gap. When he died, different parts of his body became various natural elements. . . . His body fleas became the human race."

[8] From South America an Inca legend explains how a mythical creator gave speech to each nation. "He gave to each nation the language it was to speak . . . He gave

8. According to Inca mythology, how did languages come about?

*A*ssyro-Babylonian Gods and Goddesses

Anu—the supreme god, reigning over the heavens; father of Ishtar

Asshur—national warrior-god of the Assyrians, also god of fertility

Ea—god of water. Father of Marduk. Warned Utnapishtim of the flood

Enlil (Bel)—lord of the air; later paralleled in Greek mythology by Zeus. Assimilated by the Babylonians into Marduk (Bel)

Ishtar—divine personification of the planet Venus; sacred prostitution a part of her cult. She was Astarte in Phoenicia, Atargatis in Syria, Ashtoreth in the Bible (1 Kings 11:5, 33), Aphrodite in Greece, Venus in Rome

Marduk—first among the Babylonian gods; "absorbed all the other gods and took over all their various functions." Called Merodach by the Israelites

Shamash—sun-god of light and justice. Forerunner of the Greek Apollo

Sin—moon-god, member of the triad that included Shamash (the sun) and Ishtar (the planet Venus)

Tammuz (Dumuzi)—the harvest-god. Ishtar's lover

(Based on the *New Larousse Encyclopedia of Mythology*)

being and soul to each one as well [as] the men and the women and commanded each nation to sink below the earth. Thence each nation passed underground and came up in the places to which he assigned them." (*The Fables and Rites of the Yncas*, by Cristóbal de Molina of Cuzco, quoted in *South American Mythology*) In this case it appears that the Bible's account of the confusion of languages at Babel is the factual kernel for this Inca myth. (Genesis 11:1-9) But now let us turn our attention to the Deluge described in the Bible at Genesis 7:17-24.

The Flood—Fact or Myth?

[9] Taking us back to some 4,500 years ago, to about 2,500 B.C.E., the Bible tells us that rebel spirit sons of God materialized in human form and "went taking wives for themselves." This unnatural interbreeding produced the violent Nephilim, "the mighty ones who were of old, the men of fame." Their lawless conduct affected the pre-Flood world to the point that Jehovah said: "'I am going to wipe men whom I have created off the surface of the ground . . . because I do regret that I have made them.' But Noah found favor in the eyes of Jehovah." The account then continues with the specific and practical steps Noah had to take to save himself, as well as his family and a variety of animal kinds, from the Flood.—Genesis 6: 1-8, 13–8:22; 1 Peter 3:19, 20; 2 Peter 2:4; Jude 6.

[10] The record of pre-Flood events related in Genesis is

---

9. (a) What does the Bible tell us about pre-Flood conditions on the earth? (b) What did Noah and his family have to do to be delivered from the Flood?
10. Why should the Bible account of the Flood not be viewed as a myth?

Clay tablet in cuneiform writing that presents part of the Epic of Gilgamesh

branded as myth by modern critics. Yet, the history of Noah was accepted and believed by faithful men, such as Isaiah, Ezekiel, Jesus Christ, and the apostles Peter and Paul. It is also supported by the fact that it is reflected in so many mythologies worldwide, including the ancient Epic of Gilgamesh as well as the myths of China and of the Aztecs, Incas, and Maya. With the Bible record in mind, let us now consider the Assyro-Babylonian

mythology and its references to a flood.*—Isaiah 54:9;
Ezekiel 14:20; Matthew 24:37; Hebrews 11:7.

The Flood and the God-Man Gilgamesh

[11] Going back in history possibly some 4,000 years,
we encounter the famous Akkadian myth called the
Epic of Gilgamesh. Our knowledge of this is based main-
ly on a cuneiform text that came from the library of
Ashurbanipal, who reigned 668-627 B.C.E., in ancient
Nineveh.

[12] It is the story of the exploits of Gilgamesh, described
as being two-thirds god and one-third man, or a demi-
god. One version of the epic states: "In Uruk he built
walls, a great rampart, and the temple of blessed Eanna
for the god of the firmament Anu, and for Ishtar the goddess of love . . . , our lady of love and war." (See box,
page 45, for a listing of Assyro-Babylonian gods and goddesses.) However, Gilgamesh was not exactly a pleasant creature to have around. The inhabitants of Uruk
complained to the gods: "His lust leaves no virgin to her
lover, neither the warrior's daughter nor the wife of the
noble."

[13] What action did the gods take in response to the
people's protest? The goddess Aruru created Enkidu to be
the human rival of Gilgamesh. However, instead of being

---

* For a more detailed discussion of the proofs of the Flood as
history, see *Insight on the Scriptures,* Volume 1, pages 327-8, 609-12,
published by the Watchtower Society.

---

11. On what is our knowledge of the Epic of Gilgamesh based?
12. Who was Gilgamesh, and why was he not popular? (Compare Genesis 6:1, 2.)
13. (a) What action did the gods take, and what did Gilgamesh
do? (b) Who was Utnapishtim?

enemies, they became close friends. In the course of the epic, Enkidu died. Shattered, Gilgamesh cried: "When I die, shall I not be like Enkidu? Woe has entered my belly. Fearing death, I roam over the steppe." He wanted the secret of immortality and set out to find Utnapishtim, the deluge survivor who had been given immortality with the gods.

[14] Gilgamesh eventually finds Utnapishtim, who tells him the story of the flood. As found in Epic tablet XI, known as the Flood Tablet, Utnapishtim recounts instructions given to him concerning the flood: "Tear down (this) house, build a ship! Give up possessions, seek thou life. . . . Aboard the ship take thou the seed of all living things." Does this not sound somewhat similar to the Bible's reference to Noah and the Flood? But Utnapishtim cannot bestow immortality upon Gilgamesh. Gilgamesh, disappointed, returns home to Uruk. The account concludes with his death. The overall message of the epic is the sadness and frustration of death and the hereafter. Those ancient people did not find the God of truth and hope. However, the epic's link to the Bible's simple account of the pre-Flood era is quite evident. Now let us turn to the Flood account as it appears in other legends.

Flood Legend in Other Cultures

[15] Even earlier than the account in the Epic of Gilgamesh is the Sumerian myth that presents "Ziusudra, the counterpart of the biblical Noah, who is described as a pious, a god-fearing king, constantly on the lookout for

14. (a) What was Utnapishtim told to do? (Compare Genesis 6: 13-16.) (b) What was the outcome of the epic journey of Gilgamesh?
15. Why is the Sumerian flood legend of interest to us?

Anubis, the jackal-headed god, weighs a heart-soul, on the left scale, against Maat, the goddess of truth and justice, symbolized by a feather; Thoth writes the result on a tablet before announcing it to Osiris

divine revelations in dreams or incantations." (*Ancient Near Eastern Texts Relating to the Old Testament*) According to the same source, this myth "offers the closest and most striking parallel to biblical material as yet uncovered in Sumerian literature." The Babylonian and Assyrian civilizations, which came later, were influenced by the Sumerian.

[16] The book *China—A History in Art* tells us that one of the ancient rulers of China was Yü, "the conqueror of the Great Flood. Yü channeled flood waters into rivers and seas to resettle his people." Mythology expert Joseph Campbell wrote about the Chinese "Period of the Great Ten," saying: "To this important age, which terminates in a Deluge, ten emperors were assigned in the early Chou-

16. From what source could the Chinese flood legends have come?

time mythology. Hence, it appears that what we are viewing here may be a local transformation of the series of the old Sumerian king list." Campbell then cited other items from Chinese legends that appeared to "reinforce the argument for a Mesopotamian source." That takes us back to the same basic source of many myths. However, the story of the Flood also appears in the Americas, for example, in Mexico during the period of the Aztecs in the 15th and 16th centuries C.E.

[17] Aztec mythology spoke of four previous ages, during the first of which the earth was inhabited by giants. (That is another reminder of the Nephilim, the giants referred to in the Bible at Genesis 6:4.) It included a primeval flood legend in which "the waters above merge with those below, obliterating the horizons and making of everything a timeless cosmic ocean." The god controlling rain and water was Tlaloc. However, his rain was not obtained cheaply but was given "in exchange for the blood of sacrificed victims whose flowing tears would simulate and so stimulate the flow of rain." (*Mythology —An Illustrated Encyclopedia*) Another legend states that the fourth era was ruled by Chalchiuhtlicue, the water-goddess, whose universe perished by a flood. Men were saved by becoming fish!

[18] Similarly, the Incas had their Flood legends. British writer Harold Osborne states: "Perhaps the most ubiquitous features in South American myth are the stories of a deluge . . . Myths of a deluge are very widespread among both the highland peoples and the tribes of the tropical lowlands. The deluge is commonly connected with the

---

17. What flood legends did the Aztecs have?
18. What accounts are prevalent in South American mythology? (Compare Genesis 6:7, 8; 2 Peter 2:5.)

creation and with an epiphany [manifestation] of the creator-god. . . . It is sometimes regarded as a divine punishment wiping out existing humankind in preparation for the emergence of a new race."

[19] Likewise, the Maya in Mexico and Central America had their Flood legend that involved a universal deluge, or *haiyococab,* which means "water over the earth." Catholic bishop Las Casas wrote that the Guatemalan Indians "called it *Butic,* which is the word which means flood of many waters and means the final judgment, and so they believe that another *Butic* is about to come, which is another flood and judgment, not of water, but of fire." Many more flood legends exist around the world, but the few already quoted serve to confirm the kernel of the legend, the historical event related in the book of Genesis.

The All-Pervasive Immortal Soul Belief

[20] However, not all myths have a basis in fact or in the Bible. In his search for God, man has clutched at straws, deluded by the illusion of immortality. As we will see throughout this book, the belief in an immortal soul or variations thereof is a legacy that has come down to us through the millenniums. The people of the ancient Assyro-Babylonian culture believed in an afterlife. The *New Larousse Encyclopedia of Mythology* explains: "Under the earth, beyond the abyss of the Apsu [full of fresh water and encircling the earth], lay the infernal dwelling-place to which men descended after death. It was the 'Land of no return' . . . In these regions of eternal darkness

---

19. Describe the Maya flood legend.
20. What was the Assyro-Babylonian belief regarding the afterlife?

the souls of the dead—*edimmu*—'clad, like birds, in a garment of wings' are all jumbled together." According to the myth, this subterranean world was ruled over by the goddess Ereshkigal, "Princess of the great earth."

[21] The Egyptians likewise had their idea of an immortal soul. Before the soul could reach a happy haven, it had to be weighed against Maat, the goddess of truth and justice, who was symbolized by the feather of truth. Either Anubis, the jackal-headed god, or Horus, the falcon, helped in the procedure. If approved by Osiris, that soul would go on to share bliss with the gods. (See illustration, page 50.) As is so often the case, here we find the common thread of the Babylonian immortal soul concept shaping people's religion, lives, and actions.

[22] The old Chinese mythology included a belief in survival after death and the need to keep ancestors happy. Ancestors were "conceived as living and powerful spirits, all vitally concerned about the welfare of their living descendants, but capable of punitive anger if displeased." The dead were to be given every aid, including companions in death. Thus, "some Shang kings . . . were buried with anywhere from a hundred to three hundred human victims, who were to be his attendants in the next world. (This practice links ancient China with Egypt, Africa, Japan, and other places, where similar sacrifices were made.)" (*Man's Religions,* by John B. Noss) In these cases belief in an immortal soul led to human sacrifices.—Contrast Ecclesiastes 9:5, 10; Isaiah 38:18, 19.

---

21. According to Egyptian belief, what happened to the dead?
22. What was the Chinese concept of the dead, and what was done to help them?

²³ The Greeks, having formulated many gods in their mythology, were also concerned with the dead and their destination. According to the myths, the one put in charge of that realm of murky darkness was the son of Cronus and brother of the gods Zeus and Poseidon. His name was Hades, and his realm was named after him. How did the souls of the dead reach Hades?*

²⁴ Writer Ellen Switzer explains: "There were . . . frightening creatures in the underworld. There was Charon, who rowed the ferry that transported those who had recently died from the land of the living to the underworld. Charon required payment for his ferry service [across the river Styx], and the Greeks often buried their dead with a coin under the tongue to make sure that they had the proper fare. Dead souls who could not pay were kept on the wrong side of the river, in a kind of no-man's-land, and might return to haunt the living."#

²⁵ The Greek mythology of the soul went on to influence the Roman concept, and the Greek philosophers, such as Plato (about 427-347 B.C.E.), strongly influenced

---

* "Hades" appears in the Christian Greek Scriptures ten times, not as a mythological person, but as the common grave of mankind. It is the Greek equivalent of the Hebrew *she'ohl'.*—Compare Psalm 16:10; Acts 2:27, *Kingdom Interlinear.*—See *Insight on the Scriptures,* Volume 1, pages 1015-16, published by the Watchtower Society.

Interestingly, Utnapishtim, the hero of the Epic of Gilgamesh, had his boatman, Urshanabi, who took Gilgamesh over the waters of death to meet the flood survivor.

---

23. (a) In Greek mythology, who and what were Hades? (b) What is Hades according to the Bible?
24. (a) According to Greek mythology, what happened in the underworld? (b) What similarity to the Epic of Gilgamesh was there in Greek mythology?
25. Who were influenced by Greek thinking regarding the soul?

**Chalchiuhtlicue, Aztec goddess of fresh water;
an owl-shaped vessel that has a cavity where it is believed
sacrificed hearts were deposited**

early apostate Christian thinkers who accepted the immortal soul teaching into their doctrine, even though it had no Biblical basis.

[26] The Aztecs, Incas, and Maya also believed in an immortal soul. Death was as much a mystery to them as it was to other civilizations. They had their ceremonies and beliefs to help them reconcile themselves to it. As the archaeological historian Victor W. von Hagen explains in his book *The Ancient Sun Kingdoms of the Americas:* "The dead were in reality living: they had merely passed from one phase to another; they were invisible, impalpable, invulnerable. The dead . . . had become the unseen members of the clan."—Contrast Judges 16:30; Ezekiel 18:4, 20.

[27] The same source tells us that "the [Inca] Indian believed in immortality; in fact he believed one never died, . . . the dead body merely became undead and it took on the influences of the unseen powers." The Maya too

26, 27. How did the Aztecs, Incas, and Maya view death?

believed in a soul and in 13 heavens and 9 hells. Thus, wherever we turn, people have wanted to deny the reality of death, and the immortal soul has been the crutch to lean on.—Isaiah 38:18; Acts 3:23.

[28] Africa's mythologies likewise include references to a surviving soul. Many Africans live in awe of the souls of the dead. The *New Larousse Encyclopedia of Mythology* states: "This belief is bound up with another—the continuing existence of the soul after death. Magicians are able to call on souls to aid their powers. The souls of the dead often transmigrate into the bodies of animals, or may even be reincarnated in plants." As a consequence, the Zulu will not kill some snakes that they believe to be the spirits of relatives.

[29] The Masai of southeastern Africa believe in a creator called 'Ng ai, who places a guardian angel by each Masai as a protection. At the moment of death, the angel takes the warrior's soul to the hereafter. The previously quoted *Larousse* supplies a Zulu death-legend involving the first man, Unkulunkulu, who for this myth had become the supreme being. He sent the chameleon to tell mankind, "Men shall not die!" The chameleon was slow and got distracted on the way. So Unkulunkulu sent a different message by means of a lizard, saying, "Men shall die!" The lizard got there first, "and ever since no man has escaped death." With variations, this same legend exists among the Bechuana, Basuto, and Baronga tribes.

[30] As we pursue the study of mankind's search for

28. What are some beliefs that have prevailed in Africa?
29. Explain the legends of some tribes of southern Africa. (Compare Genesis 2:15-17; 3:1-5.)
30. In this book what will we further see about the soul?

God, we will see even further how important the myth of the immortal soul has been and still is to mankind.

Sun Worship and Human Sacrifices

[31] The mythology of Egypt embraces an extensive pantheon of gods and goddesses. As in so many other ancient societies, while the Egyptians searched for God, they gravitated toward worshiping that which sustained their daily life—the sun. Thus, under the name of Ra (Amon-Ra), they venerated the sovereign lord of the sky, who took a boat ride every day from east to west. When night fell, he followed a dangerous course through the underworld.

[32] Human sacrifices were a common feature in the sun worship of the Aztec, Inca, and Maya religions. The Aztecs celebrated a constant cycle of religious festivals, with

31. (a) What did the Egyptians believe about the sun-god Ra? (b) How does that contrast with what the Bible says? (Psalm 19: 4-6)
32. Describe one of the festivals to the fire-god Xiuhtecutli (Huehueteotl).

The Egyptian triad: from left, Horus, Osiris, and Isis

The Intihuatana, inset, the sun's "hitching post," perhaps used in connection with sun worship at Machu Picchu

Inca sun worship was practiced at Machu Picchu, Peru

human sacrifices to their various gods, especially in the worship of the sun-god Tezcatlipoca. Also, in the festival of the fire-god Xiuhtecutli (Huehueteotl), "prisoners of war danced together with their captors and . . . were whirled about a dazzling fire and then dumped into the coals, fished out while still alive to have their still palpitating hearts cut out to be offered to the gods."—*The Ancient Sun Kingdoms of the Americas.*

[33] Farther south, the Inca religion had its own sacrifices and myths. In ancient Inca worship, children and animals were offered to the sun-god Inti and to Viracocha, the creator.

Mythical Gods and Goddesses

[34] The most prominent of the Egyptian triads is that made up of Isis, symbol of divine motherhood; Osiris, her brother and consort; and Horus, their son, usually represented by a falcon. Isis is sometimes portrayed in Egyptian statues offering her breast to her child in a pose very reminiscent of Christendom's virgin-and-child statues and paintings, which came on the scene over two thousand years later. In time Isis' husband, Osiris, achieved popularity as the god of the dead because he offered hope of an eternally happy life for the souls of the dead in the hereafter.

[35] Egypt's Hathor was the goddess of love and joy, music and dancing. She became the queen of the dead, helping them with a ladder to achieve heaven. As the *New*

---

33. (a) What did Inca worship include? (b) What does the Bible say about human sacrifices? (Compare 2 Kings 23:5, 11; Jeremiah 32:35; Ezekiel 8:16.)
34. Who made up the most prominent Egyptian triad, and what roles did they play?
35. Who was Hathor, and what was her chief annual festival?

Gods of the Roman Soldier

Rome was famous for its disciplined army. The cohesion of its empire depended on the morale and the effectiveness of the military legions. Was religion a factor to be reckoned with? Yes, and fortunately for us, the Romans left behind clear evidence of their occupation in the form of highways, fortresses, aqueducts, coliseums, and temples. For example, in Northumbria, in the north of England, there is the famous Hadrian's Wall, built about 122 C.E. What have excavations revealed about Roman garrison activity and the role of religion?

In the Housesteads Museum, located near the excavated ruins of a Roman garrison on Hadrian's Wall, an exhibit states: "The religious life of a Roman soldier was divided into three parts. Firstly . . . the cult of the Deified Emperors and the worship of the protecting gods of Rome such as Jupiter, Victory and Mars. An altar was dedicated to Jupiter every year on the pa-

rade ground of each fort. All soldiers were expected to participate in the festivals celebrating the birthdays, accession days and victories of the Deified Emperors." How similar to the customs of armies of today, in which chaplains, altars, and flags are a regular part of army worship.

But what was the second feature of the Roman soldier's religious life? It was the worship of the protecting gods and the guardian spirit of their particular unit "as well as the gods brought from their native lands."

"Finally there were the cults followed by the individual. As long as a soldier fulfilled his obligations to the official cults he was free to worship any god he wished." That sounds like a very liberal freedom-of-worship situation, but "exceptions were those religions, of which Druidism was one, whose practices were considered inhumane, and those whose loyalty to the State was suspect, for example Christianity."—Compare Luke 20: 21-25; 23:1, 2; Acts 10:1, 2, 22.

Interestingly, in 1949 a temple to Mithras was discovered in a bog at Carrawburgh, quite close to Hadrian's Wall. (See photo.) Archaeologists estimate that it was built about 205 C.E. It contains a sun-god image, altars, and a Latin inscription that states, in part, "To the invincible god Mithras."

Egypt's Gods and the Ten Plagues

Jehovah executed judgment on Egypt's impotent gods by means of the Ten Plagues.—Exodus 7:14–12:32.

Plague	Description
1	**Nile and other waters turned to blood.** Nile-god Hapi disgraced
2	**Frogs.** Frog-goddess Heqt powerless to prevent it
3	**Dust turned to gnats.** Thoth, lord of magic, could not help the Egyptian magicians
4	**Gadflies on all Egypt** except Goshen where Israel dwelt. No god was able to prevent it—not even Ptah, creator of the universe, or Thoth, lord of magic
5	**Pestilence on livestock.** Neither sacred cow-goddess Hathor nor Apis the bull could prevent this plague
6	**Boils.** Healer deities Thoth, Isis, and Ptah unable to help
7	**Thunder and hail.** Exposed the impotence of Reshpu, controller of lightning, and Thoth, god of rain and thunder
8	**Locusts.** This was a blow to the fertility-god Min, protector of crops
9	**Three days of darkness.** Ra, the preeminent sun-god, and Horus, a solar god, disgraced
10	**Death of the firstborn** including Pharaoh's, who was considered to be a god incarnate. Ra (Amon-Ra), sun-god and sometimes represented as a ram, was unable to impede it

Larousse Encyclopedia of Mythology explains, she was celebrated with great festivals, "above all on New Year's Day, which was the anniversary of her birth. Before dawn the priestesses would bring Hathor's image out on to the terrace to expose it to the rays of the rising sun. The rejoicing which followed was a pretext for a veritable carnival, and the day ended in song and intoxication." Have things changed all that much in New Year celebrations thousands of years later?

[36] The Egyptians also had many animal gods and goddesses in their pantheon, such as Apis the bull, Banaded the ram, Heqt the frog, Hathor the cow, and Sebek the crocodile. (Romans 1:21-23) It was in this religious setting that the Israelites found themselves in captivity as

---

36. (a) What was the religious setting for Israel in the 16th century B.C.E.? (b) What special significance did the Ten Plagues have?

Representations of Horus the falcon, Apis the bull, and Heqt the frog. The Egyptian gods were unable to prevent the plagues that Jehovah sent, including turning the Nile into blood

slaves in the 16th century B.C.E. To release them from Pharaoh's stubborn grip, Jehovah, the God of Israel, had to send ten different plagues against Egypt. (Exodus 7:14–12:36) Those plagues amounted to a calculated humiliation of the mythological gods of Egypt.—See box, page 62.

³⁷ Now let us move on to the gods of ancient Greece and Rome. Rome borrowed many gods from ancient Greece, along with their virtues and vices. (See boxes, pages 43 and 66.) For example, Venus and Flora were brazen prostitutes; Bacchus was a drunkard and reveler; Mercury was a highway robber; and Apollo was a seducer of women. It is reported that Jupiter, the father of the gods, committed adultery or incest with about 59 women! (What a reminder of the rebel angels who cohabited with women before the Flood!) Since worshipers tend to reflect the conduct of their gods, is it any wonder that Roman emperors such as Tiberius, Nero, and Ca-

37. (a) What kind of characters were some of the Roman gods? (b) How did the conduct of the gods affect their followers? (c) What experience did Paul and Barnabas have in Lystra?

Greek deities, from left, Aphrodite; Zeus carrying Ganymede, cupbearer of the gods; and Artemis

ligula led debauched lives as adulterers, fornicators, and murderers?

38 In their religion, the Romans incorporated gods from many traditions. For example, they took up with enthusiasm the worship of Mithras, the Persian god of light, who became their sun-god (see box, pages 60-1), and the Syrian goddess Atargatis (Ishtar). They converted the Grecian Artemis the huntress into Diana and had their own variations of the Egyptian Isis. They also adopted the Celtic triple goddesses of fertility.—Acts 19: 23-28.

39 For the practice of their public cults at hundreds of shrines and temples, they had a variety of priests, all of whom "came under the authority of the Pontifex Maximus [Supreme Pontiff], who was the head of the state religion." (*Atlas of the Roman World*) The same atlas states that one of the Roman ceremonies was the taurobolium, in which "the worshiper stood in a pit and was bathed in the blood of a bull sacrificed over him. He emerged from this rite in a state of purified innocence."

Christian Myths and Legends?

40 According to some modern critics, Christianity also embraces myths and legends. Is that really so? Many scholars reject as myths the virgin birth of Jesus, his miracles, and his resurrection. Some even say he never existed but that his myth is a carryover from more ancient mythology and sun worship. As mythology expert Joseph Campbell wrote: "Several scholars have suggested,

---

38. (a) Describe the kind of worship practiced in Rome. (b) How did religion influence the Roman soldier?
39. (a) Who ruled the Roman priesthood? (b) Describe one of the Roman religious ceremonies.
40. How do many scholars view the events of early Christianity?

therefore, that there was never either John [the Baptizer] or Jesus, but only a water-god and a sun-god." But we need to remember that many of these same scholars are atheists and thus reject totally any belief in God.

[41] However, this skeptical point of view flies in the face of historical evidence. For example, the Jewish historian Josephus (c.37-c.100 C.E.) wrote: "To some of the Jews the destruction of Herod's army seemed to be divine vengeance, and certainly a just vengeance, for his treatment of John, surnamed the Baptist. For Herod had put him to death, though he was a good man."—Mark 1:14; 6: 14-29.

41, 42. What evidence is there to support the historicity of early Christianity?

*M*ythology and Christianity

Worship of the mythical gods of ancient Greece and Rome was in full sway when Christianity came on the scene nearly two thousand years ago. In Asia Minor the Greek names still prevailed, which explains why the people of Lystra (in present-day Turkey) called the Christian healers Paul and Barnabas "gods," referring to them as Hermes and Zeus respectively, rather than as the Roman Mercury and Jupiter. The account says that "the priest of Zeus, whose temple was before the city, brought bulls and garlands to the gates and was desiring to offer sacrifices with the crowds." (Acts 14:8-18) Only with difficulty did Paul and Barnabas convince the crowd not to make sacrifices to them. It illustrates how seriously those people took their mythology back then.

[42] This same historian also testified to the historical existence of Jesus Christ, when he wrote that there arose "a certain Jesus, a wizard of a man, if indeed he may be called a man . . . whom his disciples call a son of God." He continued by saying that "Pilate had sentenced him . . . And even now the race of those who are called 'Messianists' after him is not extinct."*—Mark 15:1-5, 22-26; Acts 11:26.

[43] Therefore, the Christian apostle Peter could write with total conviction as an eyewitness of Jesus' transfiguration, saying: "No, it was not by following artfully contrived false stories [Greek, *my'thos*] that we acquainted you with the power and presence of our Lord Jesus Christ, but it was by having become eyewitnesses of his magnificence. For he received from God the Father honor and glory, when words such as these were borne to him by the magnificent glory: 'This is my son, my beloved, whom I myself have approved.' Yes, these words we heard borne from heaven while we were with him in the holy mountain."—2 Peter 1:16-18.#

[44] In this conflict between man's "expert" opinion and God's Word, we must apply the principle stated earlier: "What, then, is the case? If some did not express faith, will their lack of faith perhaps make the faithfulness of God without effect? Never may that happen! But let God be found true, though every man be found a liar, even as

---

* According to the traditional text of Josephus, footnote, page 48 of the Harvard University Press edition, Volume IX.
# For further information on Christianity, see Chapter 10.

---

43. What basis did the apostle Peter have for believing in Christ?
44. What Bible principle should prevail in any conflict between man's opinions and the Word of God?

it is written: 'That you might be proved righteous in your words and might win when you are being judged.'"—Romans 3:3, 4.

Common Threads

⁴⁵ This brief review of some of the world's mythologies has served to indicate some common features, many of which can be traced back to Babylon, the Mesopotamian cradle of most religions. There are common threads, whether in the facts of creation, or in accounts about a period when demigods and giants occupied the land and a deluge destroyed the wicked, or in the basic religious concepts of sun-worship and an immortal soul.

⁴⁶ From a Biblical viewpoint, we can explain these common threads when we recall that after the Flood, at God's behest mankind spread out from Babel in Mesopotamia more than 4,200 years ago. Although they separated, forming families and tribes with different languages, they started off with the same basic understanding of prior history and religious concepts. (Genesis 11:1-9) Over the centuries, this understanding became distorted and adorned in each culture, resulting in many of the fictions, legends, and myths that have come down to us today. These myths, divorced from Bible truth, failed to bring mankind nearer to the true God.

⁴⁷ However, mankind have also expressed their religious sentiments in various other ways—spiritism, shamanism, magic, ancestor worship, and so on. Do they tell us anything about mankind's search for God?

---

45. What are some of the common threads found in world mythology?
46, 47. (a) What Biblical explanation can we offer for the common origin and threads of mythology? (b) What further aspects of ancient worship will we cover?

CHAPTER 4.

Searching for the Unknown Through **Magic** and **Spiritism**

"MEN of Athens, I behold that in all things you seem to be more given to the fear of the deities than others are." (Acts 17:22) That was what the Christian apostle Paul told a crowd assembled on the Areopagus, or Mars' Hill, in the ancient city of Athens, Greece. Paul made that remark because earlier he had seen that "the city was full of idols." (Acts 17:16) What had he seen?

² Without a doubt, Paul had seen a variety of Greek and Roman gods in that cosmopolitan city, and it was obvious that the life of the people was wrapped up in their worship of the deities. For fear that by chance they might neglect to venerate any important or powerful deity who could thus become incensed, the Athenians even included "an Unknown God" in their worship. (Acts 17:23) That clearly demonstrated their fear of the deities.

³ Of course, fear of the deities, especially of unknown ones, is not limited to the Athenians of the first century. For thousands of years, it has dominated nearly all mankind. In many parts of the world, almost every aspect of

---

1. What did Paul tell the Athenians on the Areopagus? Why?
2. What demonstrated the Athenians' fear of the deities?
3. Is the fear of deities limited to the Athenians?

the people's life is directly or indirectly involved with some deity or with spirits. As we have seen in the previous chapter, the mythologies of the ancient Egyptians, Greeks, Romans, Chinese, and others were deeply rooted in ideas about gods and spirits, which played an important role in personal and national affairs. During the Middle Ages, stories about alchemists, sorcerers, and witches were rampant throughout the realm of Christendom. And the situation is much the same today.

Rites and Superstitions Today

[4] Whether people are aware of it or not, many things that they do are linked with superstitious practices or beliefs, some having to do with deities or spirits. For example, did you know that birthday observance has its origin in astrology, which attaches great importance to one's exact birth date? What about the birthday cake? It appears to be related to the Greek goddess Artemis, whose birthday was celebrated with moon-shaped honey cakes topped with candles. Or did you know that wearing black at funerals was originally a ruse to escape the attention of evil spirits said to be lurking on such occasions? Some black Africans paint themselves white, and mourners in other lands wear unusual colors so that the spirits will not recognize them.

[5] Besides these popular customs, people everywhere have their superstitions and fears. In the West, breaking a mirror, seeing a black cat, walking under a ladder, and, depending on where you are, Tuesday or Friday the 13th

---

4. What are some popular customs that are apparently linked to deities or spirits?
5. What are some common superstitions that you know of?

**Broken mirrors, black cats, and some numbers
are a basis for superstitions. The Chinese character for "four"
sounds like "death" in Chinese and Japanese**

are all viewed as omens foreboding something evil. In the East, the Japanese wear their kimono with the left side folded over the right, for the other way is reserved for corpses. Their houses are built with no windows or doors facing the northeast so that the demons, which are said to come from that direction, will not find the entrance. In the Philippines, people remove the shoes of the dead and place them beside the legs before the burial so that "Saint" Peter will welcome them. Old folks tell youngsters to behave by pointing out that the figure on the moon is "Saint" Michael, watching and writing down their deeds.

⁶ Belief in spirits and deities, however, is not limited to seemingly harmless customs and superstitions. In both primitive and modern societies, people have resorted to various means in order to control or appease the fearsome spirits and to gain the favor of the benevolent ones. Naturally, we may first think of people in remote jungles and mountains who consult spirit mediums, medicine men, and shamans (priests of magic) when sick or otherwise in dire straits. But people in cities large and small also go to astrologers, psychic readers, fortune-tellers, and soothsayers to inquire about the future or to obtain help in making important decisions. Some, even though nominally belonging to one religion or another, pursue such practices with enthusiasm. Many others have made spiritism, black magic, and the occult their religion.

⁷ What is the source or origin of all these practices and superstitions? Are they just different ways of approach to God? And most important, what do they do for those who follow them? To find the answers to these questions, we must look back into the history of man and get a glimpse of his early ways of worship.

Reaching for the Unknown

⁸ Contrary to what evolutionists may claim, a human possesses a spiritual dimension that makes him different from and superior to the lower creatures. He is born with the urge to search out the unknown. He is ever struggling with questions such as: What is the meaning of life? What happens after one dies? What is man's relationship to the

---

6. To what extent are people involved with spiritism today?
7. What questions do we need to consider?
8. What unique quality sets humans apart from lower creatures?

material world and, in fact, to the universe? He is also driven by the desire to reach out to something higher or more powerful than himself in order to gain some control over his environment and his life.—Psalm 8:3, 4; Ecclesiastes 3:11; Acts 17:26-28.

[9] Ivar Lissner in his book *Man, God and Magic* put it this way: "One can only marvel at the perseverance with which man has striven, throughout his history, to reach outside himself. His energies were never directed solely toward the necessities of life. He was forever questing, groping his way further, aspiring to the unattainable. This strange and inherent urge in the human being is his spirituality."

[10] Of course, those who do not believe in God do not view matters quite that way. They generally attribute this human tendency to man's needs, psychological or otherwise, as we have seen in Chapter 2. However, is it not our common experience that when faced with danger or a desperate situation, most people's first response is to appeal to God or some higher power for help? This is just as true today as it was in times past. Thus, Lissner went on to say: "No one who has carried out research among the oldest primitive peoples can fail to understand that they all conceive of God, that they possess a lively awareness of a supreme being."

[11] How they endeavored to satisfy that inborn desire to reach out to the unknown was quite another matter.

---

9. How does one scholar describe "spirituality"?
10. What shows that man has a natural urge to reach out to God?
11. What is the result of man's effort to reach out to the unknown? (Compare Romans 1:19-23.)

Left, Basilica of Our Lady of Guadalupe,
Mexico, where Catholics pray for miraculous cures.
Right, Stonehenge, England, where ancient
Druids are said to have worshiped the sun

Nomadic hunters and herdsmen trembled at the power
of wild beasts. Farmers were particularly attuned to the
changes in weather and seasons. Dwellers of the jungles
reacted quite differently from people living in the deserts
or mountains. In the face of these varied fears and needs,
people developed a bewildering variety of religious practices through which they hoped to appeal to the benevolent gods and appease the fearsome ones.

[12] In spite of the great diversity, however, there are
certain common features recognizable in these religious
practices. Among them are reverence and fear of sacred
spirits and supernatural powers, the use of magic, divin-
ing the future by signs and omens, astrology, and diverse
methods of fortune-telling. As we examine these features,
we will see that they have played a major role in shaping
the religious thinking of people around the world and
throughout the ages, even including people today.

12. What common features can be seen in the religious practices
of people everywhere?

Sacred Spirits and Supernatural Powers

[13] The life of people in early times seemed to be filled with mystery. They were surrounded by inexplicable and perplexing events. For example, they could not understand why a perfectly robust person should suddenly fall ill, or why the sky should fail to give rain at the usual season, or why a bare, seemingly lifeless, tree should turn green and appear full of life at a certain time of the year. Even one's own shadow, heartbeat, and breath were mysteries.

[14] With man's inborn spiritual inclination, it was only natural that he attribute these mysterious things and happenings to some supernatural power. However, lacking proper guidance and understanding, his world soon came to be filled with souls, spirits, ghosts, and demons. For example, the Algonquian Indians of North America call a person's soul *otahchuk,* meaning "his shadow," and the Malays of Southeast Asia believe that when a man dies, his soul escapes through his nostrils. Today, belief in spirits and departed souls—and attempts to communicate with them in some fashion—is nearly universal.

[15] In the same manner, other things in the natural environment—sun, moon, stars, oceans, rivers, mountains—seemed to be alive and to exert a direct influence on human activities. Since these things appeared to occupy a world of their own, they were personified as spirits and deities, some benevolent and helpful, others wicked and harmful. Worship of created things came to occupy a prominent place in almost all religions.

---

13. What might have been puzzling to people in times past?
14, 15. Because of lack of understanding and guidance, to what did man most likely attribute the unexplainable? (Compare 1 Samuel 28:3-7.)

[16] We can find beliefs of this kind in the religions of practically every ancient civilization. The Babylonians and Egyptians worshiped their gods of the sun, moon, and constellations. Animals and wild beasts were also among their objects of veneration. The Hindus are noted for their pantheon of gods, numbering into the millions. The Chinese have always had their sacred mountains and their river gods, and they express their filial piety in ancestor worship. The ancient Druids

Some magic seemed to work

of the British Isles held oak trees as sacred, and they gave special reverence to mistletoe growing on oak. Later, the Greeks and Romans contributed their share; and belief in spirits, deities, souls, demons, and sacred objects of all sorts became solidly entrenched.

[17] Though some people today may view all such beliefs as superstitions, these ideas are still to be found in the religious practices of many people around the world. Some still believe that certain mountains, rivers, strangely shaped rocks, old trees, and numerous other things are sacred, and they worship them as objects of devotion. They build altars, shrines, and temples at these places. For example, the Ganges River is sacred to the Hindus, whose fondest wish is to bathe in it while alive and have their ashes scattered on it after death. Buddhists consider it an extraordinary experience to worship at the shrine in Buddh Gaya, India, where the Buddha is said to have gained enlightenment under a bodhi tree. Catholics go on

16. How was worship of spirits, deities, and sacred objects manifested?
17. How is worship of created things still in evidence today?

their knees to the Basilica of Our Lady of Guadalupe in Mexico or bathe in the "sacred" waters at the shrine in Lourdes, France, in search of miraculous cures. Veneration of created things rather than of the Creator is still very much in evidence today.—Romans 1:25.

The Rise of Magic

[18] Once the belief had been established that the inanimate world was full of spirits, good and bad, it led easily to the next step—attempts to communicate with the good ones for guidance and blessings and to appease the evil ones. The result was the practice of magic, which has flourished in practically every nation past and present. —Genesis 41:8; Exodus 7:11, 12; Deuteronomy 18:9-11, 14; Isaiah 47:12-15; Acts 8:5, 9-13; 13:6-11; 19:18, 19.

[19] In its most basic sense, magic is an effort to control or coerce the natural or supernatural forces to do man's bidding. Not knowing the real cause of many everyday happenings, people in earlier societies believed that the repetition of certain magical words or incantations, or the performance of some ritual, could bring about certain desired effects. What lent credibility to this sort of magic was that some of the rituals actually worked. For example, the medicine men—essentially magicians or sorcerers—of the Mentawai Islands west of Sumatra were reported to be surprisingly effective in curing people suffering from diarrhea. Their magical formula was to have the sufferers lie face down near the edge of a cliff and lick the ground from time to time. What made it work? The soil on the

---

18. To what did the belief in spirits and deities lead?
19. (a) What is magic? (b) Why does magic seem believable to many people?

cliffs contained kaolin, the white clay commonly used in some of today's diarrhea medicines.

[20] A few successes of this kind quickly negated all the failures and established the reputation of the practitioners. They soon became members held in awe and high esteem—priests, chiefs, shamans, medicine men, witch doctors, mediums. People went to them with their problems, such as the healing and the prevention of sickness, finding lost items, identifying thieves, warding off evil influences, and meting out vengeance. Eventually there came to be a large body of superstitious practices and rituals that dealt with these matters as well as other events in life, like birth, coming of age, betrothal, marriage, death, and burial. The power and mystery of magic soon dominated every aspect of the people's lives.

Rain Dances and Spells

[21] In spite of the enormous variety in the magical practices of different peoples, the basic ideas behind them are remarkably similar. First, there is the idea that like produces like, that a desired effect can be produced by mimicking it. This is sometimes called imitative magic. For example, when shortage of rain threatened their crops, the Omaha Indians of North America danced around a vessel of water. Then one of them drank some of the water and spit it into the air in imitation of a sprinkle or shower. Or a man might roll on the ground like a wounded bear to ensure that he would be successful in his bear hunt.

[22] Other people had more elaborate rituals, including chants and offerings. The Chinese would make a large

---

20. How did magic come to dominate people's lives?
21, 22. What is meant by "imitative magic"? Illustrate.

paper or wooden dragon, their rain-god, and parade it around, or they would take the idol of their deity out of the temple and place it in the sun so that it could feel the heat and perhaps send rain. The ritual of the Ngoni people of East Africa includes pouring beer into a pot buried in the ground in a rain temple and then praying, "Master *Chauta,* you have hardened your heart towards us, what would you have us do? We must perish indeed. Give your children the rains, there is the beer we have given you." Then they drink the remaining beer. This is followed by song and dance and the shaking of branches dipped in water.

[23] Another idea behind magical practices is that objects that have belonged to a person continue to influence him even after they are separated from him. This led to the practice of casting a spell on someone by working on something that once belonged to that person. Even in 16th- and 17th-century Europe and England, people still believed in witches and wizards who could cause people harm with this kind of power. The techniques included such things as making a wax image of a person and sticking pins into it, writing his name on a piece of paper and then burning it, burying a piece of his clothing, or doing other things to his hair, fingernail cuttings, sweat, or even excrement. The extent of these and other practices can be seen by the fact that Acts of Parliament were enacted in England in 1542, 1563, and 1604 declaring witchcraft a capital offense. In one manner or another, this form of magic has been practiced by people in almost every nation throughout the ages.

23. How did witchcraft and the casting of spells develop? (Compare Leviticus 19:31; 20:6, 27; Deuteronomy 18:10-13.)

Some people consult shamans and witch doctors

Others have their séances, Ouija boards, crystal balls, tarot cards, and fortune-tellers

The Future in Signs and Omens

[24] Often magic is employed to uncover hidden information or to peer into the future by signs and omens. This is known as divination, and the Babylonians were noted for it. According to the book *Magic, Supernaturalism, and Religion,* "they were masters in the arts of prescience, predicting the future from the livers and intestines of slaughtered animals, from fire and smoke, and from the brilliancy of precious stones; they foretold events from the murmuring of springs and from the shape of plants. . . . Atmospheric signs, rain, clouds, wind, and lightning were interpreted as forebodings; the cracking of furniture and wooden panels foretold future events. . . . Flies and other insects, as well as dogs, were the carriers of occult messages."

[25] The Bible book of Ezekiel reports that on one mili-

---

24. (a) What is divination? (b) How did the Babylonians practice divination?
25. How did Ezekiel and Daniel refer to the practice of divination in ancient Babylon?

tary campaign, "the king of Babylon stood still at the crossways, at the head of the two ways, in order to resort to divination. He has shaken the arrows. He has asked by means of the teraphim; he has looked into the liver." (Ezekiel 21:21) Conjurers, sorcerers, and magic-practicing priests were also a regular part of the Babylonian court. —Daniel 2:1-3, 27, 28.

[26] People of other nations, both Oriental and Occidental, also dabbled in many forms of divination. The Greeks consulted their oracles regarding great political events as well as mundane private affairs such as marriage, travel, and children. The most famous of these was the oracle of Delphi. Answers, thought to be from the god Apollo, were provided through the priestess, or Pythia, in unintelligible sounds and were interpreted by the priests to create ambiguous verses. A classic example was the answer given to Croesus, king of Lydia, which said: "If

26. What was one form of divination popular among the Greeks?

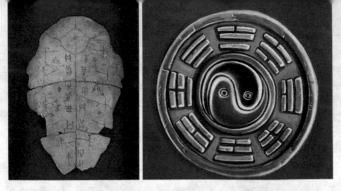

Divination in the Orient, using inscriptions on tortoiseshells and the yin-yang symbol, has a long history

Croesus crosses the Halys, he will destroy a mighty empire." It turned out that the mighty empire destroyed was his own. Croesus met defeat at the hands of Cyrus the Persian when he crossed the Halys to invade Cappadocia.

[27] In the West the craft of divination reached a peak with the Romans, who were preoccupied with omens and portents in nearly everything they did. People of every social class believed in astrology, witchcraft, talismans, fortune-telling, and many other forms of divination. And according to an authority on Roman history, Edward Gibbon, "the various modes of worship, which prevailed in the Roman world, were all considered by the people, as equally true." The famous statesman and orator Cicero was an expert in looking for omens in the flight of birds. The Roman historian Petronius observed that judging by the multitude of religions and cults in some Roman towns, there must have been more gods than people in them.

27. To what extent did the Romans engage in divination?

[28] In China, more than 100,000 pieces of oracle bones and shells dating from the second millennium B.C.E. (the Shang dynasty) have been unearthed. They were used by the Shang priests in seeking divine guidance for everything from weather to the movement of troops. The priests wrote questions in an ancient script on these bones. Then they heated the bones and examined the cracks that appeared and wrote down the answers right on the same bones. Some scholars believe that from this ancient script, Chinese writing developed.

[29] The most well-known ancient Chinese treatise on divination is the *I Ching* (Canon of Changes; pronounced *Yee-Jing*), said to be written by the first two Chou emperors, Wen Wang and Chou Kung, in the 12th century B.C.E. It contains detailed explanations of the interplay of the two opposing forces yin and yang (dark-bright, negative-positive, female-male, moon-sun, earth-heaven, and so on), which many Chinese still believe to be the controlling principles behind all life's affairs. It presents the picture that everything is ever changing and nothing is permanent. To succeed in any undertaking, one must be aware of and act in harmony with all the changes of the moment. Thus, people ask questions and cast lots and then turn to the *I Ching* for answers. Through the centuries, the *I Ching* has been the basis for all manner of fortune-telling, geomancy, and other forms of divination in China.

From Astronomy to Astrology

[30] The orderliness of the sun, moon, stars, and planets has long been a source of fascination for people on earth.

---

28. How did the Chinese practice divination in ancient times?
29. What principle of divination is set forth in *I Ching?*
30. Describe the development of early astronomy.

Star catalogs dating back to 1800 B.C.E. have been discovered in Mesopotamia. Based on such information, the Babylonians were able to predict many astronomical events, such as lunar eclipses, the rising and setting of constellations, and certain movements of the planets. The Egyptians, Assyrians, Chinese, Indians, Greeks, Romans, and other ancient people likewise observed the sky and kept detailed records of astronomical events. From these records they built their calendars and ordered their yearly activities.

[31] From the astronomical observations, it became noticeable that certain events on earth seemed to synchronize with certain celestial events. For example, the change of the seasons followed closely the movement of the sun, the tides ebbed and flowed in phase with the moon, the annual flooding of the Nile always followed the appearance of Sirius, the brightest star. The natural conclusion was that the heavenly bodies played a significant role in causing these and other events on earth. In fact, the Egyptians called Sirius the Bringer of the Nile. The notion that the stars influenced events on earth quickly led to the idea that the heavenly bodies could be counted on to foretell the future. Thus astronomy gave birth to astrology. Soon, kings and emperors kept official astrologers in their courts to consult the stars concerning important national affairs. But the common people likewise looked to the stars regarding their personal fortunes.

[32] The Babylonians, once again, come into the picture. They viewed the stars as the heavenly abodes of the gods, just as the temples were their earthly abodes. This gave

31. How did astronomy give birth to astrology?
32. In what ways did the Babylonians practice astrology?

Is Astrology Scientific?

Astrology claims that the sun, moon, stars, and planets can influence affairs on earth and that the configuration of these heavenly bodies at the moment of one's birth plays a role in one's life. However, scientific discoveries present formidable challenges:

■ The work of astronomers like Copernicus, Galileo, and Kepler has clearly demonstrated that the earth is not the center of the universe. It is also known now that often the stars that appear to be in a constellation are not really bound in a group. Some of them may be deep in space, while others may be relatively near. Thus, the zodiacal properties of the various constellations are purely imaginary.

■ The planets Uranus, Neptune, and Pluto were unknown to early astrologers because they were not discovered until the invention of the telescope. How, then, were their "influences" accounted for by the astrological charts drawn up centuries earlier? Furthermore, why should the "influence" of one planet be "good" and another "evil," when science knows now that basically they are all masses of lifeless rock or gases, hurtling in space?

■ The science of genetics tells us that the basis of our personality traits is formed, not at birth, but at conception, when one of the millions of sperm cells from the father unites with a single egg cell from the mother. Yet, astrology fixes one's horoscope by the moment of birth. This difference of about nine months should give one a completely different personality profile in astrological terms.

■ The timing of the sun's journey among the constellations as seen by an earthbound observer is today about one month behind what it was 2,000 years ago when the astrology charts and tables were drawn up. Thus, astrology would cast a person born in late June or early July as a Cancer (highly sensitive, moody, reserved). Actually, however, the sun is in the constellation Gemini at that time, which should make the person communicative, witty, chatty.

Clearly, astrology has no rational or scientific ground on which to stand.

rise to the concept of grouping the stars into constellations as well as the belief that disturbances in the heavens, such as eclipses or appearances of certain bright stars or comets, foreboded sorrow and war on earth. Hundreds of reports by astrologers to the kings were found among the artifacts unearthed in Mesopotamia. Some of these stated, for instance, that an impending lunar eclipse was a sign that a certain enemy would suffer defeat or that the appearance of a certain planet in a certain constellation would spell "great wrath" on earth.

[33] The extent to which the Babylonians relied on this form of divination can further be seen in the taunting words of the prophet Isaiah against them when foretelling Babylon's destruction: "Stand still, now, with your spells and with the abundance of your sorceries, in which you have toiled from your youth . . . Let them stand up, now, and save you, the worshipers of the heavens, the lookers at the stars, those giving out knowledge at the new moons concerning the things that will come upon you."—Isaiah 47:12, 13.

[34] From Babylon, astrology was exported to Egypt, Assyria, Persia, Greece, Rome, and Arabia. In the East, the Hindus and Chinese also had their elaborate systems of astrology. The "Magi" that the evangelizer Matthew reported came to the infant Jesus were "astrologers from eastern parts." (Matthew 2:1, 2) Some scholars believe that these astrologers might have been of the Chaldean and Medo-Persian school of astrology from Parthia, which had been a province of Persia and later became the independent Parthian Empire.

---

33. What did Isaiah say about the Babylonian "lookers at the stars"?
34. Who were the "Magi" that came to the infant Jesus?

**Many people consult horoscopes, believing
that the position of the sun, moon, planets, and stars
at the moment of birth affects their lives**

³⁵ It was the Greeks, however, who developed astrology into the form that is practiced today. In the second century C.E., Claudius Ptolemy, a Greek astronomer in Alexandria, Egypt, gathered all the existing astrological information into four books, called the *Tetrabiblos,* that have served as the basic text for astrology until now. From this, developed what is commonly called natal astrology, that is, a system for predicting a person's future by

35. What developed in astrology from the time of the Greeks?

studying his birth chart, or horoscope—a chart showing the positions of the sun, the moon, and various planets among the constellations as seen from a person's birthplace at the moment of his birth.

[36] By the 14th and 15th centuries, astrology had gained wide acceptance in the West. Universities taught it as a discipline, which required working knowledge of languages and mathematics. Astrologers were viewed as scholars. The writings of Shakespeare are full of allusions to astrological influences on human affairs. Every royal court and many noblemen retained private astrologers for ready consultation. Hardly any project—be it war, building, business, or travel—was undertaken without the stars' being consulted first. Astrology had become respectable.

[37] Even though the work of astronomers like Copernicus and Galileo, along with the advance of scientific inquiry, has greatly discredited astrology as a legitimate science, it has survived until this day. (See box, page 85.) To heads of State as well as to the man on the street, whether from technologically advanced nations or remote villages in developing countries, this mysterious craft, initiated by the Babylonians, developed by the Greeks, and further expanded by the Arabs, still wields wide influence today.

Destiny Written in the Face and the Palm

[38] If looking to the heavens for signs and omens about

---

36. What is the evidence that astrology became respectable?
37. How has advancement of science affected astrology?
38. What led to further forms of divination related to the human hand and face?

the future seems intangible, there are other more immediate and easily accessible ways available to those who dabble in the art of divination. The *Zohar,* or *Sefer hazohar* (Hebrew, Book of Splendor), a 13th-century text of Jewish mysticism, declared: "On the firmament which envelops the universe, we see many figures formed by the stars and planets. They reveal hidden things and profound mysteries. Similarly, upon our skin which encircles the human being there exist forms and traits that are the stars of our bodies." This philosophy led to further ways of divination, or foretelling the future, by examining the face and the palm of the hand for prophetic signs. Both in the East and in the West, such practices are still widespread. But it is clear that their origins are rooted in astrology and magic.

[39] **Physiognomy** is fortune-telling by examining the features of the face, such as the shape of the eyes, nose, teeth, and ears. In Strasbourg in 1531, one John of Indagine published a book on the subject in which he provided vivid engravings of faces with a variety of shapes of eyes, nose, ears, and so on, along with his interpretations. Interestingly, he quoted the words of Jesus Christ at Matthew 6:22, "If, then, your eye is simple, your whole body will be bright," as the basis for saying that large, bright, and round eyes signified integrity and good health, whereas sunken and small eyes were signs of envy, malice, and suspicion. However, in a similar book, *Compendium of Physiognomy,* published in 1533, the author Bartolommeo Cocle claimed that large and round eyes signified a fickle and lazy person.

---

39. What is physiognomy, and how has it been applied?

By shaking a fortune stick out of the container, the devotee gets a message and an interpretation

⁴⁰ According to diviners, next to the head, the hand reflects the forces from above more than any other part of the body. Thus, reading the lines of the hand to determine one's character and destiny is another popular form of divination—**chiromancy**, commonly referred to simply as palmistry. Chiromancers of the Middle Ages searched the Bible for support of their craft. They came up with verses such as "He sealeth up the hand of every man; that

---

40. (a) What is chiromancy? (b) How was the Bible appealed to for support of chiromancy?

all men may know his work" and "Length of days is in her right hand; and in her left hand riches and honour." (Job 37:7; Proverbs 3:16, *KJ*) The bumps, or mounts, of the hand were also considered because it was thought they represented the planets and thus revealed something about the individual and his future.

[41] Fortune-telling by studying the features of the face and of the hand is immensely popular in the Orient. Besides the professional readers and advisers offering their services, amateurs and do-it-yourselfers abound because books and publications of every level are widely available. People often dabble in palm reading as a source of amusement, but many take such matters seriously. In general, however, people are seldom content with employing just one means of divination. When they are faced with serious problems or important decisions, they will go to their temple, be it Buddhist, Taoist, Shinto, or other, to inquire of the gods, then to the astrologer to consult the stars, to the fortune-teller to read their palm and look at their face, and, after all of that, come home and inquire of their departed ancestors. Somewhere they hope to find an answer that seems appropriate to them.

Just Innocent Fun?

[42] It is natural that everyone should want to know what the future holds. The desire to secure good fortune and to avert what may be harmful is also universal. That is why people throughout the ages have looked to spirits and deities for guidance. In so doing, they became

---

41. How do people in the Orient practice divination?
42. To what has people's natural desire to know the future led them?

involved in spiritism, magic, astrology, and other super-stitious practices. People in the past wore amulets and talismans to protect themselves, and they turned to med-icine men and shamans for cures. People today still carry "Saint" Christopher medals or wear "good luck" charms, and they have their séances, Ouija boards, crystal balls, horoscopes, and tarot cards. Where spiritism and super-stition are concerned, mankind seems to have changed little.

[43] Many people, of course, realize that these are noth-ing but superstitions and that there is no real basis to them. And they might add that they do it just for fun. Others even argue that magic and divination are actually beneficial because they provide psychological assurance to people who might otherwise be too intimidated by the obstacles they face in life. But is all of this just innocent fun or a psychological boost? What really is the source of the spiritistic and magical practices that we have consid-ered in this chapter as well as the many others that we have not mentioned?

[44] In the course of examining the various aspects of spiritism, magic, and divination, we have noted that they are closely tied to beliefs in departed souls and the exis-tence of spirits, good and evil. Thus, fundamentally, belief in spirits, magic, and divination is based on a form of polytheism rooted in the doctrine of the immortality of the human soul. Is this a sound basis on which to build

---

43. (a) How do many feel about spiritism, magic, and divina-tion? (b) What questions about superstitious practices need an-swering?
44. Fundamentally, what can be said about the basis for all such practices?

one's religion? Would you consider worship based on such a foundation acceptable?

[45] The Christians in the first century were confronted with the same questions. They were surrounded by the Greeks and Romans, with their many gods and deities as well as their superstitious rituals. One ritual was the practice of offering food to idols and then sharing in eating the food. Should anyone who loved the true God and was interested in pleasing him participate in such rituals? Note how the apostle Paul answered that question.

[46] "Now concerning the eating of foods offered to idols, we know that an idol is nothing in the world, and that there is no God but one. For even though there are those who are called 'gods,' whether in heaven or on earth, just as there are many 'gods' and many 'lords,' there is actually to us one God the Father, out of whom all things are, and we for him." (1 Corinthians 8:4-6) To Paul and the first-century Christians, true religion was not the worship of many gods, not polytheism, but was devotion to only "one God the Father," whose name the Bible reveals when it says: "That people may know that you, whose name is Jehovah, you alone are the Most High over all the earth." —Psalm 83:18.

[47] We should note, however, that although the apostle Paul said "an idol is nothing," he did not say that the "gods" and "lords" to whom people turned with their magic, divination, and sacrifices were nonexistent. What,

45. What question about food offered to idols confronted the first-century Christians?
46. What did Paul and the early Christians believe about God?
47. How did Paul reveal the true identity of the 'gods and lords in heaven or on earth'?

then, is the point? Paul made it clear later in the same letter when he wrote: "But I say that the things which the nations sacrifice they sacrifice to demons, and not to God." (1 Corinthians 10:20) Yes, through their gods and lords, the nations were actually worshiping the demons —angelic, or spirit, creatures who rebelled against the true God and joined forces with their leader, Satan the Devil.—2 Peter 2:4; Jude 6; Revelation 12:7-9.

[48] Often people take pity on the so-called primitive people who were enslaved by their superstitions and fears. They say they are repulsed by the bloody sacrifices and savage rites. And rightly so. Yet, to this day we still hear about voodoo, satanic cults, even human sacrifices. Though these may be extreme cases, they nonetheless demonstrate that interest in the occult is still very much alive. It might begin with 'innocent fun' and curiosity, but the result is often tragedy and death. How wise it is to heed the Bible's warning: "Keep your senses, be watchful. Your adversary, the Devil, walks about like a roaring lion, seeking to devour someone."—1 Peter 5:8; Isaiah 8:19, 20.

[49] Having considered how religion began, the diversity in ancient mythologies, and the various forms of spiritism, magic, and superstition, we will now turn our attention to the more formal major religions of the world —Hinduism, Buddhism, Taoism, Confucianism, Shinto, Judaism, the churches of Christendom, and Islām. How did they get started? What do they teach? What influence do they have on their believers? These and other questions will be considered in the following chapters.

---

48. What danger from the occult still exists today, and how can it be avoided?
49. What will be the object of the investigation in the subsequent chapters of this book?

Mankind's Search for God

CHAPTER 5

Hinduism
A Search for Liberation

"In Hindu society, it is the religious custom, first thing in the morning, to bathe in a nearby river or at home if no river or stream is at hand. People believe that it makes them holy. Then, still without having eaten, they go to the local temple and make offerings of flowers and food to the local god. Some will wash the idol and decorate it with red and yellow powder.

"Nearly every home has a corner or even a room for worship of the family's favorite god. A popular god in some localities is Ganesa, the elephant god. People will especially pray to him for good fortune, as he is known as a remover of obstacles. In other places Krishna, Rama, Siva, Durga, or some other deity might take first place in devotion."—Tara C., Kathmandu, Nepal.

WHAT is Hinduism? Is it just the oversimplified Western concept of venerating animals, bathing in the Ganges, and being divided by castes? Or is there more to it? The answer: There is much more. Hinduism is a different way of understanding life, to which Western values are totally alien. Westerners tend to see life as a chronological line of events in history. Hindus see life as a self-repeating cycle in which human history is of little importance.

1. (a) Describe some Hindu customs. (b) What are some differences between the Western outlook and the Hindu outlook?

Ganesa, the elephant-headed Hindu god of good fortune,
son of Siva and Parvati

² It is no easy task to define Hinduism, since it has no definite creed, priestly hierarchy, or governing agency. However, it does have swamis (teachers) and gurus (spiritual guides). A broad definition of Hinduism given by one history book states that it is "the whole complex of beliefs and institutions that have appeared from the time when their ancient (and most sacred) scriptures, the Vedas, were composed until now." Another one states: "We might say that Hinduism is adherence to or worship of the gods Vishnu, or Shiva [Siva], or the goddess Shakti, or their incarnations, aspects, spouses, or progeny." That serves to include the cults of Rama and Krishna (incarnations of Vishnu), Durga, Skanda, and Ganesa (respectively the wife and sons of Siva). It is claimed that Hinduism has 330 million gods, yet it is said that Hinduism is not polytheistic. How can that be?

³ Indian writer A. Parthasarathy explains: "The Hindus are not polytheistic. Hinduism speaks of one God . . . The different gods and goddesses of the Hindu pantheon are mere representatives of the powers and functions of the one supreme God in the manifested world."

⁴ Hindus often refer to their faith as *sanatana dharma,* which means eternal law or order. Hinduism* is really a loose term that describes a host of religions and sects (*sampradayas*) that have developed and flourished over the millenniums under the umbrella of the complex ancient Hindu mythology. So intricate is that mythology that the *New Larousse Encyclopedia of Mythology* states:

---

* The name Hinduism is a European invention.

2, 3. (a) Why is it difficult to define Hinduism? (b) How does one Indian writer explain Hinduism and polytheism?
4. What does the term "Hinduism" cover?

"Indian mythology is an inextricable jungle of luxuriant growths. When you enter it you lose the light of day and all clear sense of direction." Nevertheless, this chapter will cover some of the features and teachings of that faith.

Hinduism's Ancient Roots

5 While Hinduism may not be as widespread as some other major religions, nevertheless, it commanded the loyalty of nearly 700 million followers by 1990, or about 1 in 8 (13%) of the world's population. However, most of these are found in India. So it is logical to ask, How and why did Hinduism become concentrated in India?

6 Some historians say that Hinduism had its roots over 3,500 years ago in a wave of migration that brought a pale-skinned, Aryan people down from the northwest into the Indus Valley, now located mainly in Pakistan and India. From there they spread into the Ganges River plains and across India. Some experts say that the religious ideas of the migrants were based on ancient Iranian and Babylonian teachings. One thread common to many cultures and also found in Hinduism is a flood legend.—See box, page 120.

7 But what form of religion was practiced in the Indus Valley before the Aryans arrived? One archaeologist, Sir John Marshall, speaks of " 'The Great Mother Goddess', some representations being pregnant female figurines, the majority being nude female figures with high collars and headdresses. . . . Next comes 'The Male God', 'recognisable at once as a prototype of the historic Siva', seated with the

---

5. How widespread is Hinduism?
6, 7. (a) According to some historians, how did Hinduism reach India? (b) How does Hinduism present its flood legend? (c) According to archaeologist Marshall, what form of religion was practiced in the Indus Valley before the Aryans arrived?

Lingams (phallic symbols) venerated by Hindus.
Siva (god of fertility) is inside one lingam and has
four heads around another

soles of his feet touching (a yoga posture), ithyphallic
(recalling the *lingam* [phallus] cult), surrounded by animals (depicting Shiva's epithet, 'Lord of Beasts'). Stone
representations of phallus and vulva abound, . . . which
point to the cult of the *lingam* and *yoni* of Shiva and his
spouse" (*World Religions—From Ancient History to the
Present*) To this day Siva is revered as the god of fertility,
the god of the phallus, or lingam. The bull Nandi is his
bearer.

[8] Hindu scholar Swami Sankarananda disagrees with
Marshall's interpretation, stating that originally the venerated stones, some known as *Sivalinga*, were symbols of
"the fire of the sky or the sun and the fire of the sun, the
rays." (*The Rigvedic Culture of the Pre-Historic Indus*) He
reasons that "the sex cult . . . did not originate as a
religious cult. It is an after-product. It is a degeneration of

8, 9. (a) How does one Hindu scholar disagree with Marshall's
theory? (b) What counterclaims are made about venerated objects of Hinduism and "Christianity"? (c) What is the basis for the
holy writings of Hinduism?

Sikhism—A Reform Religion

Golden Temple of the Sikhs, Amritsar, Punjab, India

Sikhism, symbolized by three swords and a circle, is the religion of over 17 million people. Most live in the Punjab. The Sikh Golden Temple, set in the midst of an artificial lake, is located in Amritsar, the Sikh holy city. Sikh men are easily recognized by their blue, white, or black turbans, the wearing of which is an essential part of their religious practice, as is their letting their hair grow long.

The Hindi word *sikh* means "disciple." Sikhs are disciples of their founder, Guru Nānak, and followers of the teachings of the ten gurus (Nānak and nine successors) whose writings are in the Sikh holy book, the *Guru Granth Sahib*. The religion got its start in the early 16th century when Guru Nānak wanted to take the best of Hinduism and Islām and form a united religion.

Nānak's mission can be stated in one sentence: "As there is only one God, and He is our Father; therefore, we must all be brothers." Like the Muslims, the Sikhs believe in one God and forbid the use of idols. (Psalm 115:4-9; Matthew 23:8, 9) They follow the Hindu tradition of believing in an immortal soul, reincarnation, and Karma. The Sikh place of worship is called a gurdwara.—Compare Psalm 103:12, 13; Acts 24:15.

One of Guru Nānak's great commandments was: "Always remember God, repeat His name." God is spoken of as the "True One," but no name is given. (Psalm 83: 16-18) Another commandment was "Share what you earn with the less fortunate." In line with this, there is a *langar,* or free kitchen, in every Sikh temple, where people of all kinds may freely eat. There are even free rooms where travelers may spend the night.—James 2:14-17.

The last Guru, Gobind Singh (1666-1708), established a brotherhood of Sikhs called the Khalsa, who follow what are known as the five K's, which are: *kesh,* uncut hair, symbolizing spirituality; *kangha,* a comb in the hair, symbolizing order and discipline; *kirpan,* a sword, signifying dignity, courage, and self-sacrifice; *kara,* a steel bracelet, symbolizing unity with God; *kachh,* shorts as underwear, implying modesty and worn to symbolize moral restraint. —See *The Encyclopedia of World Faiths,* page 269.

The blue turban signifies a mind as broad as the sky, with no place for prejudice

The white turban means a saintly person leading an exemplary life

The black turban is a reminder of the British persecution of the Sikhs in 1919

Other colors are a matter of taste

In ceremonial display Sikh priest relates history of sacred weapons

the original. It is the people who bring down the ideal, which is too high for them to comprehend, to their own levels." As a counterargument to Western criticism of Hinduism, he says that, based on Christian veneration of the cross, a pagan phallic symbol, "Christians . . . are the votaries of a sex cult."

[9] In the course of time, the beliefs, myths, and legends of India were put into writing, and today they form the holy writings of Hinduism. Although these sacred works are extensive, they do not attempt to propose a unified Hindu doctrine.

Hinduism's Holy Writings

[10] The oldest writings are the Vedas, a collection of prayers and hymns known as the *Rig-Veda,* the *Sama-Veda,* the *Yajur-Veda,* and the *Atharva-Veda.* They were composed during several centuries and were completed about 900 B.C.E. The Vedas were later supplemented by other writings, including the Brahmanas and the Upanishads.

[11] The Brahmanas specify how rituals and sacrifices, both domestic and public, are to be performed and go into great detail on their deep meaning. They were put into writing from about 300 B.C.E. or later. The Upanishads (literally, "sittings near a teacher"), also known as the Vedanta and written about 600-300 B.C.E., are treatises that set out the reason for all thought and action, according to Hindu philosophy. The doctrines of samsara

---

10. What are some of Hinduism's oldest writings?
11. (a) What is the difference between the Brahmanas and the Upanishads? (b) What doctrines are expressed in the Upanishads?

(transmigration of the soul) and Karma (the belief that the deeds of a former existence are the cause of one's present state in life) were expressed in these writings.

[12] Another set of writings are the Puranas, or long allegorical stories containing many Hindu myths about gods and goddesses as well as Hindu heroes. This extensive Hindu library also includes the epics of the *Ramayana* and *Mahabharata*. The first is the story of "Lord Rama . . . the most glorious of all characters found in scriptural literature," according to A. Parthasarathy. The *Ramayana* is one of the most popular writings for Hindus, dating from about the fourth century B.C.E. It is the story of the hero Rama, or Ramachandra, viewed by Hindus as a model son, brother, and husband. He is considered to be the seventh avatar (incarnation) of Vishnu, and his name is often invoked as a greeting.

[13] According to Bhaktivedanta Swami Prabhupāda, founder of the International Society for Krishna Consciousness, *"Bhagavad-gītā* [part of the *Mahabharata*] is the supreme instruction of morality. The instructions of *Bhagavad-gītā* constitute the supreme process of religion and the supreme process of morality. . . . The last instruction of the *Gītā* is the last word of all morality and religion: surrender unto Kṛṣṇa [Krishna]."—*BG*.

[14] The *Bhagavad Gita* (Celestial Song), viewed by some as "the jewel of India's spiritual wisdom," is a battle-field conversation "between Lord Śrī Kṛṣṇa [Krishna],

12. Who was Rama, and where is his story found?
13, 14. (a) According to one Hindu source, what is the *Bhagavad Gita?* (b) What do Sruti and Smriti mean, and what is the *Manu Smriti?*

Jainism—Self-Denial and Nonviolence

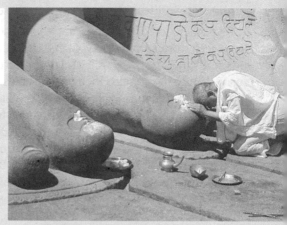

A Jain worshiping at the feet of the 57-foot-high image of the saint Gomateswara in Karnataka, India

This religion, with its ancient Indian swastika symbol, was founded in the sixth century B.C.E. by the wealthy Indian prince Nataputta Vardhamāna, better known as Vardhamana Mahāvīra (a title meaning "Great Man" or "Great Hero"). He turned to a life of self-denial and asceticism. He set out naked in search of knowledge "through the villages and plains of central India in quest of release from the cycle of birth, death, and rebirth." (*Man's Religions*, by John B. Noss) He believed that the salvation of the soul could be achieved only through extreme self-denial and self-discipline and a rigid application of ahimsa,

nonviolence to all creatures. He took ahimsa to the extreme of carrying a soft broom with which he could gently sweep away any insects that might be in his path. His respect for life was also to protect the purity and integrity of his own soul.

His followers today, in an effort to improve their Karma, lead a similar life of self-denial and respect for all other creatures. Again we see the powerful effect on human lives of the belief in the immortality of the human soul.

Today there are fewer than four million believers of this faith, and most are in the Bombay and Gujarat areas of India.

the Supreme Personality of Godhead, and Arjuna, His intimate friend and devotee, whom He instructs in the science of self-realization." However, the *Bhagavad Gita* is only one part of the extensive Hindu holy library. Some of these writings (Vedas, Brahmanas, and the Upanishads) are viewed as Sruti, or "heard," and are therefore considered to be directly revealed sacred writ. Others, such as the epics and the Puranas, are Smriti, or "remembered," and thus composed by human authors, although derived from revelation. One example is the *Manu Smriti*, which sets out Hindu religious and social law, in addition to explaining the basis for the caste system. What are some of the beliefs that have arisen from these Hindu writings?

Teachings and Conduct—Ahimsa and Varna

[15] In Hinduism, as in other religions, there are certain basic concepts that influence thinking and daily conduct. An outstanding one is that of ahimsa (Sanskrit, *ahinsa*), or nonviolence, for which Mohandas Gandhi (1869-1948), known as the Mahatma, was so famous. (See box, page 113.) On the basis of this philosophy, Hindus are not supposed to kill or do violence to other creatures, which is one of the reasons why they venerate some animals, such as cows, snakes, and monkeys. The strictest exponents of this teaching of ahimsa and respect for life are the followers of Jainism (founded in the sixth century B.C.E.), who go barefoot and even wear a mask so as not to swallow accidentally any insect. (See box, page 104, and photo, page 108.) In contrast, the Sikhs are known

15. (a) Define ahimsa, and explain how Jains apply it. (b) How did Gandhi view ahimsa? (c) How do Sikhs differ from Hindus and Jains?

Simple Guide to Hindu Terms

ahimsa (Sanskrit, *ahinsa*)—non-violence; not hurting or killing anything. Basis for Hindu vegetarianism and respect for animals

ashram—a shrine or place where a **guru** (spiritual guide) teaches

ātman—spirit; associated with that which is deathless. Often mistakenly translated soul. See *jīva*

avatar—a manifestation or an incarnation of a Hindu deity

bhakti—devotion to a deity that leads to salvation

bindi—a red spot that married women wear on the forehead

Brahman—the priestly and highest level of the caste system; also the Ultimate Reality. See page 116

dharma—the ultimate law of all things; that which determines the rightness or wrongness of acts

ghat—stairway or platform by a river

guru—teacher or spiritual guide

Harijan—member of the Untouchable caste; means "people of God," compassionate name given them by Mahatma Gandhi

japa—worship of God by repetition of one of his names; a *mala*, or rosary of 108 beads, is used to keep count

jīva (**or prān, prāni**)—the personal soul or being

Karma—the principle that every action has its positive or negative consequences for the next life of the transmigrated soul

Kshatriya—the professional, governing, and warrior class and the second level of the caste system

mahant—holy man or teacher

mahatma—Hindu saint, from *maha*, high or great, and *ātman*, spirit

mantra—a sacred formula, believed to have magical power, used in initiation into a sect and repeated in prayers and incantations

maya—the world as an illusion

moksha, or mukti—release from the cycle of rebirth; the end of the soul's journey. Also known as **Nirvana**, the union of the individual with the Supreme Entity, Brahman

OM, AUM—a word symbol representing Brahman used for meditation; sound considered to be the mystic vibration; used as a sacred mantra

paramatman—the World-Spirit, the universal *ātman*, or Brahman

puja—worship

sadhu—a holy man; an ascetic or yogi

samsara—transmigration of an eternal, imperishable soul

From left, Hindu mahant; sadhu, standing in meditation; guru from Nepal

Shakti—the female power or the wife of a god, especially Siva's consort

sraddha—important rites conducted to honor ancestors and assist departed souls in attaining **moksha**

Sudra—laborer, the lowest of the four main castes

swami—teacher or higher level of spiritual guide

tilak—a mark on the forehead that symbolizes the retention of the memory of the Lord in all his activities

Trimurti—Hindi triad of **Brahma**, **Vishnu**, and **Siva**

Upanishads—early sacred poetic writings of Hinduism. Also known as Vedanta, the end of the **Vedas**

Vaisya—class of merchants and farmers; third group in the caste system

Vedas—earliest sacred poetic writings of Hinduism

Yama—the god of death; he keeps track of each one's **Karma** to determine the quality of the next life

Yoga—from the root *yuj*, meaning to join or yoke; involves the joining of the individual to the universal divine being. Popularly known as the discipline of meditation involving posture and breath control. Hinduism recognizes at least four main Yogas, or paths. See page 110

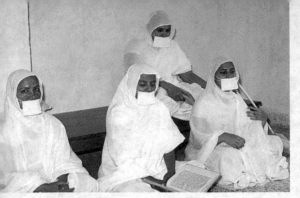

Jain nuns wearing the *mukha-vastrika*, or mouthpiece, that prevents insects from entering and being killed

for their warrior tradition, and Singh, a common last name among them, means lion.—See box, pages 100-101.

[16] A universally known aspect of Hinduism is varna, or the caste system, which divides society into rigid classes. (See box, page 113.) One cannot help noticing that Hindu society is still stratified by this system, although it is rejected by Buddhists and Jains. However, just as racial discrimination persists in the United States and elsewhere, so likewise the caste system is deeply embedded in the Indian psyche. In a way it is a form of class consciousness that, in a parallel way, can still be found today to a lesser degree in British society and in other lands. (James 2:1-9) Thus, in India a person is born into a rigid caste system, and there is almost no way out. Furthermore, the average Hindu does not seek a way out. He views it as his predetermined, inescapable lot in life, the result of his deeds in a prior existence, or Karma. But how did the caste system originate? Once again we have to turn to Hindu mythology.

16. (a) How do most Hindus view the caste system? (b) What did Gandhi say about the caste system?

Mankind's Search for God

[17] According to Hindu mythology, there were originally four major castes based on the body parts of Purusha, mankind's original father-figure. The hymns of the *Rig-Veda* state:

"When they divided Purusha how many portions did they make?

What do they call his mouth, his arms? What do they call his thighs and feet?

The Brahman [the highest caste] was his mouth, of both his arms was the Rajanya made.

His thighs became the Vaisya, from his feet the Sudra was produced."—*The Bible of the World*.

[18] Thus, the priestly Brahmans, the highest caste, were supposed to have originated from Purusha's mouth, his highest part. The governing, or warrior, class (Kshatriya or Rajanya) came from his arms. The merchant and farmer class, called the Vaisya, or Vaishya, originated from his thighs. A lower caste, the Sudra, or Shudra, or laborer class, resulted from the lowest part of the body, his feet.

[19] Over the centuries even lower castes came into existence, the outcastes and the Untouchables, or as Mahatma Gandhi called them more kindly, the Harijans, or "persons belonging to the god Vishnu." Although untouchability has been illegal in India since 1948, the Untouchables still have a very hard existence.

[20] In the course of time, the castes multiplied to match just about every profession and artisanship in Indian society. This ancient caste system, which keeps everyone

17, 18. According to Hindu mythology, how did the caste system start?
19. What other castes came into existence?
20. What are other aspects of the caste system?

Four Ways to Moksha

The Hindu faith offers at least four ways to achieve moksha, or liberation of the soul. These are known as yogas or margas, paths to moksha.

1. **Karma Yoga**—"The way of action, or *karma yoga,* the discipline of action. Basically, karma marga means performing one's dharma according to one's place in life. Certain duties are required of all people, such as ahimsa and abstention from alcohol and meat, but the specific dharma of each individual depends on that person's caste and stage in life."—*Great Asian Religions.*

This Karma is performed strictly within caste limitations. Purity of caste is maintained by neither marrying nor eating outside of one's caste, which was determined by one's Karma in a previous existence. Therefore one's caste is not viewed as an injustice but as a legacy from a previous incarnation. In Hindu philosophy men and women are not all equal. They are divided by caste and by sex and, in effect, by color. Usually the lighter the skin, the higher the caste.

2. **Jnana Yoga**—"The way of knowledge, or *jnana yoga,* the discipline of knowledge. In contrast to the way of action, karma marga, with its prescribed duties for every occasion in life, jnana marga provides a philosophical and psychological way of knowing the self and the universe. *Being, not doing, is the key to jnana marga.* [Italics ours.] Most importantly, this way makes moksha possible in this life for its practitioners." (*Great Asian Religions*) It involves introspective yoga and withdrawal from the world and the practice of austerities. It is the expression of self-control and self-denial.

3. **Bhakti Yoga**—"The most popular form of the Hindu tradition today. This is the way of devotion, bhakti marga. In contrast to karma marga . . . this path is easier, more spontaneous, and may be followed by persons of any caste, sex, or age. . . . [It] allows human emotions and desires to flow freely rather than to be overcome by yogic asceticism . . . [It] consists exclusively of devotion to divine beings." And there are traditionally 330 million to venerate. According to this tradition, to know is to love. In fact, bhakti means "emotional attachment to one's chosen god."—*Great Asian Religions.*

4. **Raja Yoga**—A method of "special postures, methods of breathing, and rhythmical repetition of the proper thought-formulas." (*Man's Religions*) It has eight steps.

in his or her social place, is in reality also racial and "includes distinct racial types varying from what is known as the [light-skinned] Aryan to the [darker-skinned] pre-Dravidian stocks." Varna, or caste, means "color." "The first three castes were Aryans, the fairest people; the fourth caste, that comprising the dark-skinned aborigines, was non-Aryan." (*Myths and Legends Series—India,* by Donald A. Mackenzie) It is a fact of India's life that the caste system, fortified by the religious teaching of Karma, has millions of people locked into perpetual poverty and injustice.

The Frustrating Cycle of Existence

[21] Another basic belief that affects Hindu ethics and conduct, and one of the most vital, is the teaching of Karma. This is the principle that every action has its consequences, positive or negative; it determines each existence of the transmigrated or reincarnated soul. As the *Garuda Purana* explains:

"A man is the creator of his own fate, and even in his foetal life he is affected by the dynamics of the works of his prior existence. Whether confined in a mountain fastness or lulling on the bosom of a sea, whether secure in his mother's lap or held high above her head, a man cannot fly from the effects of his own prior deeds. . . . Whatever is to befall a man on any particular age or time will surely overtake him then and on that date."

The *Garuda Purana* continues:

"Knowledge acquired by a man in his prior birth, wealth given away in charity in his prior existence, and works done by him in a previous incarnation, go ahead of his soul in its sojourn."

---

21. According to the *Garuda Purana,* how does Karma affect a person's destiny?

[22] On what does this belief hinge? The immortal soul is essential to the teaching of Karma, and Karma is what makes the Hindu view of the soul differ from that of Christendom. The Hindu believes that each personal soul, *jīva* or *prān,** passes through many reincarnations and possibly "hell." It must strive to unite with the "Supreme Reality," also called Brahman, or Brahm (not to be confused with the Hindu god Brahma). On the other hand, Christendom's doctrines offer the soul the options of heaven, hell, purgatory, or Limbo, depending on the religious persuasion.—Ecclesiastes 9:5, 6, 10; Psalm 146:4.

[23] As a consequence of Karma, Hindus tend to be fatalistic. They believe that one's present status and condition is the result of a previous existence and is therefore deserved, whether good or bad. The Hindu can try to establish a better record so that the next existence might be more bearable. Thus, he more readily accepts his lot in life than does a Westerner. The Hindu sees it all as the outworking of the law of cause and effect in relation to his prior existence. It is the principle of reaping what you have sown in a supposed former existence. All of this, of course, is based on the premise that man has an immortal

---

* In Sanskrit, "soul" is often translated from *ātma,* or *ātman,* but "spirit" is a more accurate translation.—See *A Dictionary of Hinduism —Its Mythology, Folklore and Development 1500 B.C.–A.D. 1500,* page 31, and the booklet *Victory Over Death—Is It Possible for You?* published by the Watchtower Bible and Tract Society of New York, Inc., in 1986.

---

22. (a) What difference is there between the Hindu options for the soul after death and those of Christendom? (b) What is the Bible teaching on the soul?
23. How does Karma affect the Hindu view of life? (Compare Galatians 6:7-10.)

Mahatma Gandhi and the Caste System

Mahatma Gandhi (1869-1948), revered Hindu leader and teacher of ahimsa

"Nonviolence is the first article of my faith. It is also the last article of my creed."—Mahatma Gandhi, March 23, 1922.

Mahatma Gandhi, famous for his nonviolent leadership in helping to achieve India's independence from Britain (granted in 1947), also campaigned to improve the lot of millions of fellow Hindus. As Indian Professor M. P. Rege explains: "He proclaimed *ahimsa* (nonviolence) as the fundamental moral value, which he interpreted as concern for the dignity and well-being of every person. He denied the authority of the Hindu scriptures when their teaching was contrary to *ahimsa*, strove valiantly for the eradication of untouchability and the hierarchical caste system, and promoted the equality of women in all spheres of life."

What was Gandhi's view of the lot of the Untouchables? In a letter to Jawaharlal Nehru, dated May 2, 1933, he wrote: "The Harijan movement is too big for mere intellectual effort. There is nothing so bad in the world. And yet I cannot leave religion and therefore Hinduism. My life would be a burden to me if Hinduism failed me. I love Christianity, Islam and many other faiths through Hinduism. . . . But then I cannot tolerate it with untouchability."—*The Essential Gandhi*.

soul that passes on to another life, whether that be as a human, an animal, or a vegetable.

^{24} So, what is the ultimate aim in the Hindu faith? To achieve moksha, which means liberation, or release, from the grinding wheel of rebirths and different existences. Therefore, it is an escape from embodied existence, not for the body, but for the "soul." "Since moksha, or release from the long series of incarnations, is the goal of every Hindu, the biggest event in his life is really his death," states one commentator. Moksha can be achieved by following the different margas, or ways. (See box, page 110.) Oh, how much of this religious teaching hangs on the ancient Babylonian concept of the immortal soul!

^{25} Yet, according to the Bible, this despising and disdaining of the material life is diametrically opposed to Jehovah God's original purpose for mankind. When he created the first human pair, he assigned them to a happy, joyful earthly existence. The Bible account tells us:

"And God proceeded to create the man in his image, in God's image he created him; male and female he created them. Further, God blessed them and God said to them: 'Be fruitful and become many and fill the earth and subdue it, and have in subjection the fish of the sea and the flying creatures of the heavens and every living creature that is moving upon the earth.' ... After that God saw everything he had made and, look! it was very good." (Genesis 1:27-31)

---

24. What is moksha, and how does the Hindu believe it is achieved?
25. How does the Hindu view of life differ from the Bible viewpoint?

The Bible prophesies an imminent era of peace and justice for the earth, an era in which each family will have its own decent dwelling, and perfect health and life will be mankind's everlasting lot.—Isaiah 65:17-25; 2 Peter 3:13; Revelation 21:1-4.

[26] The next question to answer is, Who are the gods a Hindu must please in order to achieve good Karma?

The Pantheon of Hindu Gods

[27] While Hinduism may lay claim to millions of gods, in actual practice there are certain favorite gods that have become the focal point for various sects within Hinduism. Three of the most prominent gods are included in what Hindus call Trimurti, a trinity, or triad of gods.—For other Hindu gods, see box, pages 116-17.

[28] The triad consists of Brahma the Creator, Vishnu the Preserver, and Siva the Destroyer, and each has at least one wife or consort. Brahma is wedded to Saraswati, the goddess of knowledge. Vishnu's wife is Lakshmi, while Siva's first wife was Sati, who committed suicide. She was

26. What question now needs an answer?
27, 28. (a) Which gods form the Hindu Trimurti? (b) Who are their wives or consorts? (c) Name some other Hindu gods and goddesses.

Snake worship, practiced mainly in Bengal. Manasa is the goddess of snakes

Hinduism—Some Gods and Goddesses

Aditi—mother of the gods; sky-goddess; the Infinite

Agni—god of fire

Brahma—the Creator God, the principle of creation in the universe. One of the gods of the **Trimurti** (triad)

Brahman, or Brahm—the Supreme, all-pervasive entity of the universe, represented by the sound OM or AUM. (See symbol above.) Also referred to as Atman. Some Hindus view Brahman as an impersonal Divine Principle or Ultimate Reality

Buddha—Gautama, founder of Buddhism; Hindus view him as an incarnation (avatar) of **Vishnu**

Durga—wife or Shakti of **Siva** and identified with **Kali**

Ganesa (Ganesha)—**Siva's** elephant-headed son-god, Lord of Obstacles, god of good fortune. Also called **Ganapati** and **Gajanana**

Ganga—goddess, one of **Siva's** wives and personification of the river Ganges

Hanuman—monkey god and devoted follower of **Rama**

Himalaya—abode of snow, father of **Parvati**

Kali—**Siva's** black consort (Shakti) and bloodthirsty goddess of destruction. Often portrayed with large red tongue hanging out

Krishna—the playful eighth incarnation of **Vishnu** and the deity of the *Bhagavad Gita*. His lovers were the gopis, or milkmaids

Lakshmi—goddess of beauty and good fortune; **Vishnu's** consort

Manasa—goddess of snakes

Manu—ancestor of the human race; saved from the flood's destruction by a great fish

Mitra—god of light. Known as Mithras to the Romans

Nandi—the bull, **Siva's** vehicle or mode of transport

Nataraja—**Siva** in dance posture encompassed by a ring of flames

Parvati or **Uma**—goddess consort of **Siva**. Also takes the form of goddess **Durga** or **Kali**

Prajapati—Creator of the universe, Lord of Creatures, father of gods, demons, and all other creatures. Later known as **Brahma**

Purusha—cosmic man. The four main castes were made from his body

Radha—consort of **Krishna**

Rama, Ramachandra—the seventh incarnation of the god **Vishnu.** The epic narrative *Ramayana* relates the story of **Rama** and his wife **Sita**

Saraswati—goddess of knowledge and consort of **Brahma** the Creator

From top left, clockwise, Nataraja (dancing Siva), Saraswati, Krishna, Durga (Kali)

Shashti—goddess who protects women and children in childbirth

Siva—god of fertility, death, and destruction; a member of the **Trimurti.** Symbolized by the trident and the phallus

Soma—both a god and a drug; the elixir of life

Vishnu—god the preserver of life; third member of the **Trimurti**

(Based on listing in *Mythology—An Illustrated Encyclopedia*)

Vishnu, with his wife Lakshmi, on the coils
of the serpent Ananta with the four-headed Brahma
on a lotus growing from Vishnu's navel

the first woman to enter sacrificial fire, and thus she
became the first suttee. Following her mythological example, thousands of Hindu widows over the centuries have
sacrificed themselves on their husband's funeral pyre,
although this practice is now illegal. Siva also has another
wife known by several names and titles. In her benign
form, she is Parvati and Uma, as well as Gauri, the Golden
One. As Durga or Kali, she is a terrifying goddess.

²⁹ Brahma, although central to Hindu mythology, does
not occupy a place of importance in the worship of the

29. How is Brahma viewed by Hindus? (Compare Acts 17:22-31.)

average Hindu. In fact very few temples are dedicated to him, even though he is called Brahma the Creator. However, Hindu mythology attributes the assignment of creating the material universe to a supreme being, source, or essence—Brahman, or Brahm, identified with the sacred syllable OM or AUM. All three members of the triad are considered part of that "Being," and all other gods are viewed as different manifestations. Whichever god is then worshiped as supreme, that deity is thought to be all-embracing. So while Hindus openly venerate millions of gods, most acknowledge only one true God, who can take many forms: male, female, or even animal. Therefore, Hindu scholars are quick to point out that Hinduism is actually monotheistic, not polytheistic. Later Vedic thinking, however, discards the concept of a supreme being, replacing it with an impersonal divine principle or reality.

[30] Vishnu, a benevolent solar and cosmic deity, is the center of worship for the followers of Vaishnavism. He appears under ten avatars, or incarnations, including Rama, Krishna, and the Buddha.* Another avatar is Vishnu Narayana, "represented in human form asleep on the coiled serpent Shesha or Ananta, floating on the cosmic waters with his wife, the goddess Lakshmi, seated at his feet while the god Brahma arises from a lotus growing out of Vishnu's navel."—*The Encyclopedia of World Faiths.*

---

* A tenth and future avatar is that of Kalki Avatara "depicted as a magnificent youth riding a great white horse with a meteor-like sword raining death and destruction on all sides." "His coming will re-establish righteousness on earth, and the return of an age of purity and innocence."—*Religions of India; A Dictionary of Hinduism.*—Compare Revelation 19:11-16.

---

30. What are some of the avatars of Vishnu?

³¹ Siva, also commonly called Mahesha (Supreme Lord) and Mahadeva (Great God), is Hinduism's second-greatest god, and the worship rendered to him is called Saivism. He is described as "the great ascetic, the master yogin who sits wrapped in meditation on the slopes of the Himalayas, his body smeared with ashes and his head covered in matted hair." He is also noted "for his eroticism, as the bringer of fertility and the supreme lord of creation, *Mahadeva.*" (*The Encyclopedia of World Faiths*) Worship is rendered to Siva by means of the lingam, or phallic representation.—See photos, page 99.

31. What kind of god is Siva?

*H*indu Legend of the Flood

"In the morning they brought to Manu [mankind's ancestor and first lawgiver] water for washing . . . When he was washing himself, a fish [Vishnu in his incarnation as Matsya] came into his hands.

"It spoke to him the word, 'Rear me, I will save thee!' 'Wherefrom wilt thou save me?' 'A flood will carry away all these creatures: from that I will save thee!' 'How am I to rear thee?'"

The fish instructed Manu on how to care for him. "Thereupon it said, 'In such and such a year that flood will come. Thou shalt then attend to me (to my advice) by preparing a ship; and when the flood has risen thou shalt enter into the ship, and I will save thee from it.'"

Manu followed the fish's instructions, and during the flood the fish pulled the ship to a "northern mountain. It then said, 'I have saved thee. Fasten the ship to a tree; but let not the water cut thee off, whilst thou art on the mountain. As the water subsides, thou mayest gradually descend!'"—*Satapatha-Brahmana;* compare Genesis 6:9–8:22.

[32] Like many other world religions, Hinduism has its supreme goddess, who can be attractive or terrifying. In her more pleasant form, she is known as Parvati and Uma. Her fearsome character is displayed as Durga or Kali, a bloodthirsty goddess who delights in blood sacrifices. As the Mother Goddess, Kali Ma (Black Earth-Mother), she is the chief deity for the Shakti sect. She is depicted as naked to the hips and wearing adornments of corpses, snakes, and skulls. In times past, strangled human victims were offered to her by believers known as *thugi,* from which came the English word "thug."

Hinduism and the River Ganges

[33] We cannot speak of Hinduism's pantheon of gods without mentioning its most sacred river—the Ganges. Much of Hindu mythology is directly related to the river Ganges, or *Ganga Ma* (Mother Ganga), as devout Hindus call it. (See map, page 123.) They recite a prayer that includes 108 different names for the river. Why is the Ganges so revered by sincere Hindus? Because it is so closely associated with their daily survival and with their ancient mythology. They believe that it formerly existed in the heavens as the Milky Way. Then how did it come to be a river?

[34] With some variations most Hindus would explain it like this: Maharajah Sagara had 60,000 sons who were killed by the fire of Kapila, a manifestation of Vishnu. Their souls were condemned to hell unless the goddess Ganga would come down from heaven to cleanse them

32. (a) What forms does the goddess Kali take? (b) How was an English word derived from her worship?
33. Why is the Ganges sacred to Hindus?
34. According to Hindu mythology, what is one explanation of how the river Ganges came to exist?

and release them from the curse. Bhagīratha, a great-grandson of Sagara, interceded with Brahma to allow the sacred Ganga to come down to the earth. One account continues: "Ganga replied. 'I am so mighty a torrent I would shatter the earth's foundations.' So [Bhagīratha], after doing penance for a thousand years, went to the god Shiva, the greatest of all ascetics, and persuaded him to stand high above the earth amidst the rock and ice of the Himalayas. Shiva had matted hair piled on his head, and he allowed Ganga to thunder down from the skies into his locks, which absorbed gently the earth-threatening shock. Ganga then trickled softly out on to the earth and flowed down from the mountains and across the plains, bringing water and therefore life to the dry earth."—*From the Ocean to the Sky,* by Sir Edmund Hillary.

[35] The followers of Vishnu have a somewhat different version of how the Ganges was started. According to an ancient text, the *Vishnu Purana,* their version is:

"From this region [the holy seat of Vishnu] proceeds the river Ganges, that removes all sins . . . She issues from the nail of the great toe of Vishnu's left foot."

Or as Vishnu's followers say in Sanskrit: *"Visnu-padabja-sambhuta,"* which means "Born of the lotus-like foot of Vishnu."

[36] Hindus believe that the Ganges has the power to release, purify, cleanse, and cure believers. The *Vishnu Purana* states:

"Saints, who are purified by bathing in the waters of this

---

35. How do the followers of Vishnu explain the river's existence?
36. What do Hindus believe about the power of the waters of the Ganges?

The Ganges runs over 1,500 miles from the Himalayas to Calcutta and its delta in Bangladesh

Ganga Ma, on top of Siva's head, descends through his hair

Calcutta

INDIA

Devout Hindus at a ghat, bathing in the Ganges at Varanasi, or Benares

river, and whose minds are devoted to Kesava [Vishnu], obtain final liberation. The sacred river, when heard of, desired, seen, touched, bathed in, or hymned, day by day purifies all beings. And those who living even at a distance . . . exclaim 'Ganga and Ganga' are relieved of the sins committed during the three previous existences."

The Brahmandapurana states:

"Those who bathe devoutly once in the pure currents of the Ganga, their tribes are protected by Her from hundreds of thousands of dangers. Evils accumulated through generations are destroyed. Just by bathing in the Ganga one gets immediately purified."

[37] Indians flock to the river to perform puja, or worship, by offering flowers, chanting prayers, and receiving from a priest the tilak, the spot of red or yellow paste on the forehead. Then they wade into the waters to bathe. Many will also drink the water, even though it is heavily polluted by sewage, chemicals, and cadavers. Yet such is the spiritual attraction of the Ganges that it is the ambition of millions of Indians to bathe at least once in their 'holy river,' polluted or not.

[38] Others bring the bodies of their loved ones to be burned on pyres by the riverside, and then the ashes may be strewn in the river. They believe that this guarantees eternal bliss for the departed soul. Those too poor to pay for a funeral pyre just push the shrouded body off into the river, where it is attacked by scavenger birds or just decomposes. This brings us to the question, In addition to what we have considered already, what does Hinduism teach about life after death?

37, 38. Why do millions of Hindus flock to the Ganges?

[39] The *Bhagavad Gita* gives an answer when it says: "As the embodied soul continually passes, in this body, from boyhood to youth, and then to old age, the soul similarly passes into another body at death."—Chapter 2, text 13.

[40] One Hindu comment on this text states: "Since every living entity is an individual soul, each is changing his body at every moment, manifesting sometimes as a child, sometimes as a youth, and sometimes as an old man —although the same spirit soul is there and does not undergo any change. This individual soul finally changes the body itself, in transmigrating from one to another, and since it is sure to have another body in the next birth —either material or spiritual—there was no cause for lamentation by Arjuna on account of death."

[41] Notice that the commentary states that "every living entity is an individual soul." Now that statement agrees with what the Bible says at Genesis 2:7:

"And Jehovah God proceeded to form the man out of dust from the ground and to blow into his nostrils the breath of life, and the man came to be a living soul."

But an important distinction has to be made: Is man constituted a living soul with all his functions and faculties, or does he *have* a soul apart from his bodily functions? Is man a soul, or does he have a soul? The following quotation clarifies the Hindu concept.

[42] Chapter 2, text 17, of the *Bhagavad Gita* states:

39, 40. What does one Hindu commentator say about the soul?
41. According to the Bible, what distinction regarding the soul has to be made?
42. How do Hinduism and the Bible differ on the understanding of the soul?

"That which pervades the entire body is indestructible. No one is able to destroy the imperishable soul."

This text is then explained:

"Each and every body contains an individual soul, and the symptom of the soul's presence is perceived as individual consciousness."

Therefore, while the Bible states that man *is* a soul, Hindu teaching states that he *has* a soul. And there is a world of difference here that deeply affects the teachings that are a consequence of these viewpoints.—Leviticus 24:17, 18.

[43] The teaching of the immortal soul is ultimately drawn from ancient Babylon's stagnant pool of religious knowledge. It logically leads into the 'life after death' consequences that are featured in the teachings of so many religions—reincarnation, heaven, hell, purgatory, Limbo, and so forth. For the Hindu, heaven and hell are intermediate waiting places before the soul gets its next reincarnation. Of special interest is the Hindu concept of hell.

Hindu Teaching of Hell

[44] One text from the *Bhagavad Gita* states:

"O Kṛṣṇa [Krishna], maintainer of the people, I have heard by authorities that those who destroy family traditions dwell . . . in hell."—Chapter 1, text 43.

A commentary says: "Those who are very sinful in their earthly life have to undergo different kinds of punishment on hellish planets." However, there is one shade of difference with Christendom's eternal hellfire torment: "This punishment . . . is not eternal." Then, what exactly is the Hindu hell?

---

43. (a) What is the origin of the immortal soul teaching? (b) What are its consequences?
44. How do we know that Hinduism teaches that there is a hell of conscious torment?

[45] The following is a description of the fate of a sinner, taken from the *Markandeya Purana:*

"Then the emissaries of Yama [god of the dead] quickly bind him with dreadful nooses and drag him to the south, trembling with the stroke of the rod. Then he is dragged by the emissaries of Yama, sending out dreadful, inauspicious yells through grounds rough with [the plant] Kusa, thorns, ant-hills, pins and stones, glowing with flames at places, covered with pits, blazing with the heat of the sun and burning with its rays. Dragged by the dreadful emissaries and eaten by hundreds of jackals, the sinful person goes to Yama's house through a fearful passage. . . .

"When his body is burnt he experiences a great burning sensation; and when his body is beaten or cut he feels great pain.

"His body being thus destroyed, a creature, although walking into another body, suffers eternal misery on account of his own adverse actions. . . .

"Then to have his sins washed off he is taken to another such hell. After having gone through all the hells the sinner takes upon a beastly life. Then going through the lives of worms, insects, and flies, beasts of prey, gnats, elephants, trees, horses, cows, and through diverse other sinful and miserable lives, he, coming to the race of men, is born as a hunchback, or an ugly person or a dwarf or a Chandala Pukkasa."

[46] Compare that with what the Bible says about the dead:

"For the living are conscious that they will die; but as for the dead, they are conscious of nothing at all, neither do

---

45. How are the torments of the Hindu hell described?
46, 47. What does the Bible say about the condition of the dead, and what conclusions can we draw?

they anymore have wages, because the remembrance of them has been forgotten. Also, their love and their hate and their jealousy have already perished, and they have no portion anymore to time indefinite in anything that has to be done under the sun. All that your hand finds to do, do with your very power, for there is no work nor devising nor knowledge nor wisdom in Sheol, the place to which you are going."—Ecclesiastes 9:5, 6, 10.

[47] Of course, if as the Bible says, man does not *have* a soul but *is* a soul, then there is no conscious existence after death. There is no bliss, and there is no suffering. All the illogical complications of the "hereafter" disappear.*

Hinduism's Rival

[48] This necessarily brief review of Hinduism has shown that it is a religion of polytheism based on monotheism —belief in Brahman, the Supreme Being, source, or essence, symbolized by the syllable OM or AUM, and with many facets or manifestations. It is also a religion that teaches tolerance and encourages kindness toward animals.

[49] On the other hand, some elements of Hindu teaching, such as Karma and the injustices of the caste system, together with the idolatry and the conflicts in the myths, have made some thinking people question the validity of that faith. One such doubter arose in northeastern India about the year 560 B.C.E. He was Siddhārtha Gautama. He established a new faith that failed to prosper in India yet flourished elsewhere, as our next chapter will explain. That new faith was Buddhism.

---

* The Bible teaching of a resurrection of the dead has no relationship to the immortal soul doctrine. See Chapter 10.

48, 49. (a) In review, what are some Hindu teachings? (b) Why have some questioned the validity of Hinduism? (c) Who arose to challenge Hindu thought?

CHAPTER 6

Buddhism—A Search for Enlightenment Without God

S CARCELY known outside Asia at the turn of the 20th century, Buddhism today has assumed the role of a world religion. In fact, many people in the West are quite surprised to find Buddhism thriving right in their own neighborhood. Much of this has come about as a result of the international refugee movement. Sizable Asian communities have established themselves in Western Europe, North America, Australia, and other places. As more and more immigrants put down roots in their new land, they also bring along their religion. At the same time, more of the people in the West are coming face-to-face with Buddhism for the first time. This, along with the permissiveness and spiritual decline in the traditional churches, has caused some people to become converts to the "new" religion.—2 Timothy 3:1, 5.

[2] Thus, according to the *1989 Britannica Book of the Year,* Buddhism claims a worldwide membership of some 300 million, with about 200,000 each in Western Europe and North America, 500,000 in Latin America, and 300,-000 in the Soviet Union. Most of Buddhism's adherents,

---

1. (a) How has Buddhism manifested itself in Western society? (b) What are the causes of this Western development?
2. Where are Buddhism's followers to be found today?

however, are still found in Asian countries, such as Sri Lanka, Myanmar (Burma), Thailand, Japan, Korea, and China. Who, though, was the Buddha? How did this religion get started? What are the teachings and practices of Buddhism?

A Question of Reliable Source

[3] "What is known of the Buddha's life is based mainly on the evidence of the canonical texts, the most extensive and comprehensive of which are those written in Pali, a language of ancient India," says the book *World Religions —From Ancient History to the Present*. What this means is that there is no source material of his time to tell us anything about Siddhārtha Gautama, the founder of this religion, who lived in northern India in the sixth century B.C.E. That, of course, presents a problem. However, more serious is the question of when and how the "canonical texts" were produced.

[4] Buddhist tradition holds that soon after the death of Gautama, a council of 500 monks was convened to decide what was the authentic teaching of the Master. Whether such a council actually did take place is a subject of much debate among Buddhist scholars and historians. The important point we should note, however, is that even Buddhist texts acknowledge that the authentic teaching decided upon was not committed to writing but memorized by the disciples. Actual writing of the sacred texts had to wait for a considerable time.

[5] According to Sri Lankan chronicles of the fourth and

---

3. What source material is available on the Buddha's life?
4. How was the authentic teaching of the Buddha preserved at first?
5. When were the Pali texts put down in writing?

▲ Chengteh, northern China   Kofu, Japan ▲
▼ New York City, U.S.A.   Chiang Mai, Thailand ▼

Buddhist temples vary in style worldwide

sixth centuries C.E., the earliest of these Pali "canonical texts" were put in writing during the reign of King Vatta-gamani Abhaya in the first century B.C.E. Other accounts of the Buddha's life did not appear in writing until per-haps the first or even the fifth century C.E., nearly a thou-sand years after his time.

[6] Thus, observes the *Abingdon Dictionary of Living Religions,* "The 'biographies' are both late in origin and replete with legendary and mythical material, and the oldest canonical texts are the products of a long process of oral transmission that evidently included some revision and much addition." One scholar even "contended that not a single word of the recorded teaching can be ascribed with unqualified certainty to Gautama himself." Are such criticisms justified?

The Buddha's Conception and Birth

[7] Consider the following excerpts from *Jataka,* part of the Pali canon, and *Buddha-charita,* a second-century C.E. Sanskrit text on the life of the Buddha. First, the account of how the Buddha's mother, Queen Maha-Maya, came to conceive him in a dream.

> "The four guardian angels came and lifted her up, together with her couch, and took her away to the Himalaya Mountains. . . . Then came the wives of these guardian angels, and conducted her to Anotatta Lake, and bathed her, to remove every human stain. . . . Not far off was Silver Hill, and in it a golden mansion. There they spread a divine couch with its head towards the east, and laid her down upon it. Now the future Buddha had become a superb white elephant . . . He ascended Silver Hill, and . . . three times he walked round his mother's couch, with his right side towards it, and striking her on her right side, he seemed to enter her womb. Thus the conception took place in the midsummer festival."

---

6. What criticisms are voiced against the "canonical texts"? (Compare 2 Timothy 3:16, 17.)
7. According to Buddhist texts, how did the Buddha's mother come to conceive him?

Stone relief, Dream of Maya, from Gandhara, Pakistan, depicts the future Buddha as a haloed white elephant entering the right side of Queen Maya to impregnate her

[8] When the queen told the dream to her husband, the king, he summoned 64 eminent Hindu priests, fed and clothed them, and asked for an interpretation. This was their answer:

> "Be not anxious, great king! . . . You will have a son. And he, if he continue to live the household life, will become a universal monarch; but if he leave the household life and retire from the world, he will become a Buddha, and roll back the clouds of sin and folly of this world."

[9] Thereafter, 32 miracles were said to have occurred:

> "All the ten thousand worlds suddenly quaked, quivered, and shook. . . . The fires went out in all the hells; . . . diseases ceased among men; . . . all musical instruments gave forth their notes without being played upon; . . . in the mighty ocean the water became sweet; . . . the whole ten thousand worlds became one mass of garlands of the utmost possible magnificence."

---

8. What was predicted regarding the Buddha's future?
9. What extraordinary events were said to have followed the pronouncement regarding the Buddha's future?

Buddhist monks and worshipers in a temple in New York City

¹⁰ Then came the unusual birth of the Buddha in a garden of sal trees called Lumbini Grove. When the queen wanted to take hold of a branch of the tallest sal tree in the grove, the tree obliged by bending down to within her reach. Holding on to the branch and standing, she gave birth.

> "He issued from his mother's womb like a preacher descending from his preaching-seat, or a man coming down a stair, stretching out both hands and both feet, unsmeared by any impurity from his mother's womb. . . . "

10. How do Buddhist sacred texts describe the Buddha's birth?

Mankind's Search for God

"As soon as he is born, the [future Buddha] firmly plants both feet flat on the ground, takes seven strides to the north, with a white canopy carried above his head, and surveys each quarter of the world, exclaiming in peerless tones: In all the world I am chief, best and foremost; this is my last birth; I shall never be born again."

[11] There are also equally elaborate stories regarding his childhood, his encounters with young female admirers, his wanderings, and just about every event in his life. Not surprisingly, perhaps, most scholars dismiss all these accounts as legends and myths. A British Museum official even suggests that because of the "great body of legend and miracle, . . . a historical life of the Buddha is beyond recovery."

[12] In spite of these myths, a traditional account of the Buddha's life is widely circulated. A modern text, *A Manual of Buddhism,* published in Colombo, Sri Lanka, gives the following simplified account.

"On the full-moon day of May in the year 623 B.C. there was born in the district of Nepal an Indian Sakyan Prince, by name Siddhattha Gotama.* King Suddhodana was his father, and Queen Mahā Māyā was his mother. She died a

---

* This is the transliteration of the Pali spelling of his name. From Sanskrit the transliteration is Siddhārtha Gautama. His birth date, however, has been variously given as 560, 563, or 567 B.C.E. Most authorities accept the 560 date or at least put his birth in the sixth century B.C.E.

---

11. What conclusion have some scholars drawn regarding the accounts about the Buddha's life as found in the sacred texts?
12, 13. (a) What is the traditional account of the Buddha's life? (b) What is commonly accepted regarding when the Buddha was born? (Compare Luke 1:1-4.)

few days after the birth of the child and Mahā Pajāpati Gotamī became his foster-mother.

"At the age of sixteen he married his cousin, the beautiful Princess Yasodharā.

"For nearly thirteen years after his happy marriage he led a luxurious life, blissfully ignorant of the vicissitudes of life outside the palace gates.

"With the march of time, truth gradually dawned upon him. In his 29th year, which witnessed the turning point of his career, his son Rāhula was born. He regarded his off-spring as an impediment, for he realized that all without exception were subject to birth, disease, and death. Comprehending thus the universality of sorrow, he decided to find out a panacea for this universal sickness of humanity.

"So renouncing his royal pleasures, he left home one night . . . cutting his hair, donned the simple garb of an ascetic, and wandered forth as a Seeker of Truth."

[13] Clearly these few biographical details are in stark contrast to the fantastic accounts found in the "canonical texts." And except for the year of his birth, they are commonly accepted.

The Enlightenment—How It Happened

[14] What was the aforementioned "turning point of his career"? It was when, for the first time in his life, he saw a sick man, an old man, and a dead man. This experience caused him to agonize over the meaning of life—Why were men born, only to suffer, grow old, and die? Then, it was said that he saw a holy man, one who had renounced the world in pursuit of truth. This impelled Gautama to give up his family, his possessions, and his princely name and spend the next six years seeking the answer from

---

14. What was the turning point of Gautama's life?

Hindu teachers and gurus, but without success. The accounts tell us that he pursued a course of meditation, fasting, Yoga, and extreme self-denial, yet he found no spiritual peace or enlightenment.

[15] Eventually he came to realize that his extreme course of self-denial was as useless as the life of self-indulgence that he had led before. He now adopted what he called the Middle Way, avoiding the extremes of the life-styles that he had been following. Deciding that the answer was to be found in his own consciousness, he sat in meditation under a pipal, or Indian fig tree. Resisting attacks and temptations by the devil Mara, he continued steadfast in his meditation for four weeks (some say seven weeks) until he supposedly transcended all knowledge and understanding and reached enlightenment.

[16] By this process, in Buddhist terminology, Gautama became the Buddha—the Awakened, or Enlightened, One. He had attained the ultimate goal, Nirvana, the state of perfect peace and enlightenment, freed from desire and suffering. He has also become known as Sakyamuni (sage of the Sakya tribe), and he often addressed himself as Tathagata (one who thus came [to teach]). Different Buddhist sects, however, hold different views on this subject. Some view him strictly as a human who found the path to enlightenment for himself and taught it to his followers. Others view him as the final one of a series of Buddhas to have come into the world to preach or revive the dharma (Pali, *Dhamma*), the teaching or way of the Buddha. Still others view him as a bodhisattva, one who

---

15. How did Gautama finally reach his supposed enlightenment?
16. (a) What did Gautama become? (b) What different views are held regarding the Buddha?

had attained enlightenment but postponed entering Nirvana in order to help others in their pursuit of enlightenment. Whatever it is, this event, the Enlightenment, is of central importance to all schools of Buddhism.

The Enlightenment—What Is It?

[17] Having attained enlightenment, and after overcoming some initial hesitation, the Buddha set forth to teach his newfound truth, his dharma, to others. His first and probably most important sermon was given in the city of Benares, in a deer park, to five bhikkus—disciples or monks. In it, he taught that to be saved, one must avoid both the course of sensual indulgence and that of asceticism and follow the Middle Way. Then, one must understand and follow the Four Noble Truths (see box, opposite page), which can briefly be summarized as follows:

(1) All existence is suffering.

(2) Suffering arises from desire or craving.

(3) Cessation of desire means the end of suffering.

(4) Cessation of desire is achieved by following the Eightfold Path, controlling one's conduct, thinking, and belief.

[18] This sermon on the Middle Way and on the Four Noble Truths embodies the essence of the Enlightenment and is considered the epitome of all the Buddha's teaching. (In contrast, compare Matthew 6:25-34; 1 Timothy 6: 17-19; James 4:1-3; 1 John 2:15-17.) Gautama claimed no divine inspiration for this sermon but credited himself with the words "discovered by the Tathagata." It is said

---

17. (a) Where and to whom did the Buddha preach his first sermon? (b) Explain briefly the Four Noble Truths.
18. What did the Buddha say about the source of his enlightenment? (Compare Job 28:20, 21, 28; Psalm 111:10.)

that on his deathbed, the Buddha told his disciples: "Seek salvation alone in the truth; look not for assistance to anyone besides yourself." Thus, according to the Buddha, enlightenment comes, not from God, but from personal effort in developing right thinking and good deeds.

The Buddha's Four Noble Truths

The Buddha expounded his fundamental teaching in what is called the Four Noble Truths. Here we quote from the *Dhammacakkappavattana Sutta* (The Foundation of the Kingdom of Righteousness), in a translation by T. W. Rhys Davids:

■ "Now this, O Bhikkus, is the noble truth concerning suffering. Birth is attended with pain, decay is painful, disease is painful, death is painful. Union with the unpleasant is painful, painful is separation from the pleasant; and any craving that is unsatisfied, that too is painful. . . .

■ "Now this, O Bhikkus, is the noble truth concerning the origin of suffering. Verily, it is that thirst, causing the renewal of existence, accompanied by sensual delight, seeking satisfaction now here, now there—that is to say, the craving for the gratification of the passions, or the craving for life, or the craving for success. . . .

■ "Now this, O Bhikkus, is the noble truth concerning the destruction of suffering. Verily, it is the destruction, in which no passion remains, of this very thirst; the laying aside of, the getting rid of, the being free from, the harboring no longer of this thirst. . . .

■ "Now this, O Bhikkus, is the noble truth concerning the way which leads to the destruction of sorrow. Verily, it is this noble eightfold path; that is to say: right views; right aspirations; right speech; right conduct; right livelihood; right effort; right mindfulness; and right contemplation."

[19] It is not hard to see why this teaching was welcomed in the Indian society of the time. It condemned the greedy and corrupt religious practices promoted by the Hindu Brahmans, or priestly caste, on the one hand, and the austere asceticism of the Jains and other mystic cults on the other. It also did away with the sacrifices and rituals, the myriads of gods and goddesses, and the burdensome caste system that dominated and enslaved every aspect of the people's life. In short, it promised liberation to everyone who was willing to follow the Buddha's way.

Buddhism Spreading Its Influence

[20] When the five bhikkus accepted the Buddha's teaching, they became the first sangha, or order of monks. So the "Three Jewels" (Triratna) of Buddhism were completed, namely, the Buddha, the dharma, and the sangha, which were supposed to help people get on the way to enlightenment. Thus prepared, Gautama the Buddha went preaching through the length and breadth of the Ganges Valley. People from every social rank and status came to hear him, and they became his disciples. By the time of his death at age 80, he had become well-known and well respected. It was reported that his last words to his disciples were: "Decay is inherent in all component things. Work out your own salvation with diligence."

[21] In the third century B.C.E., about 200 years after the Buddha's death, appeared Buddhism's greatest champi-

---

19. Why was the Buddha's message welcomed at the time?
20. (a) What are the "Three Jewels" of Buddhism? (b) How extensive was the Buddha's preaching campaign?
21. (a) Who was instrumental in Buddhism's expansion? (b) What was the outcome of his efforts?

Images of the Buddha
with stylized gestures

▲ entering
Nirvana   teaching ▲

◀ meditating   resisting
temptation ▼

on, Emperor Aśoka, who brought most of India under his rule. Saddened by the slaughter and upheaval caused by his conquests, he embraced Buddhism and gave it State support. He erected religious monuments, convened councils, and exhorted the people to live by the precepts of the Buddha. Aśoka also sent Buddhist missionaries to all parts of India and to Sri Lanka, Syria, Egypt, and Greece. Principally by Aśoka's efforts, Buddhism grew from being an Indian sect to a world religion. Justifiably, he has been regarded by some as the second founder of Buddhism.

[22] From Sri Lanka, Buddhism spread eastward into Myanmar (Burma), Thailand, and other parts of Indochina. To the north, Buddhism spread to Kashmir and central Asia. From those areas, and as early as the first century C.E., Buddhist monks traveled across the forbidding mountains and deserts and took their religion into China. From China, it was a short step for Buddhism to spread to Korea and Japan. Buddhism was also introduced into Tibet, India's northern neighbor. Mixed with local beliefs, it emerged as Lamaism, which dominated both the religious and the political life there. By the sixth or seventh century C.E., Buddhism had become well es-

---

22. How did Buddhism come to be established throughout Asia?

By the seventh century C.E., Buddhism had spread from India to all of eastern Asia

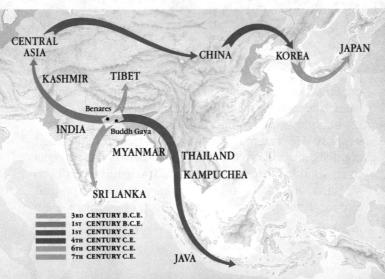

CENTRAL ASIA
KASHMIR   TIBET
Benares
INDIA   Buddh Gaya
CHINA   KOREA   JAPAN
MYANMAR   THAILAND
KAMPUCHEA
SRI LANKA

3RD CENTURY B.C.E.
1ST CENTURY B.C.E.
1ST CENTURY C.E.
4TH CENTURY C.E.
6TH CENTURY C.E.
7TH CENTURY C.E.

JAVA

tablished in all of Southeast Asia and the Far East. But what was happening in India?

[23] While Buddhism was spreading its influence in other lands, it was gradually declining back in India. Deeply involved in philosophical and metaphysical pursuits, the monks began to lose touch with their lay followers. In addition, the loss of royal patronage and the adoption of Hindu ideas and practices all hastened the demise of Buddhism in India. Even Buddhist holy places, such as Lumbini, where Gautama was born, and Buddh Gaya, where he experienced "enlightenment," fell into ruin. By the 13th century, Buddhism had virtually disappeared from India, the land of its origin.

[24] During the 20th century, Buddhism underwent another change of face. Political upheaval in China, Mongolia, Tibet, and countries in Southeast Asia dealt it a devastating blow. Thousands of monasteries and temples were destroyed and hundreds of thousands of monks and nuns were driven away, imprisoned, or even killed. Nonetheless, Buddhism's influence is still strongly felt in the thinking and habits of the people of these lands.

[25] In Europe and North America, Buddhism's idea of seeking "truth" within the individual self seems to have a wide appeal, and its practice of meditation provides an escape from the hubbub of Western life. Interestingly, in the foreword to the book *Living Buddhism,* Tenzin Gyatso, the exiled Dalai Lama of Tibet, wrote: "Perhaps today Buddhism may have a part to play in reminding western people of the spiritual dimension of their lives."

---

23. What happened to Buddhism in India?
24, 25. What further developments in Buddhism were seen in the 20th century?

[26] Although it is customary to speak of Buddhism as one religion, in reality it is divided into several schools of thought. Based on different interpretations of the nature of the Buddha and his teachings, each has its own doctrines, practices, and scriptures. These schools are further divided into numerous groups and sects, many of which are heavily influenced by local cultures and traditions.

[27] The **Theravada** (Way of the Elders), or **Hinayana** (Lesser Vehicle), school of Buddhism flourishes in Sri Lanka, Myanmar (Burma), Thailand, Kampuchea (Cambodia), and Laos. Some consider this to be the conservative school. It emphasizes gaining wisdom and working out one's own salvation by renouncing the world and living the life of a monk, devoting oneself to meditation and study in a monastery.

[28] It is a common sight in some of these lands to see groups of young men with shaved heads, in saffron robes and bare feet, carrying their alms bowls to receive their daily provision from the lay believers whose role it is to support them. It is customary for men to spend at least some part of their life in a monastery. The ultimate goal of the monastic life is to become an arhat, that is, one who has reached spiritual perfection and liberation from the pain and suffering in the cycles of rebirth. The Buddha has shown the way; it is up to each one to follow it.

[29] The **Mahayana** (Greater Vehicle) school of Buddhism is commonly found in China, Korea, Japan, and

---

26. In what ways is Buddhism divided?
27, 28. How would you describe Theravada Buddhism? (Compare Philippians 2:12; John 17:15, 16.)
29. What are the characteristics of Mahayana Buddhism? (Compare 1 Timothy 2:3, 4; John 3:16.)

Vietnam. It is so named because it emphasizes the Buddha's teaching that "truth and the way of salvation is for everyone whether one lives in a cave, a monastery, or a house . . . It is not just for those who give up the world." The basic Mahayana concept is that the love and compassion of the Buddha are so great that he would not withhold salvation from anyone. It teaches that because the

Buddhism and God

"Buddhism teaches the way to perfect goodness and wisdom without a personal God; the highest knowledge without a 'revelation'; . . . the possibility of redemption without a vicarious redeemer, a salvation in which everyone is his own saviour."—*The Message of Buddhism*, by the Bhikkhu Subhadra, as quoted in *What Is Buddhism?*

Then are Buddhists atheists? The book *What Is Buddhism?* published by the Buddhist Lodge, London, answers: "If by atheist you mean one who rejects the concept of a personal God, we are." Then it goes on to say: "A growing mind can as easily digest the idea of a Universe guided by unswerving Law, as it can the concept of a distant Personage that it may never see, who dwells it knows not where, and who has at some time created out of nothing a Universe which is permeated by enmity, injustice, inequality of opportunity, and endless suffering and strife."

Thus, in theory, Buddhism does not advocate belief in God or a Creator. However, Buddhist temples and stupas are found today in nearly every country where Buddhism is practiced, and images and relics of Buddhas and bodhisattvas have become objects of prayers, offerings, and devotion by devout Buddhists. The Buddha, who never claimed to be God, has become a god in every sense of the word.

Buddha-nature is in all of us, everyone is capable of becoming a Buddha, an enlightened one, or a bodhisattva. Enlightenment comes, not by strenuous self-discipline, but by faith in the Buddha and compassion for all living things. This clearly has greater appeal to the practical-minded masses. Because of this more liberal attitude, however, numerous groups and cults have developed.

[30] Among the many Mahayana sects that have developed in China and Japan are the **Pure Land** and **Zen** schools of Buddhism. The former centers its belief around faith in the saving power of Amida Buddha, who promised his followers a rebirth in the Pure Land, or Western Paradise, a land of joy and delight inhabited by gods and humans. From there, it is an easy step to Nirvana. By repeating the prayer "I place my faith in Amida Buddha," sometimes thousands of times a day, the devotee purifies himself in order to attain enlightenment or to gain rebirth in the Western Paradise.

[31] **Zen Buddhism** (Ch'an school in China) derived its name from the practice of meditation. The words *ch'an* (Chinese) and *zen* (Japanese) are variations of the Sanskrit word *dhyāna,* meaning "meditation." This discipline teaches that study, good works, and rituals are of little merit. One can attain enlightenment simply by contemplating such imponderable riddles as, 'What is the sound of one hand clapping?' and, 'What do we find where there is nothing?' The mystical nature of Zen Buddhism has found expression in the refined arts of flower arrangement, calligraphy, ink painting, poetry, gardening, and so

---

30. What goal do devotees of "Pure Land" Buddhism seek? (Compare Matthew 6:7, 8; 1 Kings 18:26, 29.)
31. What are the features of Zen Buddhism? (Compare Philippians 4:8.)

Mankind's Search for God

Procession in honor of the Buddha's birthday, in Tokyo, Japan. The white elephant at rear symbolizes the Buddha

on, and these have been favorably received in the West. Today, Zen meditation centers are found in many Western countries.

[32] Finally, there is **Tibetan Buddhism**, or **Lamaism**. This form of Buddhism is sometimes called Mantrayana (Mantra Vehicle) because of the prominent use of mantras, a series of syllables with or without meaning, in long recitals. Instead of emphasizing wisdom or compassion, this form of Buddhism emphasizes the use of rituals, prayers, magic, and spiritism in worship. Prayers are repeated thousands of times a day with the aid of prayer beads and prayer wheels. The complicated rituals can be learned only under oral instruction by lamas, or monastic leaders, among whom the best known are the Dalai Lama and the Panchen Lama. After the death of a lama, a search is made

32. How is Tibetan Buddhism practiced?

for a child in whom the lama is said to have been reincarnated to be the next spiritual leader. The term, however, is also generally applied to all monks, who, by one estimate, at one time numbered about one fifth of the entire population of Tibet. Lamas also served as teachers, doctors, landowners, and political figures.

[33] These principal divisions of Buddhism are in turn subdivided into many groups, or sects. Some are devoted to a particular leader, such as Nichiren in Japan, who taught that only the Mahayanan *Lotus Sutra* contains the definitive teachings of the Buddha, and Nun Ch'in-Hai in Taiwan, who has a mass following. In this respect, Buddhism is not very different from Christendom with its many denominations and sects. In fact it is common to see people who claim to be Buddhists engage in practices of Taoism, Shinto, ancestor worship, and even those of Christendom.* All these Buddhist sects claim to base their beliefs and practices on the teachings of the Buddha.

The Three Baskets and Other Buddhist Scriptures

[34] Teachings attributed to the Buddha were passed on by word of mouth and only began to be put down in writing centuries after he had passed off the scene. Thus, at best, they represent what his followers in later generations thought he said and did. This is further complicated by the fact that, by then, Buddhism had already splintered into many schools. Thus, different texts present quite different versions of Buddhism.

---

* Many Buddhists in Japan celebrate a showy "Christmas."

---

33. How are Buddhism's divisions similar to those of Christendom? (Compare 1 Corinthians 1:10.)
34. What must we bear in mind when considering the teachings of Buddhism?

[35] The earliest of the Buddhist texts were written in Pali, said to be related to the Buddha's native tongue, in about the first century B.C.E. They are accepted by the Theravada school as the authentic texts. They consist of 31 books organized into three collections called *Tipitaka* (Sanskrit, *Tripitaka*), meaning "Three Baskets," or "Three Collections." The *Vinaya Pitaka* (Basket of Discipline) deals mainly with rules and regulations for monks and nuns. The *Sutta Pitaka* (Basket of Discourses) contains the sermons, parables, and proverbs delivered by the Buddha and his leading disciples. Finally, the *Abhidhamma Pitaka* (Basket of Ultimate Doctrine) consists of commentaries on Buddhist doctrines.

[36] On the other hand, the writings of the Mahayana school are mostly in Sanskrit, Chinese, and Tibetan, and they are voluminous. The Chinese texts alone consist of over 5,000 volumes. They contain many ideas that were not in the earlier writings, such as accounts of Buddhas as numerous as the sands of the Ganges, who are said to have lived for countless millions of years, each presiding over his own Buddha world. It is no exaggeration when one writer observes that these texts are "characterized by diversity, extravagant imagination, colorful personalities, and inordinate repetitions."

[37] Needless to say, few people are able to comprehend these highly abstract treatises. As a result, these later developments have taken Buddhism far away from what the Buddha intended originally. According to the *Vinaya Pitaka*, the Buddha wanted his teachings to be

35. What are the earliest of the Buddhist sacred texts?
36. What characterizes the Mahayana Buddhist scriptures?
37. What problems were posed by the Mahayana writings? (Compare Philippians 2:2, 3.)

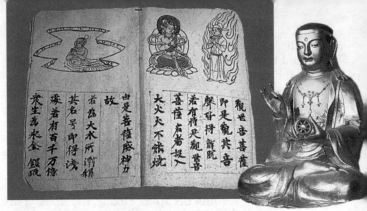

Pages of the *Lotus Sutra* (10th century), in Chinese, describe the power of the bodhisattva Kuan-yin to save from fire and flood. Bodhisattva Ksitigarbha, right, was popular in Korea in the 14th century

understood not only by the educated class but by every sort of people. To this end, he insisted that his ideas be taught in the language of the common people, not the sacred dead language of Hinduism. Thus, to the Theravada Buddhists' objection that these books were noncanonical, the Mahayana followers' reply is that Gautama the Buddha first taught the simple and ignorant, but to the learned and wise he revealed the teachings written later in the Mahayana books.

The Cycle of Karma and Samsara

[38] Although Buddhism freed the people from the shackles of Hinduism to a certain extent, its fundamental ideas are still a legacy of the Hindu teachings of Karma and samsara. Buddhism, as it was originally taught by the

---

38. (a) How do Buddhist and Hindu teachings compare? (b) What is the Buddhist concept of the soul in theory and in practice?

Buddha, differs from Hinduism in that it denies the existence of an immortal soul but speaks of the individual as "a combination of physical and mental forces or energies."* Nonetheless, its teachings are still centered on the ideas that all humanity is wandering from life to life through countless rebirths (samsara) and suffering the consequences of actions past and present (Karma). Even though its message of enlightenment and liberation from this cycle may appear attractive, some ask: How sound is the foundation? What proof is there that all sufferings are the result of one's actions in a previous life? And, in fact, what evidence is there that there is any past life?

[39] One explanation about the law of Karma says:

"Kamma [Pali equivalent of Karma] is a law in itself. But it does not follow that there should be a lawgiver. Ordinary laws of nature, like gravitation, need no lawgiver. The law of Kamma too demands no lawgiver. It operates in its own field without the intervention of an external, independent ruling agency."—*A Manual of Buddhism*

[40] Is this sound reasoning? Do laws of nature really need no lawgiver? Rocket expert Dr. Wernher von Braun once stated: "The natural laws of the universe are so precise that we have no difficulty building a spaceship to fly to the moon and can time the flight with the precision of a fraction of a second. These laws must have been set by somebody." The Bible also speaks about the law of cause

---

* Buddhist doctrines, such as anatta (no self), deny the existence of an unchanging or eternal soul. However, most Buddhists today, particularly those in the Far East, believe in the transmigration of an immortal soul. Their practice of ancestor worship and belief in torment in a hell after death clearly demonstrate this.

---

39. How does one Buddhist text explain the law of Karma?
40. (a) What does the existence of natural laws indicate? (b) What does the Bible say about cause and effect?

and effect. It tells us, "God is not one to be mocked. For whatever a man is sowing, this he will also reap." (Galatians 6:7) Instead of saying this law needs no lawgiver, it points out that "God is not one to be mocked," indicating that this law was set in motion by its Maker, Jehovah.

⁴¹ In addition, the Bible tells us that "the wages sin pays is death," and "he who has died has been acquitted from his sin." Even courts of justice recognize that no one is to suffer double jeopardy for any crime. Why, then, should a person who has already paid for his sins by dying be reborn only to suffer anew the consequences of his past acts? Furthermore, without knowing what past acts one is being punished for, how can one repent and improve? Could this be considered justice? Is it consistent with mercy, which is said to be the Buddha's most outstanding quality? In contrast, the Bible, after stating that "the wages sin pays is death," goes on to say: "But the gift God gives is everlasting life by Christ Jesus our Lord." Yes, it promises that God will do away with all corruption, sin, and death and will bring freedom and perfection for all mankind.—Romans 6:7, 23; 8:21; Isaiah 25:8.

⁴² As for rebirth, here is an explanation by the Buddhist scholar Dr. Walpola Rahula:

"A being is nothing but a combination of physical and mental forces or energies. What we call death is the total non-functioning of the physical body. Do all these forces and energies stop altogether with the non-functioning of the body? Buddhism says 'No.' Will, volition, desire, thirst to exist, to continue, to become more and more, is a tre-

41. (a) What comparison may be drawn between the law of Karma and the law of the courts? (b) Contrast Karma with the Bible's promise.
42. How does a Buddhist scholar explain rebirth?

mendous force that moves whole lives, whole existences, that even moves the whole world. This is the greatest force, the greatest energy in the world. According to Buddhism, this force does not stop with the non-functioning of the body, which is death; but it continues manifesting itself in another form, producing re-existence which is called rebirth."

[43] At the moment of conception, a person inherits 50 percent of his genes from each parent. Therefore there is no way by which he can be 100 percent like someone in a previous existence. Indeed, the process of rebirth cannot be supported by any known principle of science. Frequently, those who believe in the doctrine of rebirth cite as proof the experience of people who claim to recollect faces, events, and places that they have not formerly known. Is this logical? To say that a person who can recount things in bygone times must have lived in that era, one would also have to say that a person who can foretell the future—and there are many who claim to do so—must have lived in the future. That, obviously, is not the case.

[44] More than 400 years before the Buddha, the Bible spoke of a life-force. Describing what happens at a person's death, it says: "Then the dust returns to the earth just as it happened to be and the spirit itself returns to the true God who gave it." (Ecclesiastes 12:7) The word "spirit" is translated from the Hebrew word *ru'ach,* meaning the life-force that animates all living creatures, human and animal. (Ecclesiastes 3:18-22) However, the important

43. (a) Biologically, how is one's genetic makeup determined? (b) What "proof" is sometimes offered to support rebirth? (c) Is such "proof" of rebirth in harmony with common experience?
44. Compare the Bible's teaching regarding "spirit" with the Buddhist doctrine of rebirth.

difference is that *ru'ach* is an *impersonal* force; it does not have a will of its own or retain the personality or any of the characteristics of the deceased individual. It does not go from one person to another at death but "returns to the true God who gave it." In other words, the person's future life prospects—the hope of a resurrection—are entirely in God's hands.—John 5:28, 29; Acts 17:31.

Nirvana—Attaining the Unattainable?

[45] This brings us to the Buddha's teaching on enlightenment and salvation. In Buddhist terms, the basic idea of salvation is liberation from the laws of Karma and samsara, as well as the attaining of Nirvana. And what is Nirvana? Buddhist texts say that it is impossible to describe or explain but can only be experienced. It is not a heaven where one goes after death but an attainment that is within the reach of all, here and now. The word itself is said to mean "blowing out, extinguishing." Thus, some define Nirvana as cessation of all passion and desire; an existence free from all sensory feelings, such as pain, fear, want, love, or hate; a state of eternal peace, rest, and changelessness. Essentially, it is said to be the cessation of individual existence.

[46] The Buddha taught that enlightenment and salvation—the perfection of Nirvana—come, not from any God or external force, but from within a person by his own effort in good deeds and right thoughts. This raises the question: Can something perfect come out of something imperfect? Does not our common experience tell us, as the Hebrew prophet Jeremiah did, that "to earthling

45. What is the Buddhist concept of Nirvana?
46, 47. (a) According to Buddhist teachings, what is the source of salvation? (b) Why is the Buddhist view of the source of salvation contrary to common experience?

Buddhist scroll from Kyoto, Japan, depicts torments in "hell"

man his way does not belong. It does not belong to man who is walking even to direct his step"? (Jeremiah 10:23) If no one is able to have total control of his actions even in simple day-to-day matters, is it logical to think that anyone can work out his eternal salvation all by himself? —Psalm 146:3, 4.

[47] Just as a man mired in quicksand is not likely to free himself from it on his own, likewise all mankind is entrapped in sin and death, and no one is capable of extricating himself from this entanglement. (Romans 5:12) Yet, the Buddha taught that salvation depends solely on one's own effort. His parting exhortation to his disciples was to "rely on yourselves and do not rely on external help; hold fast to the truth as a lamp; seek salvation alone in the truth; look not for assistance to anyone besides yourself."

Enlightenment or Disillusionment?

[48] What is the effect of such a doctrine? Does it inspire its believers to true faith and devotion? The book *Living Buddhism* reports that in some Buddhist countries, even "monks give little thought to the sublimities of their religion. The attainment of Nirvāna is widely thought to be a hopelessly unrealistic ambition, and meditation is seldom practised. Apart from desultory study of the Tipitaka, they devote themselves to being a benevolent and harmonious influence in society." Similarly, *World Encyclopedia* (Japanese), in commenting on the recent resurgence of interest in Buddhist teachings, observes: "The more the study of Buddhism becomes specialized, the more it departs from its original purpose—to guide the people. From this point of view, the recent trend in

---

48. (a) How does one book describe the effect of complicated Buddhist ideas such as Nirvana? (b) What has been the outcome of recent interest in Buddhist teachings in some areas?

Buddhists today worship before, as seen clockwise from top left, a lingam in Bangkok, Thailand; the Buddha's Tooth relic in Kandy, Sri Lanka; images of the Buddha in Singapore and New York

the rigorous study of Buddhism does not necessarily mean the revival of a living faith. Rather, it must be observed that when a religion becomes the object of complicated metaphysical scholarship, its real life as a faith is losing its power."

⁴⁹ The fundamental concept of Buddhism is that knowledge and understanding lead to enlightenment and salvation. But the complicated doctrines of the various schools of Buddhism have only produced the abovementioned "hopelessly unrealistic" situation, beyond the grasp of most believers. For them, Buddhism has been reduced to doing good and following a few rituals and simple precepts. It does not come to grips with life's perplexing questions, such as: Where do we come from? Why are we here? And what is the future for man and the earth?

⁵⁰ Some sincere Buddhists have recognized the confu-

---

49. For many, what has Buddhism become?
50. What question comes to mind in view of the experiences of some sincere Buddhists? (Compare Colossians 2:8.)

A Buddhist woman praying before family altar, and children participating in temple service

sion and disillusionment that arise from the complicated doctrines and burdensome rituals of Buddhism as it is practiced today. The humanitarian efforts of Buddhist groups and associations in some countries may have brought relief from pain and suffering to many. But as a source of true enlightenment and liberation for all, has Buddhism lived up to its promise?

Enlightenment Without God?

[51] Accounts of the life of the Buddha relate that on one occasion he and his disciples were in a forest. He picked up a handful of leaves and said to his disciples: "What I have taught you is comparable to the leaves in my hand, what I have not taught you is comparable to the amount of leaves in the forest." The implication, of course, was that the Buddha had taught only a fraction of what he knew. However, there is one important omission—Gautama the Buddha had next to nothing to say about God; neither did he ever claim to be God. In fact, it is said that he told his disciples, "If there is a God, it is inconceivable that He would be concerned about my day-to-day affairs," and "there are no gods who can or will help man."

[52] In this sense, Buddhism's role in mankind's search for the true God is minimal. *The Encyclopedia of World Faiths* observes that "early Buddhism appears to have taken no account of the question of God, and certainly did not teach or require belief in God." In its emphasis on each person's seeking salvation on his own, turning inward to his own mind or consciousness for

---

51. (a) What does one anecdote tell about the Buddha's teachings? (b) What important omission is evident in the Buddha's teachings? (Compare 2 Chronicles 16:9; Psalm 46:1; 145:18.)
52. (a) What is Buddhism's view of God? (b) What has Buddhism ignored?

enlightenment, Buddhism is really agnostic, if not atheistic. (See box, page 145.) In trying to throw off Hinduism's shackles of superstition and its bewildering array of mythical gods, Buddhism has swung to the other extreme. It ignored the fundamental concept of a Supreme Being, by whose will everything exists and operates. —Acts 17:24, 25.

[53] Because of this self-centered and independent way of thinking, the result is a veritable labyrinth of legends, traditions, complex doctrines, and interpretations generated by the many schools and sects over the centuries. What was meant to bring a simple solution to the complicated problems of life has resulted in a religious and philosophical system that is beyond the comprehension of most people. Instead, the average follower of Buddhism is simply preoccupied with worshiping idols and relics, gods and demons, spirits and ancestors, and performing many other rituals and practices that have little to do with what Gautama the Buddha taught. Clearly, seeking enlightenment without God does not work.

[54] At about the same time that Gautama the Buddha was searching for the way to enlightenment, in another part of the continent of Asia there lived two philosophers whose ideas came to influence millions of people. They were Lao-tzu and Confucius, the two sages venerated by generations of Chinese and others. What did they teach, and how did they influence mankind's search for God? That is what we will consider in the next chapter.

---

53. What can be said about seeking enlightenment without God? (Compare Proverbs 9:10; Jeremiah 8:9.)
54. The teachings of what other Oriental religious thinkers will be considered next?

CHAPTER 7.

Taoism and Confucianism—A Search for Heaven's Way

Taoism, Confucianism, and Buddhism constitute the three major religions of China and the Far East. Unlike Buddhism, however, Taoism and Confucianism have not become world religions but have basically remained in China and wherever Chinese culture has asserted its influence. Though no official figures of the current number of their followers in China are available, Taoism and Confucianism together have dominated the religious life of nearly one quarter of the world's population for the past 2,000 years.

'LET a hundred flowers bloom; let a hundred schools contend.' That saying, made famous by Mao Tse-tung of the People's Republic of China in a speech in 1956, was actually a paraphrase of the expression that Chinese scholars have used to describe the era in China from the fifth to the third centuries B.C.E., called the Warring States period. By this time the mighty Chou dynasty (c. 1122-256 B.C.E.) had deteriorated into a system of

1. (Include introduction.) (a) Where are Taoism and Confucianism practiced, and how extensive are they? (b) To what time period do we now turn to examine these teachings?

loosely bound feudal states that were engaged in continuous warfare, much to the distress of the common people.

[2] The turmoil and suffering brought about by the wars seriously weakened the authority of the traditional ruling class. The common people were no longer content with submitting themselves to the whims and wiles of the aristocracy and silently suffering the consequences. As a result, long-suppressed ideas and aspirations burst forth like "a hundred flowers." Different schools of thought advanced their ideas on government, law, social order, conduct, and ethics, as well as on subjects such as agriculture, music, and literature, as the means for restoring some normalcy to life. They came to be known as the "hundred schools." Most of them did not produce a lasting effect. Two schools, however, gained such prominence that they have influenced life in China for

2. (a) What led to the "hundred schools" of thought? (b) What remains of the "hundred schools" development?

*P*ronunciation of Chinese Words

To be consistent with most scholarly work, the Wade-Giles form of transliteration of Chinese words is used in this book. The English equivalents in sound are given below:

ch	*j,* as in Tao Te *Ching* (*jing*)
ch'	*ch,* as in *Ch'in* (*chin*) dynasty
hs	*sh,* as in Ta *Hsüeh* (*shu-eh*), *The Great Learning*
j	*r,* as in *jen* (*ren*), human-heartedness
k	*g,* as in the Buddhist goddess *Kuan*-yin (*gwan-yin*)
k'	*k,* as in *K'ung*-fu-tzu (*kung-fu-tzu*), or Confucius
t	*d,* as in *Tao* (*dao*), the Way
t'	*t,* as in *T'ang* (*tang*) dynasty

over 2,000 years. They were what eventually came to be known as Taoism and Confucianism.

Tao—What Is It?

[3] To understand why Taoism (pronounced *dow*-ism; rhymes with *now*) and Confucianism came to wield such a deep and lasting influence on the Chinese people, as well as on those of Japan, Korea, and other surrounding nations, it is necessary to have some understanding of the fundamental Chinese concept of Tao. The word itself means "way, road, or path." By extension, it can also mean "method, principle, or doctrine." To the Chinese, the harmony and orderliness they perceived in the universe were manifestations of Tao, a sort of divine will or legislation existing in and regulating the universe. In other words, instead of believing in a Creator God, who controls the universe, they believed in a providence, a will of heaven, or simply heaven itself as the cause of everything.

Tao, 'the way a person should go'

[4] Applying the concept of Tao to human affairs, the Chinese believed that there is a natural and correct way to do everything and that everything and everyone has its proper place and its proper function. They believed, for example, that if the ruler performed his duty by dealing justly with the people and looking after

3. (a) What is the Chinese concept of Tao? (b) Instead of a Creator, what did the Chinese believe was the cause of all things? (Compare Hebrews 3:4.)
4. How did the Chinese apply the concept of Tao to human affairs? (Compare Proverbs 3:5, 6.)

the sacrificial rituals pertaining to heaven, there would be peace and prosperity for the nation. Similarly, if people were willing to seek out the way, or Tao, and follow it, everything would be harmonious, peaceful, and effective. But if they were to go contrary to or resist it, the result would be chaos and disaster.

[5] This idea of going with Tao and not interfering with its flow is a central element of Chinese philosophical and religious thinking. It may be said that Taoism and Confucianism are two different expressions of the same concept. Taoism takes a mystical approach and, in its original form, advocates inaction, quietness, and passivity, shunning society and returning to nature. Its basic idea is that everything will come out right if people will sit back, do nothing, and let nature take its course. Confucianism, on the other hand, takes a pragmatic approach. It teaches that social order will be maintained when every person plays his intended role and does his duty. To that end, it codifies all human and social relationships—ruler-subject, father-son, husband-wife, and so on—and provides guidelines for all of them. Naturally, this brings up the following questions: How did these two systems come into existence? Who were their founders? How are they practiced today? And what have they done as far as man's search for God is concerned?

Taoism—A Philosophical Start

[6] In its early stages, Taoism was more a philosophy

---

5. (a) What is Taoism's approach to Tao? (b) What is Confucianism's approach to Tao? (c) What questions need to be answered?
6. (a) What is known about the founder of Taoism? (b) How did the founder of Taoism come to be known as Lao-tzu?

Lao-tzu, the philosopher of Taoism, on the back of a buffalo

than a religion. Its founder, Lao-tzu, was dissatisfied with the chaos and turmoil of the times and sought relief by shunning society and returning to nature. Not a great deal is known about the man, who is said to have lived in the sixth century B.C.E., although even that is uncertain. He was commonly called Lao-tzu, which means "Old Master" or "Old One," because, as legend has it, his pregnant mother carried him for so long that when he was born, his hair had already turned white.

[7] The only official record about Lao-tzu is in *Shih Chi* (Historical Records), by Ssu-ma Ch'ien, a respected court historian of the second and first centuries B.C.E. According to this source, Lao-tzu's real name was Li Erh. He served as a clerk in the imperial archives at Loyang, central China. But more significantly, it gives this account about Lao-tzu:

> "Lao Tzu resided in Chou most of his life. When he foresaw the decay of Chou, he departed and came to the frontier. The custom-house officer Yin Hsi said: 'Sir, since it pleases you to retire, I request you for my sake to write a book.' Thereupon Lao Tzu wrote a book of two parts consisting of five thousand and odd words, in which he discussed the concepts of the Way [Tao] and

7. What do we learn about Lao-tzu from "Historical Records"?

the Power [Te]. Then he departed. No one knows where he died."

[8] Many scholars doubt the authenticity of this account. In any case, the book that was produced is known as *Tao Te Ching* (generally translated "The Classic of the Way and the Power") and is considered the principal text of Taoism. It is written in terse, cryptic verses, some of which are only three or four words long. Because of this and because the meaning of some characters has changed considerably since the time of Lao-tzu, the book is subject to many different interpretations.

A Glimpse of "Tao Te Ching"

[9] In *Tao Te Ching*, Lao-tzu expounded on Tao, the ultimate way of nature, and applied it to every level of human activity. Here we quote from a modern translation

8. (a) What book was Lao-tzu said to have produced? (b) Why is the book subject to many different interpretations?
9. How did Lao-tzu describe Tao in *Tao Te Ching?*

Taoist temple to Matsu, "Holy Mother in Heaven," in Taiwan

by Gia-fu Feng and Jane English to get a glimpse of *Tao Te Ching*. Regarding Tao, it says the following:

"[There was] something mysteriously formed,
Born before heaven and earth. . . .
Perhaps it is the mother of ten thousand things.
I do not know its name.
Call it Tao."—Chapter 25.

"All things arise from Tao.
They are nourished by Virtue [Te].
They are formed from matter.
They are shaped by environment.
Thus the ten thousand things all respect Tao
    and honor Virtue [Te]."—Chapter 51.

[10] What can we deduce from these enigmatic passages? That to Taoists, Tao is some mysterious cosmic force that is responsible for the material universe. The objective of Taoism is to search out the Tao, leave behind the world, and become at one with nature. This concept is also reflected in the Taoists' view on human conduct. Here is an expression of this ideal in *Tao Te Ching*:

"Better stop short than fill to the brim.
Oversharpen the blade, and the edge will soon blunt.
Amass a store of gold and jade, and no one can protect it.
Claim wealth and titles, and disaster will follow.
Retire when the work is done.
This is the way of heaven."—Chapter 9.

[11] These few examples show that at least initially, Taoism was basically a school of philosophy. Reacting to the injustices, suffering, devastation, and futility that resulted from the harsh rule of the feudal system of the

---

10. (a) What is the objective of Taoism? (b) How is this Taoist view applied to human conduct?
11. How can the Taoist ideal be described?

time, Taoists believed that the way to find peace and harmony was to go back to the tradition of the ancients before there were kings and ministers who dominated the common people. Their ideal was to live the tranquil, rural life, in union with nature.—Proverbs 28:15; 29:2.

Taoism's Second Sage

[12] The philosophy of Lao-tzu was carried one step further by Chuang Chou, or Chuang-tzu, meaning "Master Chuang" (369-286 B.C.E.), who was considered the most eminent successor to Lao-tzu. In his book, *Chuang Tzu*, he not only elaborated on the Tao but also expounded on the ideas of yin and yang, first developed in the *I Ching*. (See page 83.) In his view, nothing is really permanent or absolute, but everything is in a state of flux between two opposites. In the chapter "Autumn Flood," he wrote:

"Nothing in the universe is permanent, as everything lives only long enough to die. Only Tao, having no beginning or end, lasts forever.... Life can be likened to a fleet horse galloping at full speed—it changes constantly and continuously, in every fraction of a second. What should you do? What should you not do? It really does not make any difference."

[13] Because of this philosophy of inertia, the Taoist view is that there is no point in anyone doing anything to interfere with what nature has set in motion. Sooner or later, everything will return to its opposite. No matter how unbearable a situation is, it will soon become better. No matter how pleasant a situation is, it will soon fade away. (In contrast, see Ecclesiastes 5:18, 19.) This philo-

---

12. (a) Who was Chuang Chou? (b) What did he add to Lao-tzu's original teachings?
13. (a) With Chuang-tzu's elaboration, what is the Taoist view of life? (b) What dream of Chuang-tzu's is best remembered?

sophical view of life is typified in a dream of Chuang-tzu's by which the common folk best remember him:

> "Once Chuang Chou dreamt he was a butterfly, a butterfly flitting and fluttering about, happy with himself and doing as he pleased. He didn't know he was Chuang Chou. Suddenly he woke up and there he was, solid and unmistakable Chuang Chou. But he didn't know if he was Chuang Chou who had dreamt he was a butterfly, or a butterfly dreaming he was Chuang Chou."

[14] The influence of this philosophy is seen in the style of the poetry and painting developed by Chinese artists of later generations. (See page 171.) Taoism, however, was not to remain as a passive philosophy for long.

From Philosophy to Religion

[15] In their attempt to be at one with nature, Taoists became obsessed with its agelessness and resilience. They speculated that perhaps by living in harmony with Tao, or nature's way, one could somehow tap into the secrets of nature and become immune to physical harm, diseases, and even death. Although Lao-tzu did not make this an issue, passages in *Tao Te Ching* seemed to suggest this idea. For example, chapter 16 says: "Being at one with the Tao is eternal. And though the body dies, the Tao will never pass away."*

[16] Chuang-tzu also contributed to such speculations.

---

* Lin Yutang's translation of this passage reads: "Being in accord with Tao, he is eternal, and his whole life is preserved from harm."

---

14. In what fields is the Taoist influence reflected?
15. (a) To what idea did the fascination with nature lead the Taoists? (b) What statements in *Tao Te Ching* contributed to such an idea?
16. How did the writings of Chuang-tzu add to the magical beliefs of Taoism?

For instance, in a dialogue in *Chuang Tzu,* one mythical character asked another, "You are of a high age, and yet you have a child's complexion. How is this?" The latter replied: "I have learnt Tao." Regarding another Taoist philosopher, Chuang-tzu wrote: "Now Liehtse could ride upon the wind. Sailing happily in the cool breeze, he would go on for fifteen days before his return. Among mortals who attain happiness, such a man is rare."

[17] Stories like these fired the imagination of Taoists, and they started to experiment with meditation, dieting, and breathing exercises that supposedly could delay bodily decay and death. Soon, legends began to circulate about immortals who could fly on clouds and appear and disappear at will and who lived on sacred mountains or remote islands for countless years, sustained by dew or magical fruits. Chinese history reports that in 219 B.C.E., the Ch'in emperor, Shih Huang-Ti, sent a fleet of ships with 3,000 boys and girls to find the legendary island of P'eng-lai, the abode of the immortals, to bring back the herb of immortality. Needless to say, they did not return with the elixir, but tradition says that they populated the islands that came to be known as Japan.

[18] During the Han dynasty (206 B.C.E.–220 C.E.), the magical practices of Taoism reached a new peak. It was said that Emperor Wu Ti, though promoting Confucianism as the official State teaching, was much attracted to the Taoist idea of physical immortality. He was particularly taken up with concocting 'immortality pills' by alchemy. In the Taoist view, life results when the opposing yin

---

17. What Taoist practices resulted from earlier speculations, and what was the outcome? (Compare Romans 6:23; 8:6, 13.)
18. (a) What is the Taoist idea behind 'immortality pills'? (b) What other magical practices were developed by Taoism?

Misty mountains, tranquil waters, swaying trees, and retiring scholars —popular themes in Chinese landscape paintings—reflect Taoist ideal of living in harmony with nature

and yang (female and male) forces combine. Thus, by fusing lead (dark, or yin) and mercury (bright, or yang), the alchemists were imitating the process of nature, and the product, they thought, would be an immortality pill. Taoists also developed Yogalike exercises, breath-control techniques, dietary restrictions, and sexual practices that were believed to strengthen one's vital energy and prolong one's life. Their paraphernalia included magic talismans that were said to render one invisible and invulnerable to weapons or enable one to walk on water or fly through space. They also had magic seals, usually containing the yin-yang symbol, affixed on buildings and over doorways to repel evil spirits and wild beasts.

[19] By the second century C.E., Taoism became organized. A certain Chang Ling, or Chang Tao-ling, established a Taoist secret society in western China and practiced magical cures and alchemy. Because each member was levied a fee of five pecks of rice, his movement came to be known as the Five-Pecks-of-Rice Taoism (*wu-tou-mi tao*).* Claiming that he received a personal revelation from Lao-tzu, Chang became the first "celestial master." Finally, it was said that he succeeded in making the elixir of life and ascended alive to heaven, riding a tiger, from Mount Lung-hu (Dragon-Tiger Mountain) in Kiangsi Province. With Chang Tao-ling there started a centuries-long succession of Taoist "celestial masters," each said to be a reincarnation of Chang.

Meeting the Challenge of Buddhism

[20] By the seventh century, during the T'ang dynasty (618-907 C.E.), Buddhism was making inroads into Chinese religious life. As a countermeasure, Taoism promoted itself as a religion with Chinese roots. Lao-tzu was deified, and Taoist writings were canonized. Temples, monasteries, and nunneries were built, and orders of monks and nuns were established, more or less in the Buddhist fashion. In addition, Taoism also adopted into its own pantheon many of the gods, goddesses, fairies, and immortals of Chinese folklore, such as the Eight Immortals (*Pa Hsien*), the god of the hearth (*Tsao Shen*), city gods (*Ch'eng Huang*), and guardians of the door (*Men*

---

* A peck is a dry measure equaling two gallons.

---

19. How did Taoism become organized?
20. How did Taoism attempt to counteract Buddhism's influence?

Ancient Taoist carving, left, of god of Long Life with the Eight Immortals. Right, Taoist priest in full regalia officiating at a funeral

Shen). The result was an amalgam embracing elements of Buddhism, traditional superstitions, spiritism, and ancestor worship.—1 Corinthians 8:5.

[21] As time wore on, Taoism slowly degenerated into a system of idolatry and superstition. Each person simply worshiped his favorite gods and goddesses at the local temples, petitioning them for protection against evil and for help in attaining earthly fortune. The priests were for hire to conduct funerals; select favorable sites for graves,

21. Eventually, into what did Taoism transform itself, and how?

houses, and businesses; communicate with the dead; ward off evil spirits and ghosts; celebrate festivals; and perform sundry other rituals. Thus, what started off as a school of mystic philosophy had transformed itself into a religion deeply mired in belief in immortal spirits, hellfire, and demigods—ideas drawn from the stagnant pool of false beliefs of ancient Babylon.

China's Other Prominent Sage

²² While we have traced the rise, development, and decay of Taoism, we should recall that it was just one of the "hundred schools" that blossomed in China during the period of the Warring States. Another school that eventually came to prominence, in fact, dominance, was Confucianism. But why did Confucianism come to such prominence? Of all Chinese sages, Confucius is undoubtedly the best-known outside of China, but who really was he? And what did he teach?

²³ Regarding Confucius, we again turn to the *Shih Chi* (Historical Records) of Ssu-ma Ch'ien. In contrast to the brief sketch on Lao-tzu, we find an extended biography of Confucius. Here are some personal details quoted from a translation by the Chinese scholar Lin Yutang:

"Confucius was born in the town of Tsou, in the county of Ch'angping, in the country of Lu. . . . [His mother] prayed at the hill Nich'iu and begat Confucius in answer to her prayer, in the twenty-second year of Duke Hsiang of Lu (551 B.C.). There was a noticeable convolution on

---

22. What school of thought came to dominance in China, and what questions do we need to consider?
23. What personal details regarding Confucius are given in the "Historical Records"?

Mankind's Search for God

his head at his birth, and that was why he was called 'Ch'iu' (meaning a "hill"). His literary name was Chung-ni, and his surname was K'ung."*

24 Shortly after his birth, his father died, but his mother, though poor, managed to provide him with a proper education. The boy developed a keen interest in history, poetry, and music. According to *The Analects,* one of the Confucian *Four Books,* he devoted himself to scholarly study when he reached age 15. At age 17, he was given a minor government post in his native state of Lu.

---

* The word "Confucius" is a Latin transliteration of the Chinese *K'ung-fu-tzu,* meaning "K'ung the Master." Jesuit priests who came to China in the 16th century coined the Latinized name when they recommended to the pope of Rome that Confucius be canonized as a "saint" of the Roman Catholic Church.

---

24. What happened during the early life of Confucius?

Confucianism—Philosophy or Religion?

Because Confucius made few comments about God, many people view Confucianism as only a philosophy and not a religion. Yet, what he said and did showed that he was religious. This can be seen in two respects. First, he had a reverent fear for a supreme cosmic spiritual power, what the Chinese call *T'ien,* or Heaven, which he regarded as the source of all virtue and moral goodness and whose will, he felt, directs all things. Second, he placed great emphasis on meticulous observance of the rites and ceremonies relating to the worship of heaven and the spirits of departed ancestors.

Though Confucius never advocated these views as a form of religion, to generations of Chinese they have become what religion is all about.

[25] His financial status apparently improved, so that he married at the age of 19 and had a son the next year. In his middle 20's, however, his mother died. That evidently had quite an effect on him. Being a meticulous observer of ancient traditions, Confucius retired from public life and mourned his mother at her grave for 27 months, thus furnishing the Chinese with a classic example of filial piety.

Confucius the Teacher

[26] Thereafter, he left his family and took up the occupation of a wandering teacher. The subjects he taught included music, poetry, literature, civics, ethics, and science, or what there was of it at that time. He must have made quite a name for himself, for it was said that at one time he had as many as 3,000 students.

[27] In the Orient, Confucius is revered principally as a master teacher. In fact the epitaph on his grave in Ch'ü-fou, Shantung Province, reads simply "Ancient, Most Holy Teacher." One Western writer describes his teaching method this way: "He walked about from 'place to place accompanied by those who were absorbing his views of life.' Whenever the journey took them any distance he rode in an ox cart. The slow pace of the animal enabled his pupils to follow on foot, and it is evident that the subject of his lectures was frequently suggested by events occurring on the road." Interestingly, Jesus at a later date, and independently, used a similar method.

---

25. How did the death of Confucius' mother affect him? (Compare Ecclesiastes 9:5, 6; John 11:33, 35.)
26. What profession did Confucius take up after the death of his mother?
27. What is known about Confucius as a teacher? (Compare Matthew 6:26, 28; 9:16, 17; Luke 12:54-57; John 4:35-38.)

Confucian Four Books and Five Classics

正其心。心所發的一欲正其心者。必先正其身。

家。必須先整齊自己的家。欲齊其家者。自己的多。先修其身。

至。所知善惡判別得極明切而后意誠。意誠能誠心所發判判的不欺矇致知在格物。

誠懇看善自己的而后心正。誠懇看善自己的而后心正。知至。自己意誠的而后身修。

治。然後纔可以治國。國治國家的而后天下平。然後天下平。

皆以修身爲本。一切事都要修其本亂。如果不能修身。

所厚者薄。深也就是把親近看得輕而其所薄者厚。天如下把

Five Classics, above, and a portion, left, of *The Great Learning* (one of the Four Books), quoted on page 181

The Four Books

1. ***The Great Learning*** (*Ta Hsüeh*), the basis of a gentleman's education, the first text studied by school-boys in old China

2. ***The Doctrine of the Mean*** (*Chung Yung*), a treatise on the development of human nature through moderation

3. ***The Analects*** (*Lun Yü*), a collection of Confucius' sayings, considered the main source of Confucian thought

4. ***The Book of Mencius*** (*Meng-tzu*), writings and sayings of Confucius' greatest disciple, Meng-tzu, or Mencius

The Five Classics

1. ***The Book of Poetry*** (*Shih Ching*), 305 poems providing a picture of daily life in early Chou times (1000-600 B.C.E.)

2. ***The Book of History*** (*Shu Ching*), covering 17 centuries of Chinese history beginning with the Shang dynasty (1766-1122 B.C.E.)

3. ***The Book of Changes*** (*I Ching*), a book of divination, based on interpretations of the 64 possible combinations of six whole or broken lines

4. ***The Book of Rites*** (*Li Chi*), a collection of rules on ceremonies and rituals

5. ***Annals of Spring and Autumn*** (*Ch'un Ch'iu*), a history of Confucius' native state of Lu, covering 721-478 B.C.E.

[28] What made Confucius an honored teacher among the Orientals, no doubt, was the fact that he was a good student himself, especially of history and ethics. "People were attracted to Confucius, less because he was the wisest man of his time, than because he was the most *learned* scholar, the only one of his day who could teach them about the ancient books and ancient scholarship," wrote Lin Yutang. Pointing to this love of learning as perhaps the key reason Confucianism triumphed over other schools of thought, Lin summarized the matter this way: "The Confucian teachers had something definite to teach and the Confucian pupils had something definite to learn, namely, historical learning, while the other schools were forced to air merely their own opinions."

"It Is Heaven That Knows Me!"

[29] In spite of his success as a teacher, Confucius did not consider teaching to be his lifework. He felt that his ideas on ethics and morals could save the troubled world of his day if only the rulers would apply them by employing him or his pupils in their governments. To this end, he and a small group of his closest disciples left his native state of Lu and went traveling from state to state trying to find the wise ruler who would adopt his ideas on government and social order. What was the outcome? *Shih Chi* states: "Finally he left Lu, was abandoned in Ch'i, was driven out of Sung and Wei, suffered want between Ch'en and Ts'ai." After 14 years on the road, he returned to Lu, disappointed but not broken.

---

28. According to the Chinese writer Lin Yutang, what made Confucius an honored teacher?
29. (a) What was Confucius' real ambition in life? (b) How did he try to achieve his ambition, and with what result?

[30] For the remainder of his days, he devoted himself to literary work and teaching. (See box, page 177.) Though undoubtedly he lamented his obscurity, he said: "I do not murmur against Heaven. I do not grumble against man. I pursue my studies here on earth, and am in touch with Heaven above. It is Heaven that knows me!" Finally, in the year 479 B.C.E., he died at the age of 73.

The Essence of Confucian Ideas

[31] Although Confucius excelled as a scholar and as a teacher, his influence was by no means limited to scholastic circles. In fact, the aim of Confucius was not just to teach rules of conduct or morals but also to restore peace and order to society, which was, at the time, torn apart by the constant warfare between the feudal lords. To achieve that goal, Confucius taught that everyone, from

---

30. What literary works form the basis of Confucianism?
31. What did Confucius teach was the way to achieve social order?

Confucius, China's foremost sage, is revered as a teacher of morals and ethics

the emperor to the common folk, must learn what role he was expected to play in society and live accordingly.

[32] In Confucianism this concept is known as li, which means propriety, courtesy, the order of things, and, by extension, ritual, ceremony, and reverence. In answer to the question, "What is this great *li?*" Confucius gave the following explanation:

> "Of all the things that the people live by, *li* is the greatest. Without *li,* we do not know how to conduct a proper worship of the spirits of the universe; or how to establish the proper status of the king and the ministers, the ruler and the ruled, and the elders and the juniors; or how to establish the moral relationships between the sexes, between parents and children and between brothers; or how to distinguish the different degrees of relationships in the family. That is why a gentleman holds *li* in such high regard."

[33] Hence, li is the rule of conduct by which a true gentleman (*chün-tzu,* sometimes translated "superior man") carries out all his social relations. When everyone endeavors to do so, "everything becomes right in the family, the state and the world," said Confucius, and that is when Tao, or heaven's way, is done. But how is li to be expressed? That takes us to another of the central concepts of Confucianism—jen (pronounced *ren*), humaneness or human-heartedness.

[34] While li emphasizes restraint by external rules, jen deals with human nature, or the inner person. The Confucian concept, especially as expressed by Confucius'

32, 33. (a) What was the Confucian concept of li? (b) According to Confucius, what would be the result of practicing li?
34. What is the Confucian concept of jen, and how does it help in dealing with social ills?

Mankind's Search for God

**Celebrations, with music, at Sung Kyun Kwan,
a 14th-century Confucian educational center in Seoul, Korea,
perpetuate Confucian rituals**

principal disciple, Mencius, is that human nature is basically good. Thus, the solution to all social ills lies in self-cultivation, and that starts with education and knowledge. The opening chapter of *The Great Learning* says:

"When true knowledge is achieved, then the will becomes sincere; when the will is sincere, then the heart is set right . . . ; when the heart is set right, then the personal life is cultivated; when the personal life is cultivated, then the family life is regulated; when the family life is regulated, then the national life is orderly; and when the national life is orderly, then there is peace in this world. From the emperor down to the common men, all must regard the cultivation of the personal life as the root or foundation."

[35] Thus, we see that according to Confucius, the

35. (a) How can the principles of li and jen be summarized? (b) How is all of this reflected in the Chinese view of life?

Whether Buddhist, Taoist, or Confucian, the typical Chinese, from left, pays homage to ancestors at home, worships the god of wealth, and offers sacrifices at temples on festive days

observance of li will enable people to behave properly in every situation, and the cultivation of jen will make them treat everyone else kindly. The result, theoretically, is peace and harmony in society. The Confucian ideal, based on the principles of li and jen, can be summarized this way:

"Kindness in the father, filial piety in the son

Gentility in the eldest brother, humility and respect in the younger

Righteous behavior in the husband, obedience in the wife

Humane consideration in elders, deference in juniors

Benevolence in rulers, loyalty in ministers and subjects."

Mankind's Search for God

All of this helps to explain why most Chinese people, and even other Orientals, place so much emphasis on family ties, on being industrious, on education, and on knowing and acting according to one's place. For better or for worse, these Confucian concepts have been driven deep into the Chinese consciousness through centuries of inculcation.

Confucianism Became a State Cult

[36] With the rise of Confucianism, the period of the "hundred schools" came to an end. Emperors of the Han dynasty found in the Confucian teaching of loyalty to the ruler just the formula they needed to solidify the power of the throne. Under Emperor Wu Ti, whom we have already referred to in connection with Taoism, Confucianism was elevated to the status of a State cult. Only those versed in the Confucian classics were selected as State officials, and anyone hoping to enter government service had to pass nationwide examinations based on the Confucian classics. Confucian rites and rituals became the religion of the royal house.

[37] This change of events did much to elevate the position of Confucius in Chinese society. The Han emperors started the tradition of offering sacrifices at the grave of Confucius. Honorific titles were bestowed on him. Then, in 630 C.E., the T'ang emperor T'ai Tsung ordered that a State temple to Confucius be erected in every province and county throughout the empire and that sacrifices be offered regularly. For all practical purposes, Confucius was elevated to the status of a god, and Confucianism

---

36. How did Confucianism gain the status of a State cult?
37. (a) How did Confucianism become a religion? (b) Why, in reality, is Confucianism more than just a philosophy?

became a religion hardly distinguishable from Taoism or Buddhism.—See box, page 175.

The Legacy of the Wisdom of the East

[38] Since the end of dynastic rule in China in 1911, Confucianism and Taoism have come under much criticism, even persecution. Taoism was discredited on account of its magical and superstitious practices. And Confucianism has been labeled as feudalistic, promoting a slave mentality to keep people, especially women, under subjection. In spite of such official denunciations, however, the basic concepts of these religions are so deeply embedded in the Chinese mind that they still have a strong hold on many of the people.

[39] For example, under the headline "Chinese Religious Rites Rare in Beijing but Flourishing in the Coastal Regions," the Canadian newspaper *Globe and Mail* reported in 1987 that after nearly 40 years of atheistic rule in China, funeral rites, temple services, and many superstitious practices are still common in rural areas. "Most villages have a *fengshui* man, usually an elderly resident who knows how to read the forces of wind (feng) and water (shui) to determine the most propitious location for everything from the ancestral grave, a new house or living room furniture," says the report.

[40] Elsewhere, Taoism and Confucianism are found wherever traditional Chinese culture survives. In Taiwan, one man who claims to be a descendant of Chang Tao-

---

38. (a) What has happened to Taoism and Confucianism since 1911? (b) But what is still true of the basic concepts of these religions?
39. What does one news report say about superstitious religious practices in China?
40. What religious practices are seen in Taiwan?

ling presides as "celestial master" with the power to ordain Taoist priests (*Tao Shih*). The popular goddess Matsu, billed as "Holy Mother in Heaven," is worshiped as the patron saint of the island and of sailors and fishermen. As for the common people, they are mostly preoccupied with making offerings and sacrifices to the spirits of the rivers, mountains, and stars; the patron deities of all the trades; and the gods of health, good luck, and wealth.*

[41] What about Confucianism? Its role as a religion has been reduced to the status of a national monument. In China at Ch'ü-fou, the birthplace of Confucius, the State maintains the Temple of Confucius and family grounds as tourist attractions. There, according to the magazine *China Reconstructs,* performances are put on "reenacting a ritual of worship for Confucius." And in Singapore, Taiwan, Hong Kong, and other places in eastern Asia, people still celebrate Confucius' birthday.

[42] In Confucianism and Taoism, we see how a system based on human wisdom and reasoning, no matter how logical and well-meaning, ultimately falls short in the search for the true God. Why? Because it leaves out one essential element, namely, the will and requirements of a personal God. Confucianism turns to human nature as the motivating force to do good, and Taoism turns to nature itself. But this is misplaced confidence because it simply amounts to worshiping created things rather than the Creator.—Psalm 62:9; 146:3, 4; Jeremiah 17:5.

---

* One Taoist group in Taiwan, called *T'ien Tao* (Heavenly Way), claims to be an amalgam of five world religions—Taoism, Confucianism, Buddhism, Christianity, and Islām.

---

41. How is Confucianism as a religion carried on today?
42. How do Taoism and Confucianism fall short as guides in the search for the true God?

[43] On the other hand, the traditions of ancestor and idol worship, reverence for a cosmic heaven, and veneration of spirits in nature, as well as the rites and rituals connected with them, have become so deeply rooted in the Chinese way of thinking that they are accepted as the unspoken truth. Often it is very difficult to talk to a Chinese person about a personal God or Creator because the concept is so foreign to him.—Romans 1:20-25.

[44] It is undeniable that nature is filled with great marvels and wisdom and that we humans are endowed with the wonderful faculties of reason and conscience. But as pointed out in the chapter on Buddhism, the wonders we see in the natural world have caused reasoning minds to conclude that there must be a Designer or Creator. (See pages 151-2.) That being the case, then, is it not logical that we should endeavor to search out the Creator? In fact the Creator invites us to do so: "Raise your eyes high up and see. Who has created these things? It is the One who is bringing forth the army of them even by number, all of whom he calls even by name." (Isaiah 40:26) Doing so, we will come to know not only who the Creator is, namely Jehovah God, but also what he has in store for our future.

[45] Along with Buddhism, Confucianism, and Taoism, which have played a major role in the religious life of the people of the Orient, there is another religion, one unique to the people of Japan—Shinto. How is it different? What is its source? Has it led people to the true God? This we will consider in the next chapter.

---

43. How have the religious traditions of the Chinese worked against them as a whole in the search for the true God?
44. (a) How do reasoning minds react to the marvels of the way of nature? (b) What are we encouraged to do?
45. What other Oriental religion will we consider next?

CHAPTER 8

Shinto
Japan's Search for God

"Because my father was a Shinto priest, we were told to offer a glass of water and a bowl of steamed rice on the *kamidana* [Shinto household shrine] every morning before breakfast. After that act of worship, we took down the bowl of rice and ate from it. By doing so, I was confident that the gods would protect us.

"When we purchased a house, we carefully confirmed the auspicious location of the new house in relation to our old one by consulting a shaman, or a spirit medium. He cautioned us about three demon gates and instructed us to follow the purification procedure that my father prescribed. So we purified those quarters with salt once every month."—Mayumi T.

SHINTO is predominantly a Japanese religion. According-ing to the *Nihon Shukyo Jiten* (Encyclopedia of Japanese Religions), "The formation of Shintoism is almost identical with the Japanese ethnic culture, and it is a religious culture that was never practiced apart from this ethnic society." But Japanese business and cultural influences are now so widespread that it should interest us to know what religious factors have shaped Japan's history and the Japanese personality.

1. (Include introduction.) Where primarily is the Shinto religion practiced, and what does it involve for some of its believers?

² Although Shinto claims a membership of over 91,-000,000 in Japan, which amounts to about three quarters of its population, a survey reveals that only 2,000,000 people, or 3 percent of the adult population, really profess to believe in Shinto. However, Sugata Masaaki, a researcher on Shinto, says: "Shinto is so inextricably woven into the fabric of Japanese daily life that people are barely aware of its existence. To the Japanese it is less a religion than an unobtrusive environmental fixture, like the air they breathe." Even those who claim to be apathetic to religion will buy Shinto traffic safety amulets, have their weddings according to Shinto tradition, and pour their money into annual Shinto festivals.

How Did It Start?

³ The designation "Shinto" sprang up in the eighth century C.E. to distinguish the local religion from Bud-

2. To what extent does Shinto influence the lives of the Japanese people?
3, 4. How did Japanese religion first become known as Shinto?

A Shinto devotee asking gods for favors

dhism, which was being introduced into Japan. "Of course, 'the Religion of the Japanese' . . . existed before the introduction of Buddhism," explains Sachiya Hiro, a researcher of Japanese religions, "but it was a subconscious religion, consisting of customs and 'mores.' With the introduction of Buddhism, however, people became aware of the fact that those mores constituted a Japanese religion, different from Buddhism, which was a foreign religion." How did this Japanese religion evolve?

[4] It is difficult to pinpoint a date when the original Shinto, or "Religion of the Japanese," emerged. With the advent of the wetland cultivation of rice, "wetland agriculture necessitated well-organized and stable communities," explains the *Kodansha Encyclopedia of Japan,* "and agricultural rites—which later played such an important role in Shintō—were developed." Those early peoples conceived of and revered numerous gods of nature.

神道

Shinto, 'Way of the Gods'

[5] In addition to this reverence, fear of departed souls led to rites for appeasing them. This later developed into a worship of ancestral spirits. According to Shinto belief, a "departed" soul still has its personality and is stained with death pollution immediately after death. When the bereaved perform memorial rites, the soul is purified to the point of removing all malice, and it takes on a peaceful and benevolent character. In time the ancestral spirit rises to the position of an ancestral, or

5. (a) What is the Shinto view of the dead? (b) How does the Shinto view of the dead compare with that of the Bible?

guardian, deity. Thus we find that the immortal soul belief is fundamental to yet another religion and conditions the attitudes and actions of the believers.—Psalm 146:4; Ecclesiastes 9:5, 6, 10.

⁶ Gods of nature and ancestral gods were considered to be spirits "floating" in and filling the air. During festivals, people called upon the gods to descend to the specific sites sanctified for the occasion. Gods were said to take temporary residence in shintai, objects of worship such as trees, stones, mirrors, and swords. Shamans, or spirit mediums, presided over rituals to call down the gods.

⁷ Gradually, the "landing sites" of the gods, which were temporarily purified for festivals, took on a more permanent form. People built shrines for benevolent gods, those who appeared to bless them. At first they did not carve

------

6, 7. (a) How did Shintoists view their gods? (b) What is a shintai, and why is it significant in Shinto? (Compare Exodus 20: 4, 5; Leviticus 26:1; 1 Corinthians 8:5, 6.)

An entire mountain, such as Fuji, is sometimes viewed as a shintai, or object of worship

images of the gods but worshiped the shintai, in which spirits of gods were said to reside. Even an entire mountain, such as Fuji, could serve as a shintai. In time there came to be so many gods that the Japanese developed the expression *yaoyorozu-no-kami*, which literally means "eight million gods" (*"kami"* means "gods" or "deities"). Now the expression is used to signify "countless gods," since the number of deities in the Shinto religion is ever increasing.

The Sun-Goddess in Shinto Myth

Shinto myth says that far back in time, the god Izanagi "washed his left eye, and so gave birth to the great goddess Amaterasu, goddess of the Sun." Later on, Susanoo, the god of the sea plains, so frightened Amaterasu that she "hid in a rocky cave of Heaven, blocking the entrance with a boulder. The world was plunged into darkness." So the gods devised a plan to get Amaterasu out of the cave. They collected crowing cocks who herald the dawn and made a large mirror. On the sakaki trees, they hung jewels and cloth streamers. Then the goddess Ama no Uzume began to dance and drum on a tub with her feet. In her frenzied dance, she stripped off her clothes, and the gods burst out laughing. All this activity aroused the curiosity of Amaterasu, who looked out and saw herself in the mirror. The reflection drew her out of the cave, whereupon the god of Force grabbed her by the hand and brought her out into the open. "Once more the world was lit up by the rays of the Sun goddess."—*New Larousse Encyclopedia of Mythology.*—Compare Genesis 1: 3-5, 14-19; Psalm 74: 16, 17; 104:19-23.

⁸ As Shinto rituals concentrated around shrines, each clan enshrined its own guardian deity. However, when the imperial family unified the nation in the seventh century C.E., they elevated their sun-goddess, Amaterasu Omikami, to be the national deity and central figure of the Shinto gods. (See box, page 191.) In time the myth was propounded that the emperor was a direct descendant of the sun-goddess. To fortify that belief, two major Shinto writings, *Kojiki* and *Nihon shoki,* were compiled in the eighth century C.E. Using myths that exalted the imperial family as the descendants of gods, these books helped to establish the supremacy of the emperors.

A Religion of Festivals and Rituals

⁹ These two books of Shinto mythology, however, were not considered to be inspired scriptures. Interestingly, Shinto does not have a known founder or a Bible. "Shinto is a religion of a series of 'withouts,'" explains Shouichi Saeki, a Shinto scholar. "It is *without* definite doctrines and *without* detailed theology. It is as good as *without* any precepts to be observed. . . . Although I was brought up in a family that has traditionally adhered to Shinto, I have no recollection of being given serious religious education." (Italics ours.) For Shintoists, doctrines, precepts, and, at times, even what they worship are not important. "Even at the same shrine," says a Shinto researcher, "the enshrined god was often exchanged for another, and at times people who worshiped those gods

---

8. (a) According to Shinto myth, how was Amaterasu Omikami formed and forced to give light? (b) How did Amaterasu Omikami become the national deity, and how were the emperors tied in with her?
9. (a) Why is Shinto called a religion of "withouts" by one scholar? (b) How strict is Shinto regarding teachings? (Compare John 4:22-24.)

and offered prayers to them were not aware of the change."

¹⁰ What, then, is of vital importance to Shintoists? "Originally," says a book on Japanese culture, "Shinto

10. What is of vital importance to Shintoists?

*S*hinto—A Religion of Festivals

The Japanese year is full of religious festivals, or *matsuri*. The following are some of the principal ones:

■ *Sho-gatsu,* or the New Year Festival, January 1-3.

■ *Setsubun,* bean throwing inside and outside homes, while shouting, "Devils out, good luck in"; February 3.

■ *Hina Matsuri,* or Doll Festival for girls, held March 3. A platform of dolls, depicting an ancient imperial household, is displayed.

■ Boy's Festival, on May 5; *Koinobori* (carp streamers symbolizing strength) are flown from poles.

■ *Tsukimi,* admiring midautumn full moon, while offering small round rice cakes and firstfruits of crops.

■ *Kanname-sai,* or the offering of the first new rice by the emperor, in October.

■ *Niiname-sai* is celebrated by the imperial family in November, when the new rice is tasted by the emperor, who presides as chief priest of the Imperial Shinto.

■ *Shichi-go-san,* which means "seven-five-three," celebrated by Shinto families on November 15. Seven, five, and three are viewed as important transition years; children in colorful kimono visit the family shrine.

■ Many Buddhist festivals are also celebrated, including the Buddha's birthday, on April 8, and the Obon Festival, July 15, which ends with lanterns floating out on sea or stream "to guide the ancestrial spirits back to the other world."

considered acts that promoted the harmony and liveli-hood of a small community as 'good' and those that hindered such as 'bad.'" Harmony with gods, nature, and the community was considered to be of superlative value. Anything that disrupted the peaceful harmony of the community was bad regardless of its moral value.

[11] Since Shinto has no formal doctrine or teaching, its way of promoting the harmony of the community is through rituals and festivals. "What is most important in Shintoism," explains the encyclopedia *Nihon Shukyo Jiten,* "is whether we celebrate festivals or not." (See box, page 193.) Feasting together at festivals around ancestral gods contributed to a cooperative spirit among people in the rice-growing community. Major festivals were and still are related to rice cultivation. In the spring, village people call upon the "god of the paddies" to come down to their village, and they pray for a good crop. In the fall, they thank their gods for the harvest. During festivals, they carry their gods around on a *mikoshi,* or portable shrine, and have communion of rice wine (sake) and food with the gods.

[12] To be in union with the gods, however, Shintoists believe that they must be cleansed and purified from all their moral impurity and sin. This is where rituals come in. There are two ways to purify a person or an object. One is *oharai* and the other is *misogi.* In *oharai,* a Shinto priest swings a branch of the evergreen sakaki tree with paper or flax tied to its tip to purify an item or a person, whereas in *misogi,* water is used. These purification rituals

---

11. What role do festivals play in Shinto worship and daily life?
12. What kind of purification rites are performed in Shinto, and for what purpose?

Shintoists carrying a *mikoshi*, or portable shrine, and above, wearing hollyhock (*aoi*) leaves during the Aoi Festival in Kyoto

are so vital to the Shinto religion that one Japanese authority states: "It may safely be said that without these rituals, Shinto cannot stand [as a religion]."

Shinto's Adaptability

[13] Festivals and rituals have lingered with Shinto despite the transformation that the Shinto religion has gone through over the years. What transformation? One Shinto researcher likens the changes in Shinto to those of a dress-up doll. When Buddhism was introduced, Shinto clothed itself with the Buddhist teaching. When people needed moral standards, it put on Confucianism. Shinto has been extremely adaptable.

[14] Syncretism, or the fusing of the elements of one religion into another, took place very early in the history of Shinto. Although Confucianism and Taoism, known in

---

13, 14. How has Shinto adapted to other religions?

Japan as the "Way of *yin* and *yang*," had infiltrated the Shinto religion, Buddhism was the major ingredient that blended with Shinto.

[15] When Buddhism entered by way of China and Korea, the Japanese labeled their traditional religious practices as *Shinto*, or the "way of the gods." However, with the advent of a new religion, Japan was divided on whether to accept Buddhism or not. The pro-Buddhist camp insisted, 'All neighboring countries worship that way. Why should Japan be different?' The anti-Buddhist faction disputed, 'If we worship the neighboring gods, we will be provoking the anger of our own gods.' After decades of discord, the pro-Buddhists won out. By the end of the sixth century C.E., when Prince Shōtoku embraced Buddhism, the new religion had taken root.

[16] As Buddhism spread to rural communities, it encountered the local Shinto deities whose existence was strongly entrenched in the daily lives of the people. The two religions had to compromise to coexist. Buddhist monks practicing self-discipline in the mountains helped to fuse the two religions. As mountains were considered

15, 16. (a) How did Shintoists react to Buddhism? (b) How did the fusion of Shinto and Buddhism come about?

The swinging of paper or flax tied to a branch of evergreen is thought to purify man and objects, assuring them safety

A Japanese does not feel contradiction in praying before both a Shinto shrine, left, and a Buddhist altar

the dwellings of Shinto divinities, the monks' ascetic practices in the mountains gave rise to the idea of mixing Buddhism and Shinto, which also led to the building of *jinguji*, or "shrine-temples."* Gradually a fusion of the two religions took place as Buddhism took the initiative in forming religious theories.

[17] Meanwhile, the belief that Japan was a divine nation was taking root. When the Mongols attacked Japan in the 13th century, there arose belief in *kamikaze*, literally "divine wind." Twice the Mongols raided the island of Kyushu with overwhelming fleets, and twice they were

---

* In Japan the religious buildings for Shintoists are regarded as shrines and those for Buddhists, temples.

17. (a) What is the meaning of *kamikaze?* (b) How was *kamikaze* related to the belief that Japan is a divine nation?

thwarted by storms. The Japanese credited these storms, or winds (*kaze*), to their Shinto gods (*kami*), and this greatly enhanced the reputation of their gods.

[18] As confidence in Shinto deities swelled, they were viewed as being the original gods, whereas Buddhas ("enlightened ones") and bodhisattvas (Buddhas-to-be who help others achieve enlightenment; see pages 136-8, 145-6) were seen only as temporary local manifestations of the divinity. As a result of this Shinto-versus-Buddhist conflict, various schools of Shinto developed. Some emphasized Buddhism, others elevated the Shinto pantheon, and still others used a later form of Confucianism to adorn their teachings.

Emperor Worship and State Shinto

[19] After many years of compromising, Shinto theologians decided that their religion had been defiled by Chinese religious thinking. So they insisted on a return to the ancient Japanese way. A new school of Shinto, known as Restoration Shinto, emerged, with Norinaga Motoori (pronounced *Moto´ori*), an 18th-century scholar, as one of

---

18. How did Shinto compete with other religions?
19. (a) What was the aim of the Restoration Shintoists? (b) To what thinking did the teachings of Norinaga Motoori lead? (c) What does God invite us to do?

Emperor Hirohito (on dais) was worshiped as the descendant of the sun-goddess

its foremost theologians. In search of the origin of the Japanese culture, Motoori studied the classics, especially the Shinto writings called *Kojiki*. He taught the superiority of the sun-goddess Amaterasu Omikami but left the reason for natural phenomena vaguely up to the gods. In addition, according to his teaching, divine providence is unpredictable, and it is disrespectful for men to try to understand it. Ask no questions and be submissive to divine providence was his idea.—Isaiah 1:18.

[20] One of his followers, Atsutane Hirata, enlarged on Norinaga's idea and tried to purify Shinto, rid it of all "Chinese" influences. What did Hirata do? He fused Shinto with apostatized "Christian" theology! He likened *Amenominakanushi-no-kami,* a god mentioned in the *Kojiki,* to the God of "Christianity" and described this presiding god of the universe as having two subordinate gods, "the High-Producing (Takami-musubi) and the Divine-Producing (Kami-musubi), who appear to represent the male and female principles." (*Religions in Japan*) Yes, he adopted the teaching of a triune god from Roman Catholicism, although it never became the mainline Shinto teaching. Hirata's blending of so-called Christianity into Shinto, however, finally grafted Christendom's form of monotheism into the Shinto mind.—Isaiah 40: 25, 26.

[21] Hirata's theology became the basis for the 'Revere the Emperor' movement, which led to the overthrowing of the feudal military dictators, the shoguns, and to the

_____
20, 21. (a) How did one Shinto theologian try to rid Shinto of "Chinese" influence? (b) Hirata's philosophy led to the establishment of what movement?

restoration of imperial rule in 1868. With the establishment of the imperial government, Hirata's disciples were appointed to be the governmental commissioners of the Shinto worship, and they promoted a movement toward making Shinto the State religion. Under the then new constitution, the emperor, viewed as a direct descendant of the sun-goddess Amaterasu Omikami, was considered "sacred and inviolable." He thus became the supreme god of State Shinto.—Psalm 146:3-5.

Shinto "Holy Writ"

22 While Shinto had its ancient records, rituals, and prayers in the *Kojiki,* the *Nihongi,* and the *Yengishiki* writings, State Shinto needed a sacred book. In 1882 Emperor Meiji issued the Imperial Rescript to Soldiers and Sailors. Since it came down from the emperor, it was viewed by the Japanese as holy writ, and it became the basis for daily meditation for men in the armed forces. It emphasized that an individual's duty to pay his debts and obligations to the god-emperor was above any that he might have to anyone else.

23 A further addition to Shinto holy writ took place when the emperor issued the Imperial Rescript on Education on October 30, 1890. It "not only laid down fundamentals for school education but virtually became the holy scriptures of State Shinto," explains Shigeyoshi Murakami, a researcher of State Shinto. The rescript made clear that the "historical" relationship between the mythical imperial ancestors and their subjects was the basis of education. How did the Japanese view these edicts?

22, 23. (a) What two edicts were issued by the emperor? (b) Why were these edicts considered sacred?

[24] "When I was a girl the vice principal [of the school] would hold a wooden box at eye level and reverentially bring it up to the stage," recalls Asano Koshino. "The principal would receive the box and pull out the scroll on which the Imperial Rescript on Education was written. While the rescript was being read, we were to bow our heads low until we heard the concluding words, 'The Name of His Majesty and His seal.' We heard it so many times that we memorized the words." Until 1945, and by means of an educational system based on mythology, the whole nation was conditioned to dedicate itself to the emperor. State Shinto was viewed as the superreligion, and the other 13 Shinto sects teaching different doctrines were relegated to being referred to as Sect Shinto.

Japan's Religious Mission—World Conquest

[25] State Shinto was equipped with its idol as well. "Every morning, I clapped my hands toward the sun, the symbol of the goddess Amaterasu Omikami, and then faced east toward the Imperial Palace and worshiped the emperor," recalls Masato, an older Japanese man. The emperor was worshiped as god by his subjects. He was viewed as supreme politically and religiously by reason of his descent from the sun-goddess. One Japanese professor stated: "The Emperor is god revealed in men. He is manifest Deity."

[26] As a result, the teaching was developed that "the center of this phenomenal world is the Mikado's [Emperor's] land. From this center we must expand this Great

24. (a) Give an example of how the imperial rescripts were viewed by the people. (b) How did State Shinto lead to emperor worship?
25. How was the Japanese emperor viewed by the people?
26. What teaching resulted from the veneration of the emperor?

Spirit throughout the world. . . . The expansion of Great Japan throughout the world and the elevation of the entire world into the land of the Gods is the urgent business of the present and, again, it is our eternal and unchanging object." (*The Political Philosophy of Modern Shinto*, by D. C. Holtom) There was no separation of Church and State there!

[27] In his book *Man's Religions*, John B. Noss comments: "The Japanese military were not slow in availing themselves of this point of view. They made it part of their war talk that conquest was the holy mission of Japan. Certainly in such words we may see the logical outcome of a nationalism infused with all the values of religion." What tragedy was sown for the Japanese and for other peoples, based mainly on the Shinto myth of the divinity of the emperor and the mixing of religion with nationalism!

[28] The Japanese in general did not have any alternative but to worship the emperor under State Shinto and its imperial system. Norinaga Motoori's teaching of 'Ask nothing, but submit to divine providence' permeated and controlled Japanese thinking. By 1941 the whole nation was mobilized into the war effort of World War II under the banner of State Shinto and in dedication to the "living man-god." 'Japan is a divine nation,' the people thought, 'and the *kamikaze,* the divine wind, will blow when there is a crisis.' Soldiers and their families petitioned their guardian gods for success in the war.

[29] When the "divine" nation was defeated in 1945,

---

27. How was worship of the Japanese emperor used by militarists?
28. What role did Shinto have in the Japanese war effort?
29. What led to loss of faith on the part of many after World War II?

A young woman affixes to the shrine an *ema,* or wooden prayer plaque, she has bought

under the twin blows of the atomic annihilation of Hiroshima and much of Nagasaki, Shinto faced a severe crisis. Overnight, the supposedly invincible divine ruler Hirohito became simply the defeated human emperor. Japanese faith was shattered. *Kamikaze* had failed the nation. States the encyclopedia *Nihon Shukyo Jiten:* "One of the reasons was the nation's disappointment at being betrayed. . . . Worse yet, the Shinto world gave no religiously advanced and appropriate explanation of doubts that resulted from [defeat]. Thus, the religiously immature reaction of 'There is no god or Buddha' became the general trend."

The Way to True Harmony

[30] The course that State Shinto trod highlights the need for each individual to investigate the traditional beliefs to which he adheres. Shintoists may have sought a way of

---

30. (a) What lesson can be learned from the Shinto experience in World War II? (b) Why is it vital to use our power of reason with regard to our worship?

harmony with their Japanese neighbors when they supported militarism. That, of course, did not contribute to worldwide harmony, and with their breadwinners and young ones killed in battle, neither did it bring domestic harmony. Before we dedicate our lives to someone, we must make sure to whom and to what cause we are offering ourselves. "I entreat you," said a Christian teacher to Romans who had previously been given to emperor worship, "to present your bodies a sacrifice living, holy, acceptable to God, a sacred service with your power of reason." Just as the Roman Christians were to use their power of reason to choose to whom they should dedicate themselves, it is vital to use our power of reason to determine whom we should worship.—Romans 12:1, 2.

[31] For Shintoists in general, the important factor in their religion was not the specific identification of one god. "For the common people," says Hidenori Tsuji, an instructor of Japanese religious history, "gods or Buddhas did not make any difference. Be they gods or Buddhas, as long as they heard supplications for a good crop, eradication of disease, and family safety, that was sufficient for the people." But did that lead them to the true God and his blessing? History's answer is clear.

[32] In their search for a god, the Shintoists, basing their beliefs on mythology, turned a mere man, their emperor, into a god, the so-called descendant of the sun-goddess Amaterasu Omikami. Yet, thousands of years before Shinto started, the true God had revealed himself to a Semitic man of faith in Mesopotamia. Our next chapter will discuss that momentous event and its outcome.

31. (a) What has been sufficient for most Shinto believers? (b) What question needs to be answered?
32. What will our next chapter discuss?

CHAPTER 9

Judaism—Searching for God Through Scripture and Tradition

M OSES, Jesus, Mahler, Marx, Freud, and Einstein —what did all of them have in common? All were Jews, and in different ways, all have affected the history and culture of mankind. Very evidently Jews have been noteworthy for thousands of years. The Bible itself is a testimony to that.

² Unlike other ancient religions and cultures, Judaism is rooted in history, not in mythology. Yet, some might ask: The Jews are such a tiny minority, about 18 million in a world of over 5 thousand million people, why should we be interested in their religion, Judaism?

Why Judaism Should Interest Us

³ One reason is that the roots of the Jewish religion go back some 4,000 years in history and other major religions are indebted to its Scriptures to a greater or lesser degree. (See box, page 220.) Christianity, founded by Jesus (Hebrew, *Ye·shu'a'*), a first-century Jew, has its roots in the

---

1, 2. (a) Who were some prominent Jews who have affected history and culture? (b) What question might be raised by some people?
3, 4. (a) Of what do the Hebrew Scriptures consist? (b) What are some reasons we should consider the Jewish religion and its roots?

Abram (Abraham), the forefather of the Jews, worshiped Jehovah God nearly 4,000 years ago

Hebrew Scriptures. And as any reading of the Qur'ān will show, Islām also owes much to those scriptures. (Qur'ān, surah 2:49-57; 32:23, 24) Thus, when we examine the Jewish religion, we also examine the roots of hundreds of other religions and sects.

⁴ A second and vital reason is that the Jewish religion provides an essential link in mankind's search for the true God. According to the Hebrew Scriptures, Abram, the forefather of the Jews, was already worshiping the true God nearly 4,000 years ago.* Reasonably, we ask, How did the Jews and their faith develop?—Genesis 17:18.

How Did the Jews Originate?

⁵ Generally speaking, the Jewish people are descendants of an ancient, Hebrew-speaking branch of the Semitic race. (Genesis 10:1, 21-32; 1 Chronicles 1:17-28, 34; 2:

---

* Compare Genesis 5:22-24, *New World Translation of the Holy Scriptures—With References,* second footnote on verse 22.

5, 6. What, briefly, is the history of the origin of the Jews and their name?

1, 2) Nearly 4,000 years ago, their forefather Abram emi-
grated from the thriving metropolis of Ur of the Chaldeans
in Sumeria to the land of Canaan, of which God had stated:
"I will assign this land to your offspring."* (Genesis 11:
31–12:7) He is spoken of as "Abram the Hebrew" at Genesis
14:13, although his name was later changed to Abraham.
(Genesis 17:4-6) From him the Jews draw a line of descent
that begins with his son Isaac and his grandson Jacob,
whose name was changed to Israel. (Genesis 32:27-29)
Israel had 12 sons, who became the founders of 12 tribes.
One of those was Judah, from which name the word "Jew"
was eventually derived.—2 Kings 16:6.

⁶ In time the term "Jew" was applied to all Israelites, not
just to a descendant of Judah. (Esther 3:6; 9:20) Because
the Jewish genealogical records were destroyed in 70 C.E.
when the Romans razed Jerusalem, no Jew today can
accurately determine from which tribe he himself is descended. Nevertheless, over the millenniums, the ancient
Jewish religion has developed and changed. Today Judaism is practiced by millions of Jews in the Republic of
Israel and the Diaspora (dispersion around the world).
What is the basis of that religion?

Moses, the Law, and a Nation

⁷ In 1943 B.C.E.,# God chose Abram to be his special
servant and later made a solemn oath to him because of his

---

* All citations in this chapter, unless otherwise stated, are from
the modern (1985) *Tanakh, A New Translation of the Holy Scriptures,*
by scholars of The Jewish Publication Society.

The chronology here presented is based on the Bible text as the
authority. (See the book *"All Scripture Is Inspired of God and Beneficial,"* published by the Watchtower Bible and Tract Society of N.Y.,
Inc., Study 3, "Measuring Events in the Stream of Time.")

7. What oath did God make to Abraham, and why?

faithfulness in being willing to offer his son Isaac as a sacrifice, even though the sacrifice was never completed. (Genesis 12:1-3; 22:1-14) In that oath God said: "By Myself I swear, the LORD [Hebrew: יהוה, *YHWH*] declares: Because you have done this and have not withheld your son, your favored one, I will bestow My blessing upon you and make your descendants as numerous as the stars of heaven . . . All the nations of the earth shall bless themselves by your descendants ["seed," *JP*], because you have obeyed My command." This sworn oath was repeated to Abraham's son and to his grandson, and then it continued in the tribe of Judah and the line of David. This strictly monotheistic concept of a personal God dealing directly with humans was unique in that ancient world, and it came to form the basis of the Jewish religion.—Genesis 22:15-18; 26:3-5; 28:13-15; Psalm 89:4, 5, 29, 30, 36, 37 (Psalm 89:3, 4, 28, 29, 35, 36, *NW*).

Star of David—a non-Biblical symbol of Israel and Judaism

⁸ To carry out His promises to Abraham, God laid the foundation for a nation by establishing a special covenant with Abraham's descendants. This covenant was instituted through Moses, the great Hebrew leader and mediator between God and Israel. Who was Moses, and why is he so important to Jews? The Bible's Exodus account tells us that he was born in Egypt (1593 B.C.E.) to Israelite parents who were slaves in captivity along with the rest of Israel. He was the one "whom the LORD singled out" to lead His people to freedom in Canaan, the Promised Land. (Deuteronomy

8. Who was Moses, and what role did he play in Israel?

6:23; 34:10) Moses fulfilled the vital role of mediator of the Law covenant given by God to Israel, in addition to being their prophet, judge, leader, and historian.—Exodus 2:1–3:22.

⁹ The Law that Israel accepted consisted of the Ten Words, or Commandments, and over 600 laws that amounted to a comprehensive catalog of directions and guidance for daily conduct. (See box, page 211.) It involved the mundane and the holy—the physical and the moral requirements as well as the worship of God.

¹⁰ This Law covenant, or religious constitution, gave form and substance to the faith of the patriarchs. As a result, the descendants of Abraham became a nation dedicated to the service of God. Thus the Jewish religion began to take definite shape, and the Jews became a nation organized for the worship and service of their God. At Exodus 19:5, 6, God promised them: "If you will obey Me faithfully and keep My covenant, . . . you shall be to Me a kingdom of priests and a holy nation." Thus, the Israelites would become a 'chosen people' to serve God's purposes. However, the fulfillment of the covenant promises was subject to the condition "If you will obey." That dedicated nation was now obligated to its God. Hence, at a later date (the eighth century B.C.E.), God could say to the Jews: "My witnesses are *you*—declares the LORD [Hebrew: יהוה, *YHWH*]—My servant, whom I have chosen."—Isaiah 43:10, 12.

A Nation With Priests, Prophets, and Kings

¹¹ While the nation of Israel was still in the desert and heading for the Promised Land, a priesthood was

---

9, 10. (a) What was the Law that was transmitted through Moses? (b) What aspects of life were covered by the Ten Commandments? (c) What obligation did the Law covenant bring to Israel?
11. How did the priesthood and the kingship develop?

established in the line of Moses' brother, Aaron. A large portable tent, or tabernacle, became the center of Israelite worship and sacrifice. (Exodus, chapters 26-28) In time the nation of Israel arrived at the Promised Land, Canaan, and conquered it, even as God had commanded. (Joshua 1:2-6) Eventually an earthly kingship was established, and in 1077 B.C.E., David, from the tribe of Judah, became king. With his rule, both the kingship and the priesthood were firmly established at a new national center, Jerusalem. —1 Samuel 8:7.

[12] After David's death, his son Solomon built a magnificent temple in Jerusalem, which replaced the tabernacle. Because God had made a covenant with David for the kingship to remain in his line forever, it was understood that an anointed King, the Messiah, would one day come from David's line of descent. Prophecy indicated that through this Messianic King, or "seed," Israel and all the nations would enjoy perfect rulership. (Genesis 22:18, *JP*) This hope took root, and the Messianic nature of the Jewish religion became clearly crystallized.—2 Samuel 7: 8-16; Psalm 72:1-20; Isaiah 11:1-10; Zechariah 9:9, 10.

[13] However, the Jews allowed themselves to be influenced by the false religion of the Canaanites and other nations round about. As a result, they violated their covenant relationship with God. To correct them and guide them back, Jehovah sent a series of prophets who bore his messages to the people. Thus, prophecy became another unique feature of the religion of the Jews and constitutes much of the Hebrew Scriptures. In fact, 18 books of the Hebrew Scriptures bear prophets' names.—Isaiah 1:4-17.

---

12. What promise had God made to David?
13. Whom did God use to correct the backsliding of Israel? Give an example.

Ten Commandments for Worship and Conduct

Millions of people have heard of the Ten Commandments, but few have ever read them. Therefore, we reproduce the major part of their text here.

■ "You shall have no other gods besides Me.

■ "You shall not make for yourself a sculptured image, or any likeness of what is in the heavens above, or on the earth below, or in the waters under the earth. You shall not bow down to them or serve them. . . . [*At this early date, 1513 B.C.E., this command was unique in its rejection of idolatry.*]

■ "You shall not swear falsely by the name of the LORD [Hebrew: יהוה] your God . . .

■ "Remember the sabbath day and keep it holy. . . . The LORD blessed the sabbath day and hallowed it.

■ "Honor your father and your mother . . .

■ "You shall not murder.

■ "You shall not commit adultery.

■ "You shall not steal.

■ "You shall not bear false witness against your neighbor.

In spite of the unique law from God, Israel imitated the calf worship of its pagan neighbors (Golden calf, Byblos)

■ "You shall not covet your neighbor's house . . . wife . . . male or female slave . . . ox or his ass, or anything that is your neighbor's." —Exodus 20:3-14.

Although only the first four commandments are directly concerned with religious belief and worship, the other commandments showed the connection between correct conduct and a proper relationship with the Creator.

¹⁴ Outstanding among such prophets were Isaiah, Jeremiah, and Ezekiel, all of whom warned of Jehovah's impending punishment of the nation for its idolatrous worship. This punishment came about in 607 B.C.E. when, because of Israel's apostasy, Jehovah allowed Babylon, the then dominant world power, to overthrow Jerusalem and its temple and take the nation into captivity. The prophets were proved right in what they had foretold, and Israel's 70-year exile for most of the sixth century B.C.E. is a matter of historical record.—2 Chronicles 36:20, 21; Jeremiah 25: 11, 12; Daniel 9:2.

¹⁵ In 539 B.C.E., Cyrus the Persian defeated Babylon and permitted the Jews to resettle their land and rebuild the temple in Jerusalem. Although a remnant responded, the majority of the Jews remained under the influence of Babylonian society. Jews later were affected by the Persian culture. Consequently, Jewish settlements sprang up in the Middle East and around the Mediterranean. In each community a new form of worship came into being that involved the synagogue, a congregational center for the Jews in each town. Naturally, this arrangement diminished the emphasis on the rebuilt temple in Jerusalem. The far-flung Jews were now truly a Diaspora.—Ezra 2:64, 65.

Judaism Emerges With a Greek Garment

¹⁶ By the fourth century B.C.E., the Jewish community was in a state of flux and was thus prey to the waves of a

14. How did events vindicate the prophets in Israel?
15. (a) How did a new form of worship take root among the Jews? (b) What effect did the synagogues have on the worship at Jerusalem?
16, 17. (a) What new influence was sweeping across the Mediterranean world in the fourth century B.C.E.? (b) Who were instrumental in spreading Greek culture, and how? (c) How did Judaism thus emerge on the world scene?

non-Jewish culture that was engulfing the Mediterranean world and beyond. The waters emanated from Greece, and Judaism emerged from them with a Hellenistic garment.

[17] In 332 B.C.E. the Greek general Alexander the Great took the Middle East in lightning-quick conquest and was welcomed by the Jews when he came to Jerusalem.* Alexander's successors continued his plan of Hellenization, imbuing all parts of the empire with Greek language, culture, and philosophy. As a result, the Greek and Jewish cultures went through a blending process that was to have surprising results.

[18] Diaspora Jews began to speak Greek instead of Hebrew. So toward the beginning of the third century B.C.E., the first translation of the Hebrew Scriptures, called the *Septuagint,* was made into Greek, and through it, many Gentiles came to have respect for and familiarity with the Jews' religion, some even converting.# Jews, on the other hand, were becoming conversant with Greek thought and some even became philosophers, something entirely new to the Jews. One example is Philo of Alexandria of the first

---

* The first-century Jewish historian Yoseph ben Mattityahu (Flavius Josephus) relates that when Alexander arrived at Jerusalem, the Jews opened the gates to him and showed him the prophecy from the book of Daniel written over 200 years earlier that clearly described Alexander's conquests as 'the King of Greece.'—*Jewish Antiquities,* Book XI, Chapter VIII 5; Daniel 8:5-8, 21.

During the period of the Maccabees (Hasmonaeans, from 165 to 63 B.C.E.), Jewish leaders such as John Hyrcanus even forced large-scale conversion to Judaism by conquest. It is of interest that at the beginning of the Common Era, 10 percent of the Mediterranean world was Jewish. This figure clearly shows the impact of Jewish proselytism.

---

18. (a) Why was the Greek *Septuagint* translation of the Hebrew Scriptures necessary? (b) What aspect of Greek culture especially affected the Jews?

century C.E., who endeavored to explain Judaism in terms of Greek philosophy, as if the two expressed the same ultimate truths.

[19] Summing up this period of give-and-take between Greek and Jewish cultures, Jewish author Max Dimont says: "Enriched with Platonic thought, Aristotelian logic, and Euclidian science, Jewish scholars approached the Torah with new tools. . . . They proceeded to add Greek reason to Jewish revelation." The events that would take place under Roman rule, which absorbed the Greek Empire and then Jerusalem in the year 63 B.C.E., were to pave the way for even more significant changes.

Judaism Under Roman Rule

[20] The Judaism of the first century of the Common Era was at a unique stage. Max Dimont states that it was poised between "the mind of Greece and the sword of Rome." Jewish expectations were high because of political oppression and interpretations of Messianic prophecies, especially those of Daniel. The Jews were divided into factions. The Pharisees emphasized an oral law (see box, page 221) rather than temple sacrifice. The Sadducees stressed the importance of the temple and the priesthood. Then there were the Essenes, the Zealots, and the Herodians. All were at odds religiously and philosophically. Jewish leaders were called rabbis (masters, teachers) who, because of their knowledge of the Law, grew in prestige and became a new type of spiritual leader.

---

19. How does one Jewish author describe the period of the melding of Greek and Jewish cultures?
20. What was the religious situation among the Jews in the first century C.E.?

²¹ Internal and external divisions, however, continued in Judaism, especially in the land of Israel. Finally, outright rebellion broke out against Rome, and in 70 C.E., Roman troops besieged Jerusalem, laid waste the city, burned its temple to the ground, and scattered its inhabitants. Eventually, Jerusalem was decreed totally off-limits to Jews. Without a temple, without a land, with its people dispersed throughout the Roman Empire, Judaism was in need of a new religious expression if it was to survive.

²² With the destruction of the temple, the Sadducees disappeared, and the oral law that the Pharisees had championed became the centerpiece of a new, Rabbinic Judaism. More intense study, prayer, and works of piety replaced temple sacrifices and pilgrimages. Thus, Judaism could be practiced anywhere, at any time, in any cultural

---

21. What events drastically affected the Jews of the first two centuries C.E.?
22. (a) How was Judaism affected by the loss of the temple in Jerusalem? (b) How do the Jews divide the Bible? (c) What is the Talmud, and how did it develop?

A Jewish scribe copying Hebrew text

surroundings. The rabbis put this oral law into writing, in addition to composing commentaries on it, and then commentaries on the commentaries, all of which together became known as the Talmud.—See box, page 221.

[23] What was the result of these varied influences? Max Dimont says in his book *Jews, God and History* that though the Pharisees carried on the torch of Jewish ideology and religion, "the torch itself had been ignited by the Greek philosophers." While much of the Talmud was highly legalistic, its illustrations and explanations reflected the clear influence of Greek philosophy. For example, Greek religious concepts, such as the immortal soul, were expressed in Jewish terms. Truly, in that new Rabbinic era, veneration of the Talmud—by then a blend of legalistic and Greek philosophy—grew among the Jews until, by the Middle Ages, the Talmud came to be revered by the Jews more than the Bible itself.

Judaism Through the Middle Ages

[24] During the Middle Ages (from about 500 to 1500 C.E.), two distinct Jewish communities emerged —the Sephardic Jews, who flourished under Muslim rule in Spain, and the Ashkenazi Jews in Central and Eastern Europe. Both communities produced Rabbinic scholars whose writings and thoughts form the basis for Jewish religious interpretation until this day. Interestingly, many of the customs and religious practices current today in Judaism really got their start during the Middle Ages.—See box, page 231.

---

23. What shift in emphasis took place under the influence of Greek thinking?
24. (a) What two major communities emerged among the Jews during the Middle Ages? (b) How did they influence Judaism?

²⁵ In the 12th century, there began a wave of expulsions of Jews from various countries. As Israeli author Abba Eban explains in *My People—The Story of the Jews:* "In any country . . . which fell under the unilateral influence of the Catholic Church, the story is the same: appalling degradation, torture, slaughter, and expulsion." Finally, in 1492, Spain, which had once again come under Catholic rule, followed suit and ordered the expulsion of all Jews from its territory. So by the end of the 15th century, Jews had been expelled from nearly all Western Europe, fleeing to Eastern Europe and countries around the Mediterranean.

Sephardic and Ashkenazi Jews formed two communities

²⁶ Through the centuries of oppression and persecution, many self-proclaimed Messiahs rose up among the Jews in different parts of the world, all receiving acceptance to one degree or another, but ending in disillusionment. By the 17th century, new initiatives were needed to reinvigorate the Jews and pull them out of this dark period. In the mid-18th century, there appeared an answer to the despair the Jewish people felt. It was Hasidism (see box, page 226), a mixture of mysticism and religious ecstasy expressed in daily devotion and activity. In contrast, about the same time, philosopher Moses Mendelssohn, a German Jew, offered another solution, the way of Haskala, or enlightenment, which was to lead into what is historically considered to be "Modern Judaism."

25. How did the Catholic Church eventually react to the Jews in Europe?
26. (a) What led to disillusionment among the Jews? (b) What major divisions began to develop among the Jews?

From "Enlightenment" to Zionism

[27] According to Moses Mendelssohn (1729-86), Jews would be accepted if they would come out from under the restraints of the Talmud and conform to Western culture. In his day, he became one of the Jews most respected by the Gentile world. However, renewed outbursts of violent anti-Semitism in the 19th century, especially in "Christian" Russia, disillusioned the movement's followers, and many then focused on finding a political refuge for the Jews. They rejected the idea of a personal Messiah who would lead the Jews back to Israel and began to work on establishing a Jewish State by other means. This then became the concept of Zionism: "the secularization of . . . Jewish messianism," as one authority puts it.

[28] The murder of some six million European Jews in the Nazi-inspired Holocaust (1935-45) gave Zionism its final impetus and gained much sympathy for it worldwide. The Zionist dream came true in 1948 with the establishment of the State of Israel, which brings us to Judaism in our day and to the question, What do modern Jews believe?

God Is One

[29] Simply put, Judaism is the religion of a people. Therefore, a convert becomes part of the Jewish people as well as the Jewish religion. It is a monotheistic religion in the strictest sense and holds that God intervenes in human

---

27. (a) How did Moses Mendelssohn influence Jewish attitudes? (b) Why did many Jews reject the hope of a personal Messiah?
28. What events in the 20th century have affected Jewish attitudes?
29. (a) In simple terms, what is modern Judaism? (b) How is Jewish identity expressed? (c) What are some Jewish festivals and customs?

history, especially in relation to the Jews. Jewish worship involves several annual festivals and various customs. (See box, pages 230-1.) Although there are no creeds or dogmas accepted by all Jews, the confession of the oneness of God as expressed in the Shema, a prayer based on Deuteronomy 6:4 (*JP*), forms a central part of synagogue worship: "HEAR, O ISRAEL: THE LORD OUR GOD, THE LORD IS ONE."

[30] This belief in one God was passed on to Christianity and Islām. According to Dr. J. H. Hertz, a rabbi: "This sublime pronouncement of absolute monotheism was a declaration of war against all *polytheism* . . . In the same way, the Shema excludes *the trinity* of the Christian creed as a violation of the Unity of God."* But now let us turn to Jewish belief on the subject of the afterlife.

Death, Soul, and Resurrection

[31] One of the basic beliefs of modern Judaism is that man has an immortal soul that survives the death of his body. But does this originate in the Bible? The *Encyclopaedia Judaica* frankly admits: "It was probably under Greek influence that the doctrine of the immortality of the soul came into Judaism." However, this created a doctrinal dilemma, as the same source states: "Basically the two

---

* According to *The New Encyclopædia Britannica:* "The trinitarian creed of Christianity . . . sets it apart from the two other classical monotheistic religions [Judaism and Islām]." The Trinity was developed by the church even though "the Bible of Christians includes no assertions about God that are specifically trinitarian."

---

30. (a) What is the Jewish understanding of God? (b) How does the Jewish view of God conflict with that of Christendom?
31. (a) How did the doctrine of the immortal soul enter into Jewish teaching? (b) What dilemma did the teaching of the immortality of the soul cause?

The Sacred Writings of the Hebrews

The sacred Hebrew writings began with the "Tanakh." The name "Tanakh" comes from the three divisions of the Jewish Bible in Hebrew: *Torah* (Law), *Nevi'im* (Prophets), and *Kethuvim* (Writings), using the first letter of each section to form the word *TaNaKh*. These books were penned in Hebrew and Aramaic from the 16th century to the 5th century B.C.E.

Jews believe that they were written under different and diminishing degrees of inspiration. Therefore, they put them in this order of importance:

Torah—the five books of Moses, or the Pentateuch (from Greek for "five scrolls"), the Law, consisting of Genesis, Exodus, Leviticus, Numbers, and Deuteronomy. However, the term "Torah" may also be used to refer to the Jewish Bible as a whole as well as to the oral law and the **Talmud** (see next page).

Below, ancient Torah from what is known as the Tomb of Esther, Iran; right, Hebrew and Yiddish hymn of praise based on Scriptural verses

Nevi'im—the Prophets, covering from Joshua through to the major prophets, Isaiah, Jeremiah, and Ezekiel, and then through the 12 "minor" prophets from Hosea to Malachi.

Kethuvim—the Writings, consisting of the poetic works, Psalms, Proverbs, Job, The Song of Songs, and Lamentations. In addition it embraces Ruth, Ecclesiastes, Esther, Daniel, Ezra, Nehemiah, and First and Second Chronicles.

The Talmud

From the Gentile point of view, the "Tanakh," or Jewish Bible, is the most important of Jewish writings. However, the Jewish view is different. Many Jews would agree with the comment by Adin Steinsaltz, a rabbi: "If the Bible is the cornerstone of Judaism, then the Talmud is the central pillar, soaring up from the foundations and supporting the entire spiritual and intellectual edifice . . . No other work has had a comparable influence on the theory and practice of Jewish life." (*The Essential Talmud*) What, then, is the Talmud?

Orthodox Jews believe not only that God gave the written law, or Torah, to Moses at Mount Sinai but also that God revealed to him specific explanations of how to carry out that Law, and that these were to be passed on by word of mouth. This was called the oral law. Thus, the Talmud is the written summary, with later commentaries and explanations, of that oral law, compiled by rabbis from the second century C.E. into the Middle Ages.

The Talmud is usually divided into two main sections:

The **Mishnah:** A collection of commentaries supplementing Scriptural Law, based on the explanations of rabbis called Tannaim (teachers). It was put into written form in the late second and early third centuries C.E.

The **Gemara** (originally called the Talmud): A collection of commentaries on the Mishnah by rabbis of a later period (third to sixth centuries C.E.).

In addition to these two main divisions, the Talmud may also include commentaries on the Gemara made by rabbis into the Middle Ages. Prominent among these were the rabbis Rashi (Solomon ben Isaac, 1040-1105), who made the difficult language of the Talmud far more understandable, and Rambam (Moses ben Maimon, better known as Maimonides, 1135-1204), who reorganized the Talmud into a concise version ("Mishneh Torah"), thus making it accessible to all Jews.

beliefs of resurrection and the soul's immortality are contradictory. The one refers to a collective resurrection at the end of the days, i.e., that the dead sleeping in the earth will arise from the grave, while the other refers to the state of the soul after the death of the body." How was the dilemma resolved in Jewish theology? "It was held that when the individual died his soul still lived on in another realm (this gave rise to all the beliefs regarding heaven and hell) while his body lay in the grave to await the physical resurrection of all the dead here on earth."

[32] University lecturer Arthur Hertzberg writes: "In the [Hebrew] Bible itself the arena of man's life is this world. There is no doctrine of heaven and hell, only a growing concept of an ultimate resurrection of the dead at the end of days." That is a simple and accurate explanation of the Biblical concept, namely, that "the dead know nothing . . . For there is no action, no reasoning, no learning, no wisdom in Sheol [mankind's common grave], where you are going."—Ecclesiastes 9:5, 10; Daniel 12:1, 2; Isaiah 26:19.

---

32. What does the Bible say about the dead?

Hasidic Jewish family celebrating the Sabbath

[33] According to the *Encyclopaedia Judaica,* "In the rabbinic period the doctrine of the resurrection of the dead is considered one of the central doctrines of Judaism" and "is to be distinguished from the belief in ... the immortality of the soul."* Today, however, while the immortality of the soul is accepted by all factions of Judaism, the resurrection of the dead is not.

[34] In contrast with the Bible, the Talmud, influenced by Hellenism, is replete with explanations and stories and even descriptions of the immortal soul. Later Jewish mystical literature, the Kabbala, even goes so far as to teach reincarnation (transmigration of souls), which is basically an ancient Hindu teaching. (See Chapter 5.) In Israel today, this is widely accepted as a Jewish teaching, and it also plays an important role in Hasidic belief and literature. For example, Martin Buber includes in his book *Tales of the Hasidim—The Later Masters* a tale about the soul from the school of Elimelekh, a rabbi of Lizhensk: "On the Day of Atonement, when Rabbi Abraham Yehoshua would recite the Avodah, the prayer that repeats the service of the high priest in the Temple of Jerusalem, and would come to the passage: 'And thus he spoke,' he would never say those words, but would say: 'And thus I spoke.' For he had not forgotten the time his soul was in the body of a high priest of Jerusalem."

---

* In addition to Biblical authority, it was taught as an article of faith in the Mishnah (Sanhedrin 10:1) and was included as the last of Maimonides' 13 principles of faith. Until the 20th century, denial of the resurrection was viewed as heresy.

---

33. How was the doctrine of the resurrection originally viewed by Jews?
34. In contrast with the Bible's viewpoint, how does the Talmud depict the soul? What do later writers comment?

[35] Reform Judaism has gone so far as to reject belief in the resurrection. Having removed the word from Reform prayer books, it recognizes only the belief in the immortal soul. How much clearer is the Biblical idea as expressed at Genesis 2:7: "The LORD God formed man of the dust of the ground, and breathed into his nostrils the breath of life; and man became a living soul." (*JP*) The combination of the body and the spirit, or life-force, constitutes "a living soul."* (Genesis 2:7; 7:22; Psalm 146:4) Conversely, when the human sinner dies, then the soul dies. (Ezekiel 18:4, 20) Thus, at death man ceases to have any conscious existence. His life-force returns to God who gave it. (Ecclesiastes 3:19; 9:5, 10; 12:7) The truly Biblical hope for the dead is the resurrection—Hebrew: *techi·yath' ham·me·thim'*, or "revival of the dead."

[36] While this conclusion might surprise even many Jews, the resurrection has been the real hope of worshipers of the true God for thousands of years. About 3,500 years ago, faithful, suffering Job spoke of a future time when God would raise him from Sheol, or the grave. (Job 14:14, 15) The prophet Daniel was also assured that he would be raised "at the end of the days."—Daniel 12:2, 12 (13, *JP; NW*).

[37] There is no basis in Scripture for saying those faithful Hebrews believed they had an immortal soul that would

---

* "The Bible does not say we have a soul. 'Nefesh' is the person himself, his need for food, the very blood in his veins, his being." —Dr. H. M. Orlinsky of Hebrew Union College.

---

35. (a) What position has Reform Judaism taken on the immortal soul teaching? (b) What is the Bible's clear teaching about the soul?
36, 37. What did faithful Hebrews of Bible times believe about future life?

survive into an afterworld. They clearly had sufficient reason to believe that the Sovereign Lord, who counts and controls the stars of the universe, would also remember them at the time of the resurrection. They had been faithful to him and his name. He would be faithful to them. —Psalm 18:26 (25, *NW*); 147:4; Isaiah 25:7, 8; 40:25, 26.

Judaism and God's Name

[38] Judaism teaches that while God's name exists in written form, it is too holy to be pronounced.* The result has been that, over the last 2,000 years, the correct pronunciation has been lost. Yet, that has not always been the Jewish position. About 3,500 years ago, God spoke to Moses, saying: "Thus shall you speak to the Israelites: The LORD [Hebrew: יהוה, *YHWH*], the God of your fathers, the God of Abraham, the God of Isaac, and the God of Jacob, has sent me to you: This shall be My name forever, this My appellation for all eternity." (Exodus 3:15; Psalm 135:13) What was that name and appellation? The footnote to the *Tanakh* states: "The name *YHWH* (traditionally read *Adonai* "the LORD") is here associated with the root *hayah* 'to be.'" Thus, we have here the holy name of God, the Tetragrammaton, the four Hebrew consonants YHWH (Yahweh) that in their Latinized form have come to be known over the centuries in English as JEHOVAH.

[39] Throughout history, the Jews have always placed great importance on God's personal name, though emphasis on usage has changed drastically from ancient times.

---

* See Exodus 6:3 where in the *Tanakh* version of the Bible the Hebrew Tetragrammaton appears in the English text.

---

38. (a) What has happened over the centuries regarding the use of God's name? (b) What is the basis for God's name?
39. (a) Why is the divine name important? (b) Why did Jews stop pronouncing the divine name?

Judaism—A Religion of Many Voices

There are major differences between the various factions of Judaism. Traditionally, Judaism emphasizes religious practice. Debate over such matters, rather than beliefs, has caused serious tension among Jews and has led to the formation of three major divisions in Judaism.

ORTHODOX JUDAISM—This branch not only accepts that the Hebrew "Tanakh" is inspired Scripture but also believes that Moses received the oral law from God on Mount Sinai at the same time that he received the written Law. Orthodox Jews scrupulously keep the commandments of both laws. They believe that the Messiah is still to appear and to bring Israel to a golden age. Because of differences of opinion within the Orthodox group, various factions have emerged. One example is Hasidism.

Hasidim (Chasidim, meaning "the pious")—These are viewed as ultraorthodox. Founded by Israel ben Eliezer, known as Ba'al Shem Tov ("Master of the Good Name"), in the mid-18th century in Eastern Europe, they follow a teaching that highlights music and dance, resulting in mystic joy. Many of their beliefs, including reincarnation, are based on the Jewish mystical books known as the Kabbala (Cabala). Today they are led by rebbes (Yiddish for "rabbis"), or zaddikim, considered by their followers to be supremely righteous men or saints.

Hasidim today are found mainly in the United States and in Israel. They wear a particular style of Eastern European garb, mainly black, of the 18th and 19th centuries, that makes them very conspicuous, especially in a modern city setting. Today they are divided into sects that follow different prominent rebbes. One very active group is the **Lubavitchers,** who proselytize vigorously among Jews. Some groups believe that only the Messiah has the right to restore Israel as the nation of the Jews and so are opposed to the secular State of Israel.

REFORM JUDAISM (also known as "Liberal" and "Progressive")

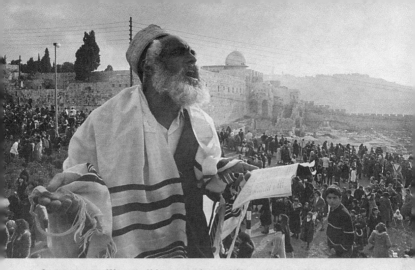

Left, Jews at Wailing Wall in Jerusalem and, above, a Jew praying, with Jerusalem in background

—The movement began in Western Europe toward the beginning of the 19th century. It is based on the ideas of Moses Mendelssohn, an 18th-century Jewish intellectual who believed Jews should assimilate Western culture rather than separate themselves from the Gentiles. Reform Jews deny that the Torah was divinely revealed truth. They view the Jewish laws on diet, purity, and dress as obsolete. They believe in what they term a "Messianic era of Universal brotherhood." In recent years they have moved back toward more traditional Judaism.

CONSERVATIVE JUDAISM—This began in Germany in 1845 as an offshoot of Reform Judaism, which, it was felt, had rejected too many traditional Jewish practices. Conservative Judaism does not accept that the oral law was received by Moses from God but holds that the rabbis, who sought to adapt Judaism to a new era, invented the oral Torah. Conservative Jews submit to Biblical precepts and Rabbinic law if these "are responsive to the modern requirements of Jewish life." (*The Book of Jewish Knowledge*) They use Hebrew and English in their liturgy and maintain strict dietary laws (kashruth). Men and women are allowed to sit together during worship, which is not allowed by the Orthodox.

As Dr. A. Cohen states in *Everyman's Talmud*: "Special reverence [was] attached to 'the distinctive Name' (*Shem Hamephorash*) of the Deity which He had revealed to the people of Israel, viz. the tetragrammaton, JHVH." The divine name was revered because it represented and characterized the very person of God. After all, it was God himself who announced his name and told his worshipers to use it. This is emphasized by the appearance of the name in the Hebrew Bible 6,828 times. Devout Jews, however, feel it is disrespectful to pronounce God's personal name.*

[40] Concerning the ancient rabbinic (not Biblical) injunction against pronouncing the name, A. Marmorstein, a rabbi, wrote in his book *The Old Rabbinic Doctrine of God*: "There was a time when this prohibition [of the use of the divine name] was entirely unknown among the Jews . . . Neither in Egypt, nor in Babylonia, did the Jews know or keep a law prohibiting the use of God's name, the Tetragrammaton, in ordinary conversation or greetings. Yet, from the third century B.C.E. till the third century A.C.E. such a prohibition existed and was partly observed." Not only was the use of the name allowed in earlier times but, as Dr. Cohen says: "There was a time when the free and open use of the Name even by the layman was advocated . . . It has been suggested that the recommendation was based on the desire to distinguish the Israelite from the [non-Jew]."

---

* The *Encyclopaedia Judaica* says: "The avoidance of pronouncing the name YHWH is . . . caused by a misunderstanding of the Third Commandment (Ex. 20:7; Deut. 5:11) as meaning 'Thou shalt not take the name of YHWH thy God in vain,' whereas it really means 'You shall not swear falsely by the name of YHWH your God.'"

---

40. What have some Jewish authorities stated regarding the use of the divine name?

[41] What, then, brought about the prohibition of the use of the divine name? Dr. Marmorstein answers: "Hellenistic [Greek-influenced] opposition to the religion of the Jews, the apostasy of the priests and nobles, introduced and established the rule not to pronounce the Tetragrammaton in the Sanctuary [temple in Jerusalem]." In their excessive zeal to avoid taking the divine name in vain, they completely suppressed its use in speech and subverted and diluted the identification of the true God. Under the combined pressure of religious opposition and apostasy, the divine name fell into disuse among the Jews.

[42] However, as Dr. Cohen states: "In the Biblical period there seems to have been no scruple against [the divine name's] use in daily speech." The patriarch Abraham "invoked the LORD by name." (Genesis 12:8) Most of the writers of the Hebrew Bible freely but respectfully used the name right down to the writing of Malachi in the fifth century B.C.E.—Ruth 1:8, 9, 17.

[43] It is abundantly clear that the ancient Hebrews did use and pronounce the divine name. Marmorstein admits regarding the change that came later: "For in this time, in the first half of the third century [B.C.E.], a great change in the use of the name of God is to be noticed, which brought about many changes in Jewish theological and philosophical lore, the influences of which are felt up to this very day." One of the effects of the loss of the name is that the

---

41. According to one rabbi, what influences brought about a prohibition of the use of God's name?
42. What does the Bible record show about the use of the divine name?
43. (a) What is abundantly clear regarding the Jewish use of the divine name? (b) What was one indirect effect of the Jews' dropping the use of the divine name?

Some Important Festivals and Customs

The majority of Jewish festivals are based on the Bible and, generally, either are seasonal festivals in connection with different harvests or are related to historical events.

■ **Shabbat** (Sabbath)—The seventh day of the Jewish week (from sundown Friday to sundown Saturday) is viewed as sanctifying the week, and the special observance of this day is an essential part of worship. Jews attend the synagogue for Torah readings and prayers.—Exodus 20:8-11.

■ **Yom Kippur**—Day of Atonement, a solemn festival characterized by fasting and self-examination. It culminates the Ten Days of Penitence that begin with Rosh Hashanah, the Jewish New Year, which falls in September according to the Jewish secular calendar.—Leviticus 16:29-31; 23:26-32.

■ **Sukkot** (above, right)—Festival of Booths, or Tabernacles, or Ingathering. Celebrates the harvest and the end of the major part of the agricultural year. Held in October. —Leviticus 23:34-43; Numbers 29: 12-38; Deuteronomy 16:13-15.

■ **Hanukkah**—Festival of Dedication. A popular festival held in December that commemorates the Maccabees' restoration of Jewish independence from Syro-Grecian domination and the rededication of the temple at Jerusalem in December 165 B.C.E. Usually distinguished by the lighting of candles for eight days.

■ **Purim**—Festival of Lots. Celebrated in late February or early March, in commemoration of the deliverance of the Jews in Persia during the fifth century B.C.E. from Haman and his genocidal plot.—Esther 9:20-28.

■ **Pesach**—Festival of Passover. Instituted to commemorate the deliverance of Israel from captivity in Egypt (1513 B.C.E.). It is the greatest and oldest of Jewish festivals. Held on Nisan 14 (Jewish calendar), it usually falls at the end of March or the beginning of April. Each Jewish family comes together to share the Passover meal, or Seder. During the following seven days, no leaven may be eaten. This period is called the Festival of Unfermented Cakes (*Matzot*). —Exodus 12:14-20, 24-27.

Some Jewish Customs

■ **Circumcision**—For Jewish boys, it is an important ceremony that takes place when the baby is eight days old. It is often called the Covenant of Abraham, since circumcision was the sign of God's covenant with him. Males who convert to Judaism must also be circumcised. —Genesis 17:9-14.

■ **Bar Mitzvah** (below)—Another essential Jewish ritual, which literally means "son of the commandment," a "term denoting both the attainment of religious and legal maturity as well as the occasion at which this status is formally assumed for boys at the age of 13 plus one day." It became a Jewish custom only in the 15th century C.E. —*Encyclopaedia Judaica*.

■ **Mezuzah** (above)—A Jewish home is usually easy to distinguish by reason of the mezuzah, or scroll case, on the right side of the doorpost as one enters. In practice the mezuzah is a small parchment on which are inscribed the words cited from Deuteronomy 6:4-9 and 11:13-21. This is rolled up inside a small case. The case is then fixed to every door of each room used for occupancy.

■ **Yarmulke** (skullcap for males) —According to the *Encyclopaedia Judaica:* "Orthodox Jewry . . . regards the covering of the head, both outside and inside the synagogue, as a sign of allegiance to Jewish tradition." Covering the head during worship is nowhere mentioned in the Tanakh, thus the Talmud mentions this as an optional matter of custom. Hasidic Jewish women either wear a head covering at all times or shave their heads and wear a wig.

concept of an anonymous God helped to create a theological vacuum in which Christendom's Trinity doctrine was more easily developed.*—Exodus 15:1-3.

[44] The refusal to use the divine name diminishes the worship of the true God. As one commentator said: "Unfortunately, when God is spoken of as 'the Lord,' the phrase, though accurate, is a cold and colorless one . . . One needs to remember that by translating YHWH or Adonay as 'the Lord' one introduces into many passages of the Old Testament a note of abstraction, formality and remoteness that is entirely foreign to the original text." (*The Knowledge of God in Ancient Israel*) How sad to see the sublime and significant name Yahweh, or Jehovah, missing from many Bible translations when it clearly appears thousands of times in the original Hebrew text!—Isaiah 43:10-12.

Do Jews Still Await the Messiah?

[45] There are many prophecies in the Hebrew Scriptures from which Jews over 2,000 years ago derived their Messianic hope. Second Samuel 7:11-16 indicated that the Messiah would be of the line of David. Isaiah 11:1-10 prophesied that he would bring righteousness and peace

---

* George Howard, an associate professor of religion and Hebrew at the University of Georgia, states: "As time went on, these two figures [God and Christ] were brought into even closer unity until it was often impossible to distinguish between them. Thus it may be that the removal of the Tetragrammaton contributed significantly to the later Christological and Trinitarian debates which plagued the church of the early centuries. Whatever the case, the removal of the Tetragrammaton probably created a different theological climate from that which existed during the New Testament period of the first century."—*Biblical Archaeology Review,* March 1978.

---

44. What are some other effects caused by the suppression of God's name?
45. What Biblical basis is there for believing in a Messiah?

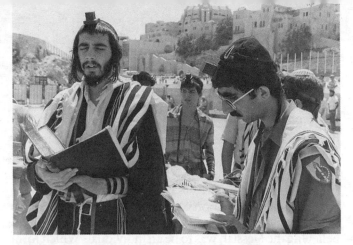

Devout Jews wearing phylacteries, or prayer scroll cases, on arm and forehead

to all mankind. Daniel 9:24-27 gave the chronology for the appearance of the Messiah and his being cut off in death.

[46] As the *Encyclopædia Judaica* explains, by the first century, Messianic expectations were high. The Messiah was expected to be "a charismatically endowed descendant of David who the Jews of the Roman period believed would be raised up by God to break the yoke of the heathen and to reign over a restored kingdom of Israel." However, the militant Messiah the Jews were expecting was not forthcoming.

[47] Yet, as *The New Encyclopædia Britannica* notes, the Messianic hope was vital in holding the Jewish people together throughout their many ordeals: "Judaism

46, 47. (a) What kind of Messiah was expected by Jews living under Roman domination? (b) What change has taken place in Jewish aspirations regarding the Messiah?

undoubtedly owes its survival, to a considerable extent, to its steadfast faith in the messianic promise and future." But with the rise of modern Judaism between the 18th and 19th centuries, many Jews ended their passive waiting for the Messiah. Finally, with the Nazi-inspired Holocaust, many lost their patience and hope. They began to view the Messianic message as a liability and so reinterpreted it merely as a new age of prosperity and peace. Since that time, although there are exceptions, Jews as a whole can hardly be said to be waiting for a personal Messiah.

[48] This change to a non-Messianic religion raises serious questions. Was Judaism wrong for thousands of years in believing the Messiah was to be an individual? Which form of Judaism will aid one in the search for God? Is it ancient Judaism with its trappings of Greek philosophy? Or is it one of the non-Messianic forms of Judaism that evolved during the last 200 years? Or is there yet another path that faithfully and accurately preserves the Messianic hope?

[49] With these questions in mind, we suggest that sincere Jews reexamine the subject of the Messiah by investigating the claims regarding Jesus of Nazareth, not as Christendom has represented him, but as the Jewish writers of the Greek Scriptures present him. There is a big difference. The religions of Christendom have contributed to the Jewish rejection of Jesus by their non-Biblical doctrine of the Trinity, which is clearly unacceptable to any Jew who cherishes the pure teaching that "THE LORD OUR GOD, THE LORD IS ONE." (Deuteronomy 6:4, *JP*) Therefore, we invite you to read the following chapter with an open mind in order to get to know the Jesus of the Greek Scriptures.

---

48. What questions can reasonably be raised about Judaism?
49. What invitation is made to sincere Jews?

CHAPTER 10

Christianity—Was Jesus the Way to God?

So far, with the exception of the chapter on Judaism, we have considered major religions that are based to a large extent on mythology. Now we will examine another religion that claims to bring mankind nearer to God—Christianity. What is the basis for Christianity —myth or historical fact?

T HE history of Christendom,* with its wars, inquisitions, crusades, and religious hypocrisy, has not helped the cause of Christianity. Devout Muslims and others point to the moral corruption and decadence of the Western, "Christian" world as a basis for rejecting Christianity. Indeed, the so-called Christian nations have lost their moral rudder and have suffered shipwreck on the rocks of faithlessness, greed, and self-indulgence.

² That the standards of original Christianity were different from the permissive mores of today is attested to by

---

* By "Christendom" we refer to the realm of sectarian activity dominated by religions that claim to be Christian. "Christianity" refers to the original form of worship and access to God taught by Jesus Christ.

---

1. (a) Why does the history of Christendom cause some to have serious doubts about Christianity? (b) What distinction do we make between Christendom and Christianity?
2, 3. (a) What contrast is there between the conduct of early Christians and that of people of modern Christendom? (b) What are some questions to be answered?

Professor Elaine Pagels in her book *Adam, Eve, and the Serpent,* wherein she states: "Many Christians of the first four centuries took pride in their sexual restraint; they eschewed polygamy and often divorce as well, which Jewish tradition allowed; and they repudiated extramarital sexual practices commonly accepted among their pagan contemporaries, practices including prostitution and homosexuality."

[3] Therefore, it is fair to ask, Is Christendom's history and its modern moral state a true reflection of the teachings of Jesus Christ? What kind of man was Jesus? Did he help to bring mankind nearer to God? Was he the promised Messiah of Hebrew prophecy? These are some of the questions we shall consider in this chapter.

Jesus—What Were His Credentials?

[4] In earlier chapters we have seen the prominent role that mythology has played in nearly all the major religions of the world. Yet, when we turned to the origins of Judaism in our previous chapter, we did not start with a myth but with the historical reality of Abraham, his forebears, and his descendants. With Christianity and its founder, Jesus, we likewise start, not with mythology, but with a historical personage.—See box, page 237.

[5] The first verse of the Christian Greek Scriptures, commonly known as the New Testament (see box, page 241), states: "The book of the history of Jesus Christ, son of David, son of Abraham." (Matthew 1:1) Is that an idle claim

---

4. In our study, what clear difference have we noted between Christianity and its roots, and the major religions of the world?
5. (a) What are three of the credentials Jesus held that prove he was the promised "seed" of Abraham? (b) Who wrote the Christian Greek Scriptures?

Was Jesus a Myth?

"Is the life story of the founder of Christianity the product of human sorrow, imagination, and hope—a myth comparable to the legends of Krishna, Osiris, Attis, Adonis, Dionysus, and Mithras?" asks historian Will Durant. He answers that in the first century, to deny that Christ had ever existed "seems never to have occurred even to the bitterest gentile or Jewish opponents of nascent Christianity."—*The Story of Civilization,* Part III, "Caesar and Christ."

The Roman historian Suetonius (c. 69-140 C.E.), in his history *The Twelve Caesars,* stated regarding the emperor Claudius: "Because the Jews at Rome caused continuous disturbances at the instigation of Chrestus [Christ], he expelled them from the city." This oc-curred about the year 52 C.E. (Compare Acts 18:1, 2.) Note that Suetonius expresses no doubt about the existence of Christ. On this factual basis and in spite of life-endangering persecution, early Christians were very active proclaiming their faith. It is hardly likely that they would have risked their lives on the basis of a myth. Jesus' death and resurrection had taken place in their lifetime, and some of them had been eyewitnesses to those events.

Historian Durant draws the conclusion: "That a few simple men should in one generation have invented so powerful and appealing a personality, so lofty an ethic and so inspiring a vision of human brotherhood, would be a miracle far more incredible than any recorded in the Gospels."

Jesus preached and performed miracles in this Galilean region of ancient Palestine

Jesus used many illustrations in his teaching—sowing seed, harvesting, fishing, finding a pearl, mixed flocks, and a vineyard, among others (Matthew 13:3-47; 25:32)

presented by Matthew, a former Jewish tax collector and an immediate disciple and biographer of Jesus? No. The following 15 verses spell out Abraham's line of descendants down to Jacob, who "became father to Joseph the husband of Mary, of whom Jesus was born, who is called Christ." Therefore, Jesus really was a descendant of Abraham, Judah, and David and as such held three of the credentials of the foretold "seed" of Genesis 3:15 and of Abraham. —Genesis 22:18; 49:10; 1 Chronicles 17:11.

[6] Another of the credentials for the Messianic Seed would be his place of birth. Where was Jesus born? Matthew tells us that Jesus was "born in Bethlehem of Judea in the days of Herod the king." (Matthew 2:1) Physician Luke's account confirms that fact, telling us regarding Jesus' future adoptive father: "Joseph also went up from Galilee, out of the city of Nazareth, into Judea, to David's city, which is called Bethlehem, because of his being a member of the house and family of David, to get registered with Mary, who had been given him in marriage as promised, at present heavy with child."—Luke 2:4, 5.

[7] Why was it important that Jesus be born in Bethlehem rather than in Nazareth or any other town? Because of a prophecy uttered during the eighth century B.C.E. by the Hebrew prophet Micah: "And you, O Bethlehem Ephrathah, the one too little to get to be among the thousands of Judah, from you there will come out to me the one who is to become ruler in Israel, whose origin is from early times, from the days of time indefinite." (Micah 5:2) Thus, by his place of birth, Jesus held another of the credentials for being the promised Seed and Messiah.—John 7:42.

6, 7. Why was Jesus' birthplace significant?

⁸ In fact, Jesus fulfilled many more prophecies from the Hebrew Scriptures, thus proving that he had all the credentials for being the promised Messiah. You can check some of these in the Bible. (See box, page 245.)* But now let us briefly examine Jesus' message and his ministry.

Jesus' Life Points the Way

⁹ The Bible account tells us that Jesus was reared as a normal Jewish youth of his time, attending the local synagogue and the temple in Jerusalem. (Luke 2:41-52) When he reached the age of 30, he started his public ministry. First he went to his cousin John, who was baptizing Jews in symbol of repentance in the river Jordan. Luke's account tells us: "Now when all the people were baptized, Jesus also was baptized and, as he was praying, the heaven was opened up and the holy spirit in bodily shape like a dove came down upon him, and a voice came out of heaven: 'You are my Son, the beloved; I have approved you.'" —Luke 3:21-23; John 1:32-34.

¹⁰ In due course, Jesus entered upon his ministry as the anointed Son of God. He went throughout Galilee and Judea preaching the message of the Kingdom of God and performing miracles, such as healing the sick. He accepted no payment and did not look for wealth or

---

* See also *Insight on the Scriptures,* published by the Watchtower Bible and Tract Society of New York, Inc., 1988, Volume 2, pages 385-9, under "Messiah."

8. What are some prophecies that Jesus fulfilled?
9. (a) How did Jesus start his public ministry? (b) How do we know that Jesus had God's approval?
10, 11. (a) What were some characteristics of Jesus' methods of preaching and teaching? (b) How did Jesus show the importance of his Father's name?

Who Wrote the Bible?

The Christian Bible consists of the 39 books of the Hebrew Scriptures (see box, page 220), called by many the Old Testament, and the 27 books of the Christian Greek Scriptures, often called the New Testament.* Thus, the Bible is a miniature library of 66 books written by some 40 men in the course of 1,600 years of history (from 1513 B.C.E. to 98 C.E.).

The Greek Scriptures include four Gospels, or accounts of the life of Jesus and the good news that he preached. Two of these were written by immediate followers of Christ, Matthew, a tax collector, and John, a fisherman. The other two were written by the early believers Mark and Luke, the physician. (Colossians 4:14) The Gospels are followed by the Acts of Apostles, an account of the early Christian missionary activity compiled by Luke. Next are 14 letters from the apostle Paul to various individual Christians and congregations, followed by letters from James, Peter, John, and Jude.

---

* The Catholic Bible includes some additional books that form the Apocrypha and that are not viewed as canonical by Jews and Protestants.

The final book is Revelation, written by John.

That so many persons of diverse backgrounds and living in different times and cultures could produce such a harmonious book is strong proof that the Bible is not simply the product of human intelligence but is inspired by God. The Bible itself states: "All Scripture is inspired of God [literally, "God-breathed"] and beneficial for teaching." Thus, the Scriptures were written under the influence of God's holy spirit, or active force.—2 Timothy 3:16, 17, *Int.*

This incomplete Roman inscription using Pontius Pilate's name in Latin (second line, "IVS PILATVS") confirms that he was an influential figure in Palestine, as the Bible states

self-aggrandizement. In fact, he said that there is more happiness in giving than there is in receiving. He also taught his disciples how to preach.—Matthew 8:20; 10:7-13; Acts 20:35.

[11] When we analyze Jesus' message and the methods he used, we see a distinct difference between his style and that of many of Christendom's preachers. He did not manipulate the masses with cheap emotionalism or with hellfire scare tactics. Rather, Jesus used simple logic and parables, or illustrations, from everyday life to appeal to the heart and the mind. His famous Sermon on the Mount is an outstanding example of his teachings and methods. Included in that sermon is Jesus' model prayer, in which he gives a clear indication of Christian priorities by putting the sanctifying of God's name in first place. (See box, pages 258-9.) —Matthew 5:1–7:29; 13:3-53; Luke 6:17-49.

By God's power, Jesus performed many miracles, including the calming of a storm ▶

[12] In his dealings with his followers and with the public in general, Jesus manifested love and compassion. (Mark 6: 30-34) While preaching the message of God's Kingdom, he also personally practiced love and humility. Thus, in the final hours of his life, he could say to his disciples: "I am giving you a new commandment, that you love one another; just as I have loved you, that you also love one another. By this all will know that you are my disciples, if you have love among yourselves." (John 13:34, 35) Therefore, the essence of Christianity in practice is self-sacrificing love

12. (a) How did Jesus manifest love in his teachings and actions? (b) How different would the world be if Christian love were truly practiced?

based on principle. (Matthew 22:37-40) In practice this means that a Christian should love even his enemies, although he may hate their evil works. (Luke 6:27-31) Think about that for a moment. What a different world this would be if everyone actually practiced that form of love! —Romans 12:17-21; 13:8-10.

[13] Yet, what Jesus taught was far more than an ethic or philosophy, such as those taught by Confucius and Lao-tzu. Furthermore, Jesus did not teach, as did the Buddha, that one can work out one's own salvation by the pathway of knowledge and enlightenment. Rather, he pointed to God as the source of salvation when he said: "For God loved the world so much that he gave his only-begotten Son, in order that everyone exercising faith in him might not be destroyed but have everlasting life. For God sent forth his Son into the world, not for him to judge the world, but for the world to be saved through him."—John 3:16, 17.

[14] By manifesting his Father's love in his own words and deeds, Jesus drew people closer to God. That is one reason why he could say: "I am the way and the truth and the life. No one comes to the Father except through me.... He that has seen me has seen the Father also. How is it you say, 'Show us the Father'? Do you not believe that I am in union with the Father and the Father is in union with me? The things I say to you men I do not speak of my own originality; but the Father who remains in union with me is doing his works.... You heard that I said to you, I am going

---

13. In what way was Jesus' teaching different from that of Confucius, Lao-tzu, and the Buddha?
14. Why could Jesus say, "I am the way and the truth and the life"?

The Messiah in Bible Prophecy

Prophecy	Event	Fulfillment
Gen. 49:10	Born of the tribe of Judah	Matt. 1:2-16; Luke 3:23-33
Ps. 132:11; Isa. 9:7	From the family of David the son of Jesse	Matt. 1:1, 6-16; 9:27; Acts 13:22, 23
Mic. 5:2	Born in Bethlehem	Luke 2:4-11; John 7:42
Isa. 7:14	Born of a virgin	Matt. 1:18-23; Luke 1:30-35
Hos. 11:1	Called out of Egypt	Matt. 2:15
Isa. 61:1, 2	Commissioned	Luke 4:18-21
Isa. 53:4	Carried our sicknesses	Matt. 8:16, 17
Ps. 69:9	Zealous for Jehovah's house	Matt. 21:12, 13; John 2:13-17
Isa. 53:1	Not believed	John 12:37, 38; Rom. 10:11, 16
Zech. 9:9; Ps. 118:26	Hailed as king and one coming in Jehovah's name	Matt. 21:1-9; Mark 11:7-11
Isa. 28:16; Ps. 118:22, 23	Rejected but becoming chief cornerstone	Matt. 21:42, 45, 46; Acts 3:14; 4:11; 1 Pet. 2:7
Ps. 41:9; 109:8	One apostle betrays him	Matt. 26:47-50; John 13:18, 26-30
Zech. 11:12	Betrayed for 30 pieces of silver	Matt. 26:15; 27:3-10; Mark 14:10, 11
Isa. 53:8	Tried and condemned	Matt. 26:57-68; 27:1, 2, 11-26
Isa. 53:7	Silent before accusers	Matt. 27:12-14; Mark 14:61; 15:4, 5
Ps. 69:4	Hated without cause	Luke 23:13-25; John 15:24, 25
Isa. 50:6; Mic. 5:1	Struck, spit upon	Matt. 26:67; 27:26, 30; John 19:3
Ps. 22:18	Lots cast for garments	Matt. 27:35; John 19:23, 24
Isa. 53:12	Numbered with sinners	Matt. 26:55, 56; 27:38; Luke 22:37
Ps. 69:21	Given vinegar and gall	Matt. 27:34, 48; Mark 15:23, 36
Ps. 22:1	Forsaken by God	Matt. 27:46; Mark 15:34
Ps. 34:20; Ex. 12:46	No bones broken	John 19:33, 36
Isa. 53:5; Zech. 12:10	Pierced	Matt. 27:49; John 19:34, 37; Rev. 1:7
Isa. 53:5, 8, 11, 12	Dies sacrificial death to carry away sins	Matt. 20:28; John 1:29; Rom. 3:24; 4:25
Isa. 53:9	Buried with the rich	Matt. 27:57-60; John 19:38-42
Jonah 1:17; 2:10	In grave parts of three days, then resurrected	Matt. 12:39, 40; 16:21; 17:23; 27:64

away and I am coming back to you. If you loved me, you would rejoice that I am going my way to the Father, because the Father is greater than I am." (John 14:6-28) Yes, Jesus was "the way and the truth and the life" because he was leading those Jewish people back to his Father, their true God, Jehovah. Therefore, with Jesus mankind's search for God suddenly took on impetus because God, in his supreme love, had sent Jesus to the earth as a beacon of light and truth to lead men to the Father.—John 1:9-14; 6:44; 8:31, 32.

יהוה

The Tetra-grammaton, or four consonants YHWH (Jehovah)

¹⁵ On the basis of the ministry and example of Jesus, the missionary Paul could later say to the Greeks in Athens: "And [God] made out of one man every nation of men, to dwell upon the entire surface of the earth, and he decreed the appointed times and the set limits of the dwelling of men, for them to seek God, if they might grope for him and really find him, although, in fact, he is not far off from each one of us. For by him we have life and move and exist." (Acts 17:26-28) Yes, God can be found if a person is willing to make the effort to search for him. (Matthew 7:7, 8) God has made himself and his love manifest in that he has furnished an earth that supports a seemingly endless variety of life. He supplies what is necessary to all mankind, whether they be righteous or unrighteous. He has also provided mankind with his written Word, the Bible, and he sent his Son as a redeeming

---

15. (a) What must we do to find God? (b) Here on earth what evidence is there of God's love?

sacrifice.* Moreover, God has provided the assistance people need to help them find the way to Him.—Matthew 5: 43-45; Acts 14:16, 17; Romans 3:23-26.

[16] Of course, Christian love must be manifested not just by words but more importantly by deeds. For that reason the apostle Paul wrote: "Love is long-suffering and kind. Love is not jealous, it does not brag, does not get puffed up, does not behave indecently, does not look for its own interests, does not become provoked. It does not keep account of the injury. It does not rejoice over unrighteousness, but rejoices with the truth. It bears all things, believes all things, hopes all things, endures all things. Love never fails."—1 Corinthians 13:4-8.

[17] Jesus also made clear how important it is to proclaim the Kingdom of the heavens—God's rule over submissive mankind.—Matthew 10:7; Mark 13:10.

Every Christian an Evangelizer

[18] In his Sermon on the Mount, Jesus emphasized to the crowds their responsibility to illuminate others by their words and actions. He said: "You are the light of the world. A city cannot be hid when situated upon a mountain. People light a lamp and set it, not under the measuring basket, but upon the lampstand, and it shines upon all those in the house. Likewise let your light shine before men, that they may see your fine works and give glory to

---

* The Bible teaching of the ransom and its importance will be clarified in Chapter 15.

16, 17. How must true Christian love be manifested?
18. (a) What was highlighted in Jesus' Sermon on the Mount? (b) What responsibility does each Christian have? (c) How did Jesus prepare his disciples for their ministry, and what message were they to preach?

your Father who is in the heavens." (Matthew 5:14-16) Jesus trained his disciples so that they would know how to preach and teach during their travels as itinerant ministers. And what was their message to be? That which Jesus himself preached, the Kingdom of God, which would rule the earth in righteousness. As Jesus explained on one occasion: "Also to other cities I must declare the good news of the kingdom of God, because for this I was sent forth." (Luke 4:43; 8:1; 10:1-12) He also stated that part of the sign identifying the last days would be that "this good news of the kingdom will be preached in all the inhabited earth for a witness to all the nations; and then the end will come." —Matthew 24:3-14.

[19] In 33 C.E., before he finally ascended to heaven, the resurrected Jesus instructed his disciples: "All authority has been given me in heaven and on the earth. Go therefore and make disciples of people of all the nations, baptizing them in the name of the Father and of the Son and of the holy spirit, teaching them to observe all the things I have commanded you. And, look! I am with you all the days until the conclusion of the system of things." (Matthew 28:18-20) This is one reason why Christianity, from its very inception, was an active, proselytizing religion that provoked the anger and jealousy of the followers of the prevailing Greek and Roman religions of that day, which were based on mythology. The persecution of Paul in Ephesus clearly illustrated that fact.—Acts 19:23-41.

[20] The questions now are, What did the message of the Kingdom of God offer concerning the dead? What hope for the dead did Christ preach? Was he offering salvation

---

19, 20. (a) Why has true Christianity always been an active, preaching religion? (b) What basic questions now require answers?

from "hellfire" for the "immortal souls" of his believers? Or what?—Matthew 4:17.

Hope of Everlasting Life

[21] Perhaps the clearest insight into the hope that Jesus preached can be gained from what he said and did when his friend Lazarus died. How did Jesus view this death? Setting out for Lazarus' home, Jesus said to his disciples: "Lazarus our friend has gone to rest, but I am journeying there to awaken him from sleep." (John 11:11) Jesus compared Lazarus' death state to sleep. In a deep sleep, we are conscious of nothing, which agrees with the Hebrew expression at Ecclesiastes 9:5: "For the living are conscious that they will die; but as for the dead, they are conscious of nothing at all."

[22] Although Lazarus had been dead four days, we note that Jesus said nothing about Lazarus' soul being in heaven, hell, or purgatory! When Jesus arrived at Bethany and Martha, Lazarus' sister, came out to meet him, he said to her, "Your brother will rise." How did she answer? Did she say he was already in heaven? Martha answered: "I know he will rise in the resurrection on the last day." That clearly shows that the Jewish hope at that time was the resurrection, a return to life here on earth.—John 11:23, 24, 38, 39.

[23] Jesus responded: "I am the resurrection and the life. He that exercises faith in me, even though he dies, will come to life; and everyone that is living and exercises faith in me will never die at all. Do you believe this?" (John 11: 25, 26) To prove his point, Jesus went to the cave where

---

21, 22. (a) To what did Jesus compare dead Lazarus' condition, and why? (b) What hope did Martha entertain for her dead brother?
23. What miracle did Jesus perform, and with what effect on the onlookers?

Lazarus was entombed and called him forth alive in the sight of his sisters, Mary and Martha, and neighbors. The account continues: "Therefore many of the Jews that had come to Mary and that beheld what he did put faith in him . . . Accordingly the crowd that was with him when he called Lazarus out of the memorial tomb and raised him up from the dead kept bearing witness." (John 11:45; 12:17) They had seen the miracle for themselves, and they believed and testified to its actuality. Jesus' religious opposers must also have believed the event, for the record tells us that the chief priests and the Pharisees plotted to kill Jesus "because this man performs many signs."—John 11:30-53.

²⁴ Where had Lazarus gone during the four days he was dead? Nowhere. He was unconscious, asleep in the tomb awaiting a resurrection. Jesus blessed him by miraculously raising him from the dead. But according to John's account, Lazarus said nothing about having been in heaven, hell, or purgatory during those four days. Why not? Simply because he had no immortal soul that could journey to such places.*—Job 36:14; Ezekiel 18:4.

²⁵ Therefore, when Jesus spoke of everlasting life, he was referring to such life either in the heavens as a trans-

---

* The expression "immortal soul" appears nowhere in the Bible. The Greek word translated "immortal" and "immortality" appears only three times and refers to a new spirit body that is put on or acquired, not something inherent. It applies to Christ and to anointed Christians, who become corulers with him in his heavenly Kingdom.—1 Corinthians 15:53, 54; 1 Timothy 6:16; Romans 8:17; Ephesians 3:6; Revelation 7:4; 14:1-5.

---

24. (a) Where had Lazarus been for four days? (b) What does the Bible say about immortality?
25. (a) When the Bible speaks of everlasting life, to what does it refer? (b) The coming of God's promised Kingdom depends on what?

The account of the raising of Lazarus to life makes no mention or even suggestion that he had an immortal soul

formed immortal spirit coruler with him in his Kingdom, or he was referring to life everlasting as a human on a paradise earth under that Kingdom rulership.* (Luke 23: 43; John 17:3) According to God's promise, his figurative dwelling with obedient mankind on earth will bring abundant blessings to the earth. All of this, of course, depends

---

* For a more detailed consideration of this Kingdom rulership, see Chapter 15.

on whether Jesus was really sent and approved by God. —Luke 22:28-30; Titus 1:1, 2; Revelation 21:1-4.

God's Approval—Reality, Not Myth

[26] How do we know that Jesus had God's approval? In the first place, when Jesus was baptized, a voice out of heaven was heard saying: "This is my Son, the beloved, whom I have approved." (Matthew 3:17) Later, confirmation of this approval was given before other witnesses. The disciples Peter, James, and John, formerly fishermen from Galilee, accompanied Jesus to a high mountain (probably Mount Hermon, which rises to 9,232 feet). There something remarkable took place before their eyes: "And [Jesus] was transfigured before them, and his face shone as the sun, and his outer garments became brilliant as the light. And, look! there appeared to them Moses and Elijah, conversing with him. . . . Look! a bright cloud overshadowed them, and, look! a voice out of the cloud, saying: 'This is my Son, the beloved, whom I have approved; listen to him.' At hearing this the disciples fell upon their faces and became very much afraid."—Matthew 17:1-6; Luke 9:28-36.

[27] This audible and visible confirmation from God served to strengthen Peter's faith enormously, for he later wrote: "No, it was not by following artfully contrived false stories [Greek: *my'thois,* myths] that we acquainted you with the power and presence of our Lord Jesus Christ, but it was by having become eyewitnesses of his magnificence. For he received from God the Father honor and glory,

---

26. What remarkable event took place in the presence of the disciples Peter, James, and John?
27. (a) What effect did the transfiguration have on the disciples? (b) How do we know that Jesus was not a myth?

when words such as these were borne to him by the magnificent glory: 'This is my son, my beloved, whom I myself have approved.' Yes, these words we heard borne from heaven while we were with him in the holy mountain." (2 Peter 1:16-18) The Jewish disciples Peter, James, and John actually saw the miracle of the transfiguration of Jesus and heard God's voice of approval out of the heavens.

Peter, James, and John knew that God's approval of Jesus was not a myth—they heard and saw it at the transfiguration

Their faith was based on a reality they had seen and heard, not on mythology or on "Jewish fables." (See box, page 237.)—Matthew 17:9; Titus 1:13, 14.*

Jesus' Death and Another Miracle

28 In the year 33 C.E., Jesus was arrested and put on trial by the Jewish religious authorities, falsely accused of blasphemy for calling himself the Son of God. (Matthew 26:3, 4, 59-67) Since those Jews did not have the legal authority to put him to death, they sent him to the Roman rulers and again accused him falsely, this time of forbidding payment of taxes to Caesar and of saying that he himself was a king. —Mark 12:14-17; Luke 23:1-11; John 18:28-31.

29 After Jesus had been passed from one ruler to another, the Roman governor Pontius Pilate, on the insistence of the religiously inspired mob, took the line of least resistance and sentenced Jesus to death. As a consequence, Jesus died in disgrace on a stake, and his body was placed in a tomb. But within three days an event took place that transformed the disconsolate disciples of Jesus into joyful believers and zealous evangelizers.—John 19:16-22; Galatians 3:13.

30 The religious leaders, suspecting that Jesus' followers would resort to trickery, went to Pilate with a request: " 'Sir, we have called to mind that that impostor said while yet alive, "After three days I am to be raised up." Therefore command the grave to be made secure until the third day,

---

* "Moses" and "Elijah" in the vision symbolized the Law and the Prophets that were fulfilled in Jesus. For a more detailed explanation of the transfiguration, see *Insight on the Scriptures*, 1988, Volume 2, pages 1120-1.

---

28. In the year 33 C.E., how was Jesus falsely accused?
29. How did Jesus die?
30. What steps did the religious leaders take to prevent a hoax?

that his disciples may never come and steal him and say to the people, "He was raised up from the dead!" and this last imposture will be worse than the first.' Pilate said to them: 'You have a guard. Go make it as secure as you know how.' So they went and made the grave secure by sealing the stone and having the guard." (Matthew 27:62-66) How secure did it prove to be?

[31] On the third day after Jesus' death, three women went to the tomb to grease the body with perfumed oil. What did they find? "And very early on the first day of the week they came to the memorial tomb, when the sun had risen. And they were saying one to another: 'Who will roll the stone away from the door of the memorial tomb for us?' But when they looked up, they beheld that the stone had been rolled away, although it was very large. When they entered into the memorial tomb, they saw a young man sitting on the right side clothed in a white robe, and they were stunned. He said to them: 'Stop being stunned. You are looking for Jesus the Nazarene, who was impaled. He was raised up, he is not here. See! The place where they laid him. But go, tell his disciples and Peter, "He is going ahead of you into Galilee; there you will see him, just as he told you."'" (Mark 16:1-7; Luke 24:1-12) In spite of the religious leaders' special guard, Jesus had been resurrected by his Father. Is that a myth or a historical fact?

[32] About 22 years after this event, Paul, a former persecutor of Christians, wrote and explained how he came to believe that Christ had been resurrected: "For I handed on to you, among the first things, that which I also received,

---

31. What happened when faithful women went to Jesus' tomb?
32. For what solid reasons did Paul believe that Jesus had been resurrected?

that Christ died for our sins according to the Scriptures; and that he was buried, yes, that he has been raised up the third day according to the Scriptures; and that he appeared to Cephas, then to the twelve. After that he appeared to upward of five hundred brothers at one time, the most of whom remain to the present, but some have fallen asleep in death. After that he appeared to James, then to all the apostles." (1 Corinthians 15:3-7) Yes, Paul had a factual basis for risking his life in the cause of the resurrected Jesus, and it included the testimony of some 500 eyewitnesses who had seen the resurrected Jesus in person! (Romans 1:1-4) Paul knew Jesus had been resurrected, and he had an even more powerful reason for saying so, as he further explained: "But last of all he appeared also to me as if to one born prematurely."—1 Corinthians 15:8, 9; Acts 9:1-19.

[33] The early Christians were willing to die as martyrs in the Roman arenas. Why? Because they knew that their faith was based on historical realities, not on myths. It was a reality that Jesus was the Christ, or the Messiah, promised in prophecy and that he had been sent to the earth by God, had received God's approval, had died on a stake as God's integrity-keeping Son, and had been resurrected from the dead.—1 Peter 1:3, 4.

[34] We recommend that you read the whole of that chapter 15 of Paul's first letter to the Corinthians to understand what Paul believed about the resurrection and why it is essential to the Christian faith. The essence of his message is expressed in these words: "However, now Christ has been raised up from the dead, the firstfruits of those

33. Why were the early Christians willing to be martyrs for their faith?
34. According to the apostle Paul, why is Jesus' resurrection so essential to the Christian faith?

who have fallen asleep in death. For since death is through a man [Adam], resurrection of the dead is also through a man. For just as in Adam all are dying, so also in the Christ all will be made alive."—1 Corinthians 15:20-22.

[35] The resurrection of Christ Jesus thus has a purpose that will eventually benefit all mankind.* It also opened the way for Jesus eventually to fulfill the rest of the Messianic prophecies. His righteous rulership from the invisible heavens must soon extend to a cleansed earth. Then there will be what the Bible describes as "a new heaven and a new earth" in which God "will wipe out every tear from their eyes, and death will be no more, neither will mourning nor outcry nor pain be anymore. The former things have passed away."—Revelation 21:1-4.

Apostasy and Persecution Expected

[36] Shortly after Jesus' death and resurrection, another miracle took place that gave strength and momentum to the preaching by those early Christians. On the day of Pentecost of the year 33 C.E., God poured out from heaven his holy spirit, or active force, upon some 120 Christians met together in Jerusalem. The result? "And tongues as if of fire became visible to them and were distributed about, and one sat upon each one of them, and they all became filled with holy spirit and started to speak with different tongues, just as the spirit was granting them to make utterance." (Acts 2:3, 4) The foreign-language-speaking

---

* For a detailed consideration of the resurrection of Jesus, see the book *The Bible—God's Word or Man's?*, published by the Watchtower Bible and Tract Society of New York, Inc., 1989, pages 78-86.

---

35. What blessings are promised by God for the earth and for mankind? (Isaiah 65:17-25)
36. What took place at Pentecost 33 C.E., and with what result?

Jesus and the Name of God

When teaching his disciples how to pray, Jesus said: *"You must pray, then, this way: 'Our Father in the heavens, let your name be sanctified. Let your kingdom come. Let your will take place, as in heaven, also upon earth.'"* —Matthew 6:9, 10.

Jesus knew the vital significance of his Father's name and gave emphasis to it. Thus, to his religious enemies, he said: *"I have come in the name of my Father, but you do not receive me; if someone else arrived in his own name, you would receive that one. . . . I told you, and yet you do not believe. The works that I am doing in the name of my Father, these bear witness about me."*—John 5:43; 10:25; Mark 12:29, 30.

In prayer to his Father, Jesus said: *"'Father, glorify your name.' Therefore a voice came out of heaven: 'I both glorified it and will glorify it again.'"*

On a later occasion, Jesus prayed: *"I have made your name manifest to the men you gave me out of the world. They were yours, and you gave them to me, and they have observed your word. And I have made your name* *known to them and will make it known, in order that the love with which you loved me may be in them and I in union with them."* —John 12:28; 17:6, 26.

As a Jew, Jesus had to be conversant with his Father's name, Jehovah, or Yahweh, for he knew the scripture that says: *"'You are my witnesses,' is the utterance of Jehovah, 'even my servant whom I have chosen, in order that you may know and have faith in me, and that you may understand that I am the same One. Before me there was no God formed, and after me there continued to be none. . . . So you are my witnesses,' is the utterance of Jehovah, 'and I am God.'"*—Isaiah 43:10, 12.

Therefore, the Jews as a nation were chosen to be Jehovah's witnesses. As a Jew, Jesus was also a witness of Jehovah.—Revelation 3:14.

Apparently by the first century, most Jews were no longer pronouncing God's revealed name. However, there are manuscripts that prove that early Christians using the Greek Septuagint translation of the Hebrew Scriptures could have seen the Hebrew Tetragrammaton used in the Greek text. As George Howard, a professor of religion and Hebrew stated: "When the Septuagint which the New Testament church used and quoted contained the Hebrew form of the divine name, the New Testament writers no doubt included the Tetragrammaton in their quotations. But when the Hebrew form for the divine name was [later] eliminated in favor of Greek substitutes in the Septuagint, it was eliminated also from the New Testament quotations of the Septuagint."

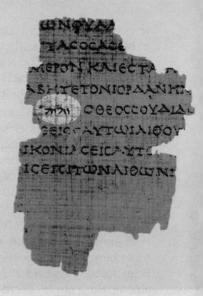

Papyrus fragment (first century B.C.E.) showing the Hebrew name of God in the Greek *Septuagint* text

Therefore, Professor Howard reasons that first-century Christians must have clearly understood texts such as Matthew 22:44, where Jesus quoted the Hebrew Scriptures to his enemies. Howard says, "The first century church probably read, 'YHWH said to my Lord'" instead of the later version, "'The Lord said to my Lord,' ... which is as ambiguous as it is imprecise."—Psalm 110:1.

That Jesus used the divine name is attested to by the Jewish accusation centuries after his death that if he performed miracles, it was "only because he had made himself master of the 'secret' name of God."—*The Book of Jewish Knowledge*.

Jesus certainly knew God's unique name. In spite of Jewish tradition at that time, Jesus would surely have used the name. He did not allow the traditions of men to overrule the law of God.—Mark 7:9-13; John 1:1-3, 18; Colossians 1:15, 16.

Jews who were in Jerusalem at that time were astonished to hear those supposedly ignorant Galilean Jews speaking in foreign tongues. The result was that many believed. The Christian message spread like wildfire as these new Jewish believers returned to their homelands.—Acts 2:5-21.

³⁷ But storm clouds soon gathered. The Romans became apprehensive of this new and apparently atheistic religion that had no idols. Starting with Emperor Nero, they brought down terrible persecution upon the Christians in the first three centuries of our Common Era.* Many Christians were condemned to die in the coliseums, to satisfy the sadistic bloodlust of the emperors and the mobs who flocked to see prisoners being thrown to wild beasts.

³⁸ Another disturbing factor in those early days was something that the apostles had prophesied. For example, Peter stated: "However, there also came to be false prophets among the people, as there will also be false teachers among you. These very ones will quietly bring in destructive sects and will disown even the owner that bought them, bringing speedy destruction upon themselves." (2 Peter 2:1-3) Apostasy! That was a falling away from true worship, a compromising with the current religious trends of the Roman world, which was saturated with Greek philosophy and thought. How did it come about? Our next chapter will answer that and related questions.—Acts 20: 30; 2 Timothy 2:16-18; 2 Thessalonians 2:3.

---

* Roman biographer Suetonius (c. 69-140 C.E.) recorded that during Nero's reign, "punishments were . . . inflicted on the Christians, a sect professing a new and mischievous religious belief."

---

37. How did some Roman rulers react to the new Christian religion?
38. What condition was prophesied that would disturb the early Christian congregation?

CHAPTER 11.

Apostasy
The Way to God Blocked

W HY are Christendom's first 400 years of history so important? For the same reason that the first few years of a child's life are important—because they are the formative years when the foundation is laid for the future personality of the individual. What do Christendom's early centuries reveal?

² Before we answer that question, let us recall a truth that Jesus Christ expressed: "Go in through the narrow gate; because broad and spacious is the road leading off into destruction, and many are the ones going in through it; whereas narrow is the gate and cramped the road leading off into life, and few are the ones finding it." The road of expediency is broad; that of right principles is narrow.—Matthew 7:13, 14.

³ At the inception of Christianity, there were two ways available to those espousing that unpopular faith—hold to the uncompromising teachings and principles of Christ and the Scriptures or gravitate toward the wide and easygoing path of compromise with the world of that time. As we will see, the history of the first 400 years shows which path the majority eventually chose.

1, 2. (a) Why are the first 400 years of Christendom's history important? (b) What truth on choices did Jesus express?
3. What two courses were available at the inception of Christianity?

The Seduction of Philosophy

[4] Historian Will Durant explains: "The Church took over some religious customs and forms common in pre-Christian [pagan] Rome—the stole and other vestments of pagan priests, the use of incense and holy water in purifications, the burning of candles and an everlasting light before the altar, the worship of the saints, the architecture of the basilica, the law of Rome as a basis for canon law, the title of *Pontifex Maximus* for the Supreme Pontiff, and, in the fourth century, the Latin language . . . Soon the bishops, rather than the Roman prefects, would be the source of order and the seat of power in the cities; the metropolitans, or archbishops, would support, if not supplant, the provincial governors; and the synod of bishops would succeed the provincial assembly. The Roman Church followed in the footsteps of the Roman state." —*The Story of Civilization: Part III—Caesar and Christ.*

4. According to historian Durant, how did pagan Rome affect the early church?

Early Christians and Pagan Rome

"As the Christian movement emerged within the Roman Empire, it challenged pagan converts, too, to change their attitudes and behavior. Many pagans who had been brought up to regard marriage essentially as a social and economic arrangement, homosexual relationships as an expected element of male education, prostitution, both male and female, as both ordinary and legal, and divorce, abortion, contraception, and exposure [to death] of unwanted infants as matters of practical expedience, embraced, to the astonishment of their families, the Christian message, which opposed these practices."—*Adam, Eve, and the Serpent,* by Elaine Pagels.

⁵ This attitude of compromise with the Roman world stands in stark contrast to the teachings of Christ and the apostles. (See box, page 262.) The apostle Peter counseled: "Beloved ones, . . . I am arousing your clear thinking faculties by way of a reminder, that you should remember the sayings previously spoken by the holy prophets and the commandment of the Lord and Savior through your apostles. You, therefore, beloved ones, having this advance knowledge, be on your guard that you may not be led away with them by the error of the law-defying people and fall from your own steadfastness." Paul clearly counseled: "Do not become unevenly yoked with unbelievers. For what fellowship do righteousness and lawlessness have? Or what sharing does light have with darkness? . . . '"Therefore get out from among them, and separate yourselves," says Jehovah, "and quit touching the unclean thing"'; '"and I will take you in."'"—2 Peter 3:1, 2, 17; 2 Corinthians 6:14-17; Revelation 18:2-5.

⁶ In spite of this clear admonition, apostate Christians of the second century took on the trappings of the pagan Roman religion. They moved away from their pure Biblical origins and instead clothed themselves with pagan Roman garb and titles and became imbued with Greek philosophy. Professor Wolfson of Harvard University explains in *The Crucible of Christianity* that in the second century, there was a great influx into Christianity of "philosophically trained gentiles." These admired the

5. How does the attitude of compromise with the pagan Roman world contrast with early Christian writings?
6, 7. (a) How were early church "fathers" influenced by Greek philosophy? (b) In which teachings did the Greek influence especially show up? (c) What warning about philosophy did Paul give?

wisdom of the Greeks and thought they saw similarities between Greek philosophy and teachings of the Scriptures. Wolfson continues: "Sometimes they variously express themselves to the effect that philosophy is God's special gift to the Greeks by way of human reason as Scripture is to the Jews by way of direct revelation." He continues: "The Fathers of the Church . . . entered upon their systematic undertaking to show how, behind the homely language in which Scripture likes to express itself, there are hidden the teachings of the philosophers couched in the obscure technical terms coined in their Academy, Lyceum, and Porch [centers for philosophical discussion]."

Christendom's Trinity Mystery Triangle

[7] Such an attitude left the way open for Greek philosophy and terminology to infiltrate Christendom's teachings, especially in the fields of Trinitarian doctrine and the belief in an immortal soul. As Wolfson states: "The [church] Fathers began to look in the stockpile of philosophic terminology for two good technical terms, of which one would be used as a designation of the reality of the distinctness of each member of the Trinity as an individual and the other would be used as a designation of their underlying common unity." Yet, they had to admit that "the conception of a triune God is a mystery which cannot be solved by human reason." In contrast, Paul had clearly recognized the danger of such contamination and 'perversion of the good news' when he wrote to the Galatian and Colossian

Christians: "Look out: perhaps there may be someone who will carry you off as his prey through the philosophy [Greek, *phi·lo·so·phi′as*] and empty deception according to the tradition of men, according to the elementary things of the world and not according to Christ."—Galatians 1: 7-9; Colossians 2:8; 1 Corinthians 1:22, 23.

Resurrection Annulled

8 As we have seen throughout this book, man has constantly struggled with the enigma of his short and finite existence that ends in death. As German author Gerhard Herm stated in his book *The Celts—The People Who Came Out of the Darkness:* "Religion is among other things a way of reconciling people to the fact that some day they must die, whether by the promise of a better life beyond the grave, rebirth, or both." Virtually every religion depends on the belief that the human soul is immortal and that after death it journeys to an afterlife or that it transmigrates to another creature.

9 Nearly all the religions of Christendom today also follow that belief. Miguel de Unamuno, a prominent 20th-century Spanish scholar, wrote about Jesus: "He believed rather in the resurrection of the flesh [such as Lazarus' case (see pages 249-52)], according to the Jewish manner, not in the immortality of the soul, according to the [Greek] Platonic manner. . . . The proofs of this can be seen in any honest book of interpretation." He concluded: "The immortality of the soul . . . is a pagan philosophical dogma." (*La Agonía Del Cristianismo* [The Agony of Christianity])

---

8. With what enigma has man struggled, and how have most religions tried to resolve it?
9. What did Spanish scholar Miguel de Unamuno conclude regarding Jesus' belief on the resurrection?

That "pagan philosophical dogma" infiltrated into Christendom's teaching, even though Christ plainly had no such thought.—Matthew 10:28; John 5:28, 29; 11:23, 24.

[10] The subtle influence of Greek philosophy was a key factor in the apostasy that followed the death of the apostles. The Greek immortal soul teaching implied a need for various destinations for the soul—heaven, hellfire, purgatory, paradise, Limbo.* By manipulating such teachings, it became easy for a priestly class to keep their flocks submissive and in fear of the Hereafter and to extract gifts and donations from them. Which leads us to another question:

* The expressions "immortal soul," "hellfire," "purgatory," and "Limbo" are nowhere found in the original Hebrew and Greek of the Bible. In contrast, the Greek word for "resurrection" (*ana'stasis*) occurs 42 times.

10. What were some consequences of belief in an immortal soul?

Christianity Versus Christendom

Porphyry, a third-century philosopher from Tyre and an opposer of Christianity, raised the question "as to whether followers of Jesus, rather than Jesus himself, were responsible for the distinctive form of the Christian religion. Porphyry (and Julian [fourth-century Roman emperor and opposer of Christianity]) showed, on the basis of the New Testament, that Jesus did not call himself God and that he preached, not about himself, but about the one God, the God of all. It was his followers who abandoned his teaching and introduced a new way of their own in which Jesus (not the one God) was the object of worship and adoration.... [Porphyry] put his finger on a troubling issue for Christian thinkers: does the Christian faith rest on the preaching of Jesus or on the ideas forged by his disciples in the generations after his death?"—*The Christians as the Romans Saw Them.*

How did Christendom's separate priestly clergy class originate?—John 8:44; 1 Timothy 4:1, 2.

How the Clergy Class Was Formed

[11] Another indication of apostasy was the retreat from the general ministry of all Christians, as Jesus and the apostles had taught, to the exclusive priesthood and hierarchy that developed in Christendom. (Matthew 5:14-16; Romans 10:13-15; 1 Peter 3:15) During the first century, after Jesus' death, his apostles, along with other spiritually qualified Christian elders in Jerusalem, served to counsel and direct the Christian congregation. None exercised superiority over the others.—Galatians 2:9.

[12] In the year 49 C.E., it became necessary for them to meet together in Jerusalem to resolve questions affecting Christians in general. The Bible account tells us that after open discussion, "the apostles and the older men [*pre·sby'te·roi*] together with the whole congregation favored sending chosen men from among them to Antioch along with Paul and Barnabas, . . . and by their hand they wrote: 'The apostles and the older men, brothers, to those brothers in Antioch and Syria and Cilicia who are from the nations: Greetings!'" Evidently the apostles and elders served as an administrative governing agency for the widespread Christian congregations.—Acts 15:22, 23.

[13] Now since that governing group in Jerusalem was the early Christian arrangement for general oversight for all Christians, what system of direction did they have in each congregation, at the local level? Paul's letter to Timothy

---

11, 12. (a) What was another sign of apostasy that arose? (b) What role was played by the apostles and elders in Jerusalem? 13. (a) What arrangement existed for immediate oversight of each of the early Christian congregations? (b) What were the qualifications for congregation elders?

Peter and the Papacy

At Matthew 16:18, Jesus said to the apostle Peter: "And I tell you, you are Peter [Greek, *Pe'tros*], and on this rock [Greek, *pe'tra*] I will build my church, and the powers of death shall not prevail against it." (*RS*) Based on this, the Catholic Church claims that Jesus built his church on Peter, who, they say, was the first of an unbroken line of bishops of Rome, and Peter's successors.

Who was the rock that Jesus indicated at Matthew 16:18, Peter or Jesus? The context shows that the point of the discussion was the identification of Jesus as "the Christ, the Son of the living God," as Peter himself confessed. (Matthew 16:16, *RS*) Logically, therefore, Jesus himself would be that solid rock foundation of the church, not Peter, who would later deny Christ three times. —Matthew 26:33-35, 69-75.

How do we know that Christ is the foundation stone? By Peter's own testimony, when he wrote: "Coming to him as to a living stone, rejected, it is true, by men, but chosen, precious, with God ... For it is contained in Scripture: 'Look! I am laying in Zion a stone, chosen, a foundation cornerstone, precious; and no one exercising faith in it will by any means come to disappointment.'" Paul also stated: "And you have been built up upon the foundation of the apostles and prophets, while Christ Jesus himself is the foundation cornerstone."—1 Peter 2:4-8; Ephesians 2:20.

There is no evidence in Scripture or history that Peter was regarded as having primacy among his peers. He makes no mention of it in his own letters, and the other three Gospels —including Mark's (apparently related by Peter to Mark)—do not even mention Jesus' statement to Peter.—Luke 22:24-26; Acts 15:6-22; Galatians 2:11-14.

There is not even any absolute proof that Peter was ever in Rome. (1 Peter 5:13) When Paul visited Jerusalem, "James and Cephas [Peter] and John, the ones who seemed to be pillars," gave him support. So at that time Peter was one of at least three pillars in the congregation. He was not a "pope," nor was he known as such or as a primate "bishop" in Jerusalem. —Galatians 2:7-9; Acts 28:16, 30, 31.

makes it clear that the congregations had overseers (Greek, *e·pi′sko·pos,* source of the word "episcopal") who were spiritual elders (*pre·sby′te·roi*), men who were qualified by their conduct and their spirituality to teach their fellow Christians. (1 Timothy 3:1-7; 5:17) In the first century, these men did not constitute a separate clergy class. They did not wear any distinctive garb. Their spirituality was their distinction. In fact, each congregation had a body of elders (overseers), not a monarchical one-man rule.—Acts 20:17; Philippians 1:1.

[14] It was only as time passed that the word *e·pi′sko·pos** (overseer, superintendent) became converted to "bishop," meaning a priest with jurisdiction over other members of the clergy in his diocese. As the Spanish Jesuit Bernardino

---

* The Greek word *e·pi′sko·pos* literally means 'one who watches over.' In Latin it became *episcopus,* and in Old English it was transformed into *"biscop"* and later, in Middle English, to "bishop."

14. (a) How were Christian overseers eventually superseded by Christendom's bishops? (b) Who strove for primacy among the bishops?

The Vatican (flag shown below) sends diplomats to the world's governments

Llorca explains: "First, there was not sufficient distinction made between the bishops and the presbyters, and attention was only paid to the meaning of the words: *bishop* is the equivalent of superintendent; *presbyter* is the equivalent of older man. . . . But little by little the distinction became clearer, designating with the name *bishop* the more important superintendents, who possessed the supreme priestly authority and the faculty to lay on hands and confer the priesthood." (*Historia de la Iglesia Católica* [History of the Catholic Church]) In fact, bishops began to function in a kind of monarchical system, especially from the beginning of the fourth century. A hierarchy, or ruling body of clergy, was established, and in time the bishop of Rome, claiming to be a successor to Peter, was acknowledged by many as the supreme bishop and pope.

¹⁵ Today the position of bishop in the different churches of Christendom is a position of prestige and power, usually well remunerated, and often identified with the elite ruling class of each nation. But between their proud and elevated situation and the simplicity of organization under Christ and the elders, or overseers, of the early Christian congregations, there is an enormous difference. And what shall we say of the gulf between Peter and his so-called successors, who have ruled in the sumptuous setting of the Vatican? —Luke 9:58; 1 Peter 5:1-3.

Papal Power and Prestige

¹⁶ Among the early congregations that accepted direction from the apostles and elders in Jerusalem was the one

15. What gulf exists between the early Christian leadership and that of Christendom?
16, 17. (a) How do we know that the early Roman congregation was not under the control of a bishop or pope? (b) How did the use of the title "pope" develop?

in Rome, where Christian truth probably arrived sometime after Pentecost 33 C.E. (Acts 2:10) Like any other Christian congregation of the time, it had elders, who served as a body of overseers without any one of them having the primacy. Certainly none of the earliest overseers in the Rome congregation were viewed by their contemporaries as bishops or as a pope, since the monarchical episcopate at Rome had not yet developed. The starting point of the monarchical, or one-man, episcopate is hard to pin down. Evidence indicates that it began to develop in the second century.—Romans 16:3-16; Philippians 1:1.

[17] The title "pope" (from the Greek *pa'pas,* father) was not used during the first two centuries. Former Jesuit Michael Walsh explains: "The first time a Bishop of Rome was called 'Pope' seems to have been in the third century, and the title was given to Pope Callistus . . . By the end of the fifth century 'Pope' usually meant the Bishop of Rome and no one else. It was not until the eleventh century, however, that a Pope could insist that the title applied to him alone."—*An Illustrated History of the Popes.*

[18] One of the first bishops of Rome to impose his authority was Pope Leo I (pope, 440-461 C.E.). Michael Walsh further explains: "Leo appropriated the once pagan title of *Pontifex Maximus,* still used by the popes today, and borne, until towards the end of the fourth century, by Roman Emperors." Leo I based his actions on the Catholic interpretation of Jesus' words found at Matthew 16:18, 19. (See box, page 268.) He "declared that because St. Peter was the first among the Apostles, St. Peter's church should be accorded primacy among the churches." (*Man's Religions*) By this

---

18. (a) Who was one of the first bishops of Rome to impose his authority? (b) On what is the papal claim of primacy based? (c) What is the proper understanding of Matthew 16:18, 19?

move, Leo I made it clear that while the emperor held temporal power in Constantinople in the East, he exercised spiritual power from Rome in the West. This power was further illustrated when Pope Leo III crowned Charlemagne emperor of the Holy Roman Empire in 800 C.E.

[19] Since 1929 the pope of Rome has been viewed by secular governments as the ruler of a separate sovereign state, Vatican City. Thus, the Roman Catholic Church, like no other religious organization, can send diplomatic representatives, nuncios, to the governments of the world. (John 18:36) The pope is honored with many titles, some of which are Vicar of Jesus Christ, Successor to the Prince of the Apostles, Supreme Pontiff of the Universal Church, Patriarch of the West, Primate of Italy, Sovereign of the Vatican City. He is carried with pomp and ceremony. He is given the honors assigned to a head of State. In contrast, note how Peter, supposedly the first pope and bishop of Rome, reacted when the Roman centurion Cornelius fell down at his feet to do obeisance to him: "Peter lifted him up, saying: 'Rise; I myself am also a man.'"—Acts 10:25, 26; Matthew 23:8-12.

[20] The question now is, How did so much power and prestige ever accrue to the apostate church of those early centuries? How was the simplicity and humility of Christ and the early Christians converted into the pride and pomp of Christendom?

Christendom's Foundation

[21] The turning point for this new religion in the Roman

19, 20. (a) How has the pope been viewed in modern times? (b) What are some of the pope's official titles? (c) What contrast can be seen between the conduct of popes and that of Peter?
21, 22. What great change supposedly took place in the life of Constantine, and how did he exploit it?

Empire was 313 C.E., the date of Emperor Constantine's so-called conversion to "Christianity." How did this conversion come about? In 306 C.E., Constantine succeeded his father and eventually, with Licinius, became coruler of the Roman Empire. He was influenced by his mother's devotion to Christianity and his own belief in divine protection. Before he went to fight a battle near Rome at the Milvian Bridge in 312 C.E., he claimed that he was told in a dream to paint the "Christian" monogram—the Greek letters *khi* and *rho*, the first two letters of Christ's name in Greek—on his soldiers' shields.* With this 'sacred talisman,' Constantine's forces defeated his enemy Maxentius.

[22] Shortly after winning the battle, Constantine claimed that he had become a believer, although he was not baptized until just prior to his death some 24 years later. He went on to obtain the support of the professed Christians in his empire by "his adoption of the [Greek letters] Chi-Rho [✗] as his emblem . . . The Chi-Rho had, however, already been used as a ligature [joining of letters] in both pagan and Christian contexts."—*The Crucible of Christianity,* edited by Arnold Toynbee.

[23] As a result, the foundation of Christendom was laid. As British broadcaster Malcolm Muggeridge wrote in his book *The End of Christendom:* "Christendom began with the Emperor Constantine." However, he also made the

---

* A popular legend says that Constantine saw a vision of a cross with the Latin words *"In hoc signo vinces"* (In this sign conquer). Some historians say it was more likely in Greek, *"En toutoi nika"* (In this conquer). The legend is doubted by some scholars because it contains anachronisms.

---

23. (a) According to one commentator, when did Christendom begin? (b) Why can we say that Christ did not found Christendom?

perceptive comment: "You might even say that Christ himself abolished Christendom before it began by stating that his kingdom was not of this world—one of the most far reaching and important of all his statements." And one most widely ignored by Christendom's religious and political rulers.—John 18:36.

[24] With Constantine's support, Christendom's religion became the official State religion of Rome. Elaine Pagels, a professor of religion, explains: "Christian bishops, once targets for arrest, torture, and execution, now received tax exemptions, gifts from the imperial treasury, prestige, and even influence at court; their churches gained new wealth, power, and prominence." They had become friends of the emperor, friends of the Roman world.—James 4:4.

Constantine, Heresy, and Orthodoxy

[25] Why was Constantine's "conversion" so significant? Because as emperor he had a powerful influence in the affairs of the doctrinally divided "Christian" church, and he wanted unity in his empire. At that time debate was raging among the Greek- and Latin-speaking bishops about "the relation between the 'Word' or 'Son' of 'God' which had been incarnate in Jesus, and 'God' himself, now called 'the Father'—his name, Yahweh, having been generally forgotten." (*The Columbia History of the World*) Some favored the Biblically supported viewpoint that Christ, the *Lo'gos*, was created and therefore subordinate to the Father. (Matthew 24:36; John 14:28; 1 Corinthians 15:25-28) Among these was Arius, a priest in Alexandria,

---

24. With Constantine's "conversion," what change came about in the church?
25. (a) By Constantine's time what theological debate was raging? (b) Before the fourth century, what situation existed with regard to the understanding of Christ's relationship to his Father?

Egypt. In fact, R. P. C. Hanson, a professor of divinity, states: "There is no theologian in the Eastern or the Western Church before the [fourth century] outbreak of the Arian Controversy, who does not in some sense regard the Son as subordinate to the Father."—*The Search for the Christian Doctrine of God.*

[26] Others considered that viewpoint of Christ's subordination to be heresy and veered more toward the worship of Jesus as "God Incarnate." Yet, Professor Hanson states that the period under question (the fourth century) "was not a history of the defence of an agreed and settled [Trinitarian] orthodoxy against the assaults of open heresy [Arianism]. On the subject which was primarily under discussion there was not as yet any orthodox doctrine." He continues: "All sides believed that they had the authority of Scripture in their favour. Each described the others as unorthodox, untraditional and unScriptural." The

26. By the early fourth century, what was the situation regarding the Trinity teaching?

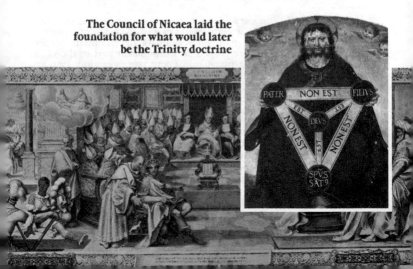

The Council of Nicaea laid the foundation for what would later be the Trinity doctrine

religious ranks were thoroughly divided on this theological issue.—John 20:17.

²⁷ Constantine wanted unity in his realm, and in 325 C.E. he called for a council of his bishops at Nicaea, located in the Eastern, Greek-speaking domain of his empire, across the Bosporus from the new city of Constantinople. It is said that anywhere from 250 to 318 bishops attended, only a minority of the total number, and most of those attending were from the Greek-speaking region. Even Pope Sylvester I was not present.* After fierce debate, out of that unrepresentative council came the Nicene Creed with its heavy bias toward Trinitarian thought. Yet it failed to settle the doctrinal argument. It did not clarify the role of God's holy spirit in Trinitarian theology. Debate raged for decades, and it required more councils and the authority of different emperors and the use of banishment to achieve eventual conformity. It was a victory for theology and a defeat for those who held to the Scriptures.—Romans 3:3, 4.

²⁸ Over the centuries, one result of the Trinity teaching

---

* *The Oxford Dictionary of Popes* states regarding Sylvester I: "Although pope for almost twenty-two years of the reign of Constantine the Great (306-37), an epoch of dramatic developments for the church, he seems to have played an insignificant part in the great events that were taking place. . . . There were certainly bishops whom Constantine made his confidants, and with whom he concerted his ecclesiastical policies; but [Sylvester] was not one of them."

---

27. (a) What did Constantine do to try to settle the debate over Jesus' nature? (b) How representative of the church was the Council of Nicaea? (c) Did the Nicene Creed settle the controversy about the developing Trinity doctrine?
28. (a) What have been some of the consequences of the Trinity doctrine? (b) Why is there no Biblical basis for the veneration of Mary as the "Mother of God"?

The veneration of Mary with a child, center, echoes much older worship of pagan goddesses—left, Egypt's Isis and Horus; right, Rome's Mater Matuta

has been that the one true God Jehovah has been submerged in the quagmire of Christendom's God-Christ theology.* The next logical consequence of that theology was that if Jesus really was God Incarnate, then Jesus' mother, Mary, was obviously the "Mother of God." Over the years, that has led to veneration of Mary in many different forms, this in spite of the total lack of texts that speak of Mary in any role of importance except as the humble biologic mother of Jesus.# (Luke 1:26-38, 46-56) Over the centuries the Mother-of-God teaching has been developed and adorned by the Roman Catholic Church, with the result that many Catholics venerate Mary far more fervently than they worship God.

---

* For a detailed consideration of the Trinity debate, see the 32-page brochure *Should You Believe in the Trinity?* published by the Watchtower Bible and Tract Society of New York, Inc., 1989.

Mary, the mother of Jesus, is mentioned by name or as his mother in 24 different texts in the four Gospels and once in Acts. She is not mentioned in any apostolic letter.

Christendom's Schisms

²⁹ Another characteristic of apostasy is that it leads to division and fragmentation. The apostle Paul had prophesied: "I know that after my going away oppressive wolves will enter in among you and will not treat the flock with tenderness, and from among you yourselves men will rise and speak twisted things to draw away the disciples after themselves." Paul had given clear counsel to the Corinthians when he stated: "Now I exhort you, brothers, through the name of our Lord Jesus Christ that you should all speak in agreement, and that there should not be divisions among you, but that you may be fitly united in the same mind and in the same line of thought." In spite of Paul's exhortation, apostasy and divisions soon took root.—Acts 20:29, 30; 1 Corinthians 1:10.

---

29. What development did Paul warn about?

Eastern Orthodox churches —Sveti Nikolaj, Sofia, Bulgaria, and, below, St. Vladimir's, New Jersey, U.S.A.

[30] Within a few decades of the death of the apostles, schisms were already evident among the Christians. Will Durant states: "Celsus [second-century opponent of Christianity] himself had sarcastically observed that Christians were 'split up into ever so many factions, each individual desiring to have his own party.' About 187 [C.E.] Irenaeus listed twenty varieties of Christianity; about 384 [C.E.] Epiphanius counted eighty."—*The Story of Civilization: Part III—Caesar and Christ.*

[31] Constantine favored the Eastern, Greek, side of his empire by having a vast new capital city built in what is today Turkey. He named it Constantinople (modern Istanbul). The result was that over the centuries the Catholic Church became polarized and split both by language and by geography—Latin-speaking Rome in the West versus Greek-speaking Constantinople in the East.

[32] Divisive debates about aspects of the still-developing Trinity teaching continued to cause turmoil in Christendom. Another council was held in 451 C.E. at Chalcedon to define the character of Christ's "natures." While the West accepted the creed issued by this council, Eastern churches disagreed, leading to the formation of the Coptic Church in Egypt and Abyssinia and the "Jacobite" churches of Syria and Armenia. The unity of the Catholic Church was constantly threatened by divisions on abstruse theological matters, especially regarding the definition of the Trinity doctrine.

---

30. What situation soon developed in the early church?
31. How did a major split develop in the Catholic Church?
32, 33. (a) What were further causes for divisions in Christendom? (b) What does the Bible say about the use of images in worship?

[33] Another cause for division was the veneration of images. During the eighth century, the Eastern bishops rebelled against this idolatry and entered into what is called their iconoclastic, or image-destroying, period. In time they returned to the use of icons.—Exodus 20:4-6; Isaiah 44:14-18.

[34] A further big test came about when the Western church added the Latin word *filioque* ("and from the Son") to the Nicene Creed to indicate that the Holy Spirit proceeded from both the Father and the Son. The end result of this sixth-century emendation was a rift when "in 876 a synod [of bishops] at Constantinople condemned the pope both for his political activities and because he did not correct the heresy of the *filioque* clause. This action was part of the East's entire rejection of the pope's claim of universal jurisdiction over the Church." (*Man's Religions*) In the year 1054, the pope's representative excommunicated the patriarch of Constantinople, who in return put a curse on the pope. That split eventually led to the formation of the Eastern Orthodox Churches—Greek, Russian, Romanian, Polish, Bulgarian, Serbian, and other self-governing churches.

[35] Another movement was also beginning to cause turmoil in the church. In the 12th century, Peter Waldo, from Lyons, France, "engaged some scholars to translate the Bible into the *langue d'oc* [a regional language] of south France. He studied the translation zealously, and concluded that Christians should live like the apostles

---

34. (a) What led to a major rift in the Catholic Church? (b) What was the end result of this rift?
35. Who were the Waldenses, and how did their beliefs differ from those of the Catholic Church?

—without individual property." (*The Age of Faith,* by Will Durant) He started a preaching movement that became known as the Waldenses. These rejected the Catholic priesthood, indulgences, purgatory, transubstantiation, and other traditional Catholic practices and beliefs. They spread into other countries. The Council of Toulouse tried to check them in 1229 by banning the possession of Scriptural books. Only books of liturgy were allowed and then only in the dead language of Latin. But more religious division and persecution was yet to come.

Persecution of the Albigenses

[36] Yet another movement got started in the 12th century in the south of France—the Albigenses (also known as Cathari), named after the town of Albi, where they had many followers. They had their own celibate clergy class, who expected to be greeted with reverence. They

36, 37. (a) Who were the Albigenses, and what did they believe? (b) How were the Albigenses repressed?

"Christian" crusaders were organized not only to free Jerusalem from Islām but also to massacre "heretics," such as the Waldenses and the Albigenses

believed that Jesus spoke figuratively in his last supper when he said of the bread, "This is my body." (Matthew 26:26, *NAB*) They rejected the doctrines of the Trinity, the Virgin Birth, hellfire, and purgatory. Thus they actively put in doubt the teachings of Rome. Pope Innocent III gave instructions that the Albigenses be persecuted. "If necessary," he said, "suppress them with the sword."

[37] A crusade was mounted against the "heretics," and the Catholic crusaders massacred 20,000 men, women, and children in Béziers, France. After much bloodshed, peace came in 1229, with the Albigenses defeated. The Council of Narbonne "forbade the possession of any part of the Bible by laymen." The root of the problem for the Catholic Church was evidently the existence of the Bible in the language of the people.

[38] The next step that the church took was to establish the Inquisition, a tribunal set up to suppress heresy. Already a spirit of intolerance possessed the people, who were superstitious and all too willing to lynch and murder "heretics." The conditions in the 13th century lent themselves to the abuse of power by the church. However, "heretics condemned by the Church were to be delivered to the 'secular arm'—the local authorities—and burned to death." (*The Age of Faith*) By leaving the actual executions to the secular authorities, the church would ostensibly be free of bloodguilt. The Inquisition started an era of religious persecution that resulted in abuses, false and anonymous denunciations, murder, robbery, torture, and the slow death of thousands who dared to believe differently from the church. Freedom of religious expression was

---

38. What was the Inquisition, and how did it function?

Tomás de Torquemada, Dominican monk, led the cruel Spanish Inquisition, which used implements of torture to extract confessions

stifled. Was there any hope for people who were seeking the true God? Chapter 13 will answer that.

[39] While all of this was happening in Christendom, a lone Arab in the Middle East took a stand against the religious apathy and idolatry of his own people. He started a religious movement in the seventh century that today commands the obedience and submission of nearly one thousand million people. That movement is Islām. Our next chapter will consider the history of its prophet-founder and explain some of his teachings and their source.

---

39. What religious movement started in the seventh century, and how?

CHAPTER 12

Islām—*The Way to God by Submission*

بسم الله الرحمن الرحيم

"I N THE name of Allah, the Beneficent, the Merciful." This sentence translates the Arabic text, above, from the Qur'ān. It continues: "Praise be to Allah, Lord of the Worlds: The Beneficent, the Merciful: Owner of the Day of Judgement. Thee (alone) we worship; Thee (alone) we ask for help. Show us the straight path: The path of those whom Thou hast favoured; Not (the path) of those who earn Thine anger nor of those who go astray."—The Qur'ān, surah 1:1-7, *MMP*.*

² These words form *Al-Fātiḥah* ("The Opening"), the first chapter, or surah, of the Muslim holy book, the Holy Qur'ān, or Koran. Since more than 1 in 6 of the world's population is Muslim and devout Muslims repeat these verses at least five times in their daily prayers, these must be among the most recited words on earth.

³ According to one source, there are over 900 million Muslims in the world, making Islām second only to the

---

* "Qur'ān" (which means "Recitation") is the spelling favored by Muslim writers and the one we will use here. It should be noted that Arabic is the original language of the Qur'ān, and in English there is no universally accepted translation. In quotations the first number represents the chapter, or surah, and the second is the verse number.

1, 2. (a) What are the opening words of the Qur'ān? (b) Why are these words significant to Muslims? (c) In what language was the Qur'ān originally written, and what does "Qur'ān" mean?
3. How widespread is Islām today?

Roman Catholic Church in numbers. It is perhaps the fastest growing major religion in the world, with an expanding Muslim movement in Africa and the Western world.

[4] The name Islām is significant to a Muslim, for it means "submission," "surrender," or "commitment" to Allāh, and according to one historian, "it expresses the innermost attitude of those who have hearkened to the preaching of Mohammed." "Muslim" means 'one who makes or does Islām.'

4. (a) What does "Islām" mean? (b) What does "Muslim" mean?

The Qur'ān and the Bible

"He has revealed to you the Book with the truth, confirming the scriptures which preceded it; for He has already revealed the Torah and the Gospel for the guidance of men, and the distinction between right and wrong."—Surah 3:2, *NJD*.

"Almost all the historical narratives of the Koran have their biblical parallels . . . Among the Old Testament characters, Adam, Noah, Abraham (mentioned about seventy times in twenty-five different sūrahs and having his name as a title for sūrah 14), Ishmael, Lot, Joseph (to whom sūrah 12 is dedicated), Moses (whose name occurs in thirty-four different sūrahs), Saul, David, Solomon, Elijah, Job and Jonah (whose name sūrah 10 bears) figure prominently. The story of the creation and fall of Adam is cited five times, the flood eight and Sodom eight. In fact the Koran shows more parallelism to the Pentateuch than to any other part of the Bible. . . .

"Of the New Testament characters Zachariah, John the Baptist, Jesus ('Īsa) and Mary are the only ones emphasized. . . .

"A comparative study of the . . . koranic and biblical narratives . . . reveals no verbal dependence [no direct quotation]."—*History of the Arabs*.

Muslim tradition says that Muḥammad ascended to heaven from this rock in the Dome of the Rock, Jerusalem

⁵ Muslims believe that their faith is the culmination of the revelations given to the faithful Hebrews and Christians of old. However, their teachings diverge from the Bible on some points, even though they cite both the Hebrew and the Greek Scriptures in the Qur'ān.* (See box, page 285.) To understand the Muslim faith better, we need to know how, where, and when this religion started.

Muḥammad's Calling

⁶ Muḥammad# was born in Mecca (Arabic, *Makkah*), Saudi Arabia, about 570 C.E. His father, ʻAbd Allāh, died before Muḥammad's birth. His mother, Āminah, died when he was about six years old. At that time the Arabs practiced

---

* Muslims believe that the Bible contains revelations of God but that some of them were falsified later.

In English the prophet's name has various spellings (Mohammed, Muḥammad, Mahomet). Most Muslim sources prefer Muḥammad, which we will use. Turkish Muslims prefer Muhammed.

---

5. (a) What do Muslims believe regarding Islām? (b) What parallels are there between the Bible and the Qur'ān?
6. (a) What was the focal point of Arab worship in Muḥammad's time? (b) What tradition existed regarding the Kaʻbah?

a form of worship of Allāh that was centered in the Mecca valley, at the sacred site of the Ka'bah, a simple cubelike building where a black meteorite was revered. According to Islāmic tradition, "the Ka'bah was originally built by Adam according to a celestial prototype and after the Deluge rebuilt by Abraham and Ishmael." (*History of the Arabs,* by Philip K. Hitti) It became a sanctuary for 360 idols, one for each day of the lunar year.

[7] As Muḥammad grew up, he questioned the religious practices of his day. John Noss, in his book *Man's Religions,* states: "[Muḥammad] was disturbed by incessant quarreling in the avowed interests of religion and honor among the Quraysh chiefs [Muḥammad belonged to that tribe]. Stronger still was his dissatisfaction with the primitive survivals in Arabian religion, the idolatrous polytheism and animism, the immorality at religious convocations and fairs, the drinking, gambling, and dancing that were fashionable, and the burial alive of unwanted infant daughters practiced not only in Mecca but throughout Arabia."—Surah 6:137.

[8] Muḥammad's call to be a prophet took place when he was about 40 years of age. He had the custom of going alone to a nearby mountain cave, called Ghār Ḥirā', for meditation, and he claimed that it was on one of these occasions that he received the call to be a prophet. Muslim tradition relates that while he was there, an angel, later identified as Gabriel, commanded him to recite in the name of Allāh. Muḥammad failed to respond, so the angel 'caught him forcefully and pressed him so hard that he

7. What religious practices disturbed Muḥammad?
8. Under what circumstances did Muḥammad's call to be a prophet take place?

could not bear it anymore.' Then the angel repeated the command. Again, Muḥammad failed to react, so the angel 'choked him' again. This occurred three times before Muḥammad started to recite what came to be viewed as the first of a series of revelations that constitute the Qur'ān. Another tradition relates that divine inspiration was revealed to Muḥammad like the ringing of a bell.—*The Book of Revelation* from Ṣaḥīḥ Al-Bukhārī.

Revelation of the Qur'ān

[9] What is said to have been the first revelation received by Muḥammad? Islāmic authorities generally agree that it was the first five verses of surah 96, entitled *Al-'Alaq,* "The Clot [of Blood]," which reads:

"In the name of Allah, the Beneficent, the Merciful.
Read: In the name of thy Lord who created.
Created man from a clot.
Read: And thy Lord is the Most Bounteous,
Who taught by the pen,
Taught man that which he knew not."
—*MMP.*

[10] According to the Arabic source *The Book of Revelation,* Muḥammad answered, "I do not know how to read." Therefore, he had to memorize the revelations so that he could repeat and recite them. The Arabs were skilled in the use of memory, and Muḥammad was no exception. How long did it take for him to receive the complete message of the Qur'ān? It is generally believed that the revelations came during a period of some 20 to 23 years, from about 610 C.E. to his death in 632 C.E.

[11] Muslim sources explain that upon receiving each

---

9. What is said to have been Muḥammad's first revelation? (Compare Revelation 22:18, 19.)
10-12. How was the Qur'ān preserved?

Muslim pilgrims at Mecca walk seven times around the Ka'bah and touch or kiss the Black Stone, lower left

revelation, Muḥammad immediately recited it to those who happened to be near. These in turn committed the revelation to memory and by recitation kept it alive. Since the manufacture of paper was unknown to the Arabs, Muḥammad had the revelations written down by scribes on the primitive materials then available, such as shoulder blades of camels, palm leaves, wood, and parchment. However, it was not until after the prophet's death that the Qur'ān took its present form, under the guidance of Muḥammad's successors and companions. This was during the rule of the first three caliphs, or Muslim leaders.

[12] Translator Muhammad Pickthall writes: "All the surahs of the Qur'an had been recorded in writing before the Prophet's death, and many Muslims had committed the whole Qur'an to memory. But the written surahs were dispersed among the people; and when, in a battle . . . a large number of those who knew the whole Qur'an by heart were killed, a collection of the whole Qur'an was made and put in writing."

[13] Islāmic life is governed by three authorities—the Qur'ān, the Ḥadīth, and the Sharī'ah. (See box, page 291.) Muslims believe that the Qur'ān in Arabic is the purest

13. (a) What are three sources of Islāmic teaching and guidance? (b) How do some Islāmic scholars view translation of the Qur'ān?

Arabic is the required language for reading the Qur'ān

form of the revelation, since, they say, it was the language used by God in speaking through Gabriel. Surah 43:3 states: "We have made it a Qur-ān in Arabic, that ye may be able to understand (and learn wisdom)." (*AYA*) Thus, any translation is viewed as only a dilution that involves a loss of purity. In fact, some Islāmic scholars refuse to translate the Qur'ān. Their viewpoint is that "to translate is always to betray," and therefore, "Muslims have always deprecated and at times prohibited any attempt to render it in another language," states Dr. J. A. Williams, lecturer on Islāmic history.

The Three Sources of Teaching and Guidance

The **Holy Qur'ān,** said to have been revealed to Muḥammad by the angel Gabriel. The Qur'ān's meaning and words in Arabic are viewed as inspired.

The **Ḥadīth,** or **Sunnah,** "the deeds, utterances and silent approval (*taqrīr*) of the Prophet . . . fixed during the second century [A.H.] in the form of written ḥadīths. A ḥadīth, therefore, is a record of an action or sayings of the Prophet." It can also be applied to the actions or sayings of any of Muḥammad's "Companions or their Successors." In a ḥadīth, only the meaning is viewed as inspired.—*History of the Arabs.*

The **Sharī'ah,** or canon law, based on principles of the Qur'ān, regulates a Muslim's entire life in the religious, political, and social senses. "All man's acts are classified under five legal categories: (1) what is considered absolute duty (*farḍ*) [involving reward for acting or punishment for failing to act]; (2) commendable or meritorious actions (*mustaḥabb*) [involving a reward but no punishment for omission]; (3) permissible actions (*jā'iz, mubāḥ*), which are legally indifferent; (4) reprehensible actions (*makrūh*), which are disapproved but not punishable; (5) forbidden actions (*ḥarām*), the doing of which calls for punishment."
—*History of the Arabs.*

Islāmic Expansion

[14] Muḥammad founded his new faith against great odds. The people of Mecca, even of his own tribe, rejected him. After 13 years of persecution and hatred, he moved his center of activity north to Yathrib, which then became known as al-Madīnah (Medina), the city of the prophet. This emigration, or the *hijrah,* in 622 C.E. marked a significant point in Islāmic history, and the date was later adopted as the starting point for the Islāmic calendar.*

[15] Eventually, Muḥammad achieved dominance when Mecca surrendered to him in January of 630 C.E. (8 A.H.) and he became its ruler. With the reins of secular and religious control in his hands, he was able to clean out the idolatrous images from the Ka'bah and establish it as the focal point for pilgrimages to Mecca that continue down to this day.—See pages 289, 303.

[16] Within a few decades of Muḥammad's death in 632 C.E., Islām had spread as far as Afghanistan and even to Tunisia in North Africa. By the early eighth century, the faith of the Qur'ān had penetrated into Spain and was at the French border. As Professor Ninian Smart stated in his book *Background to the Long Search:* "Looked at from a human point of view, the achievement of an Arabian prophet living in the sixth and seventh centuries after Christ is staggering. Humanly, it was from him that a new

---

* Thus, the Muslim year is given as A.H. (Latin, Anno Hegirae, year of the flight) rather than A.D. (Anno Domini, year of the Lord) or C.E. (Common Era).

14. What event marked a significant point early in Islāmic history?
15. How did Mecca become Islām's principal center for pilgrimage?
16. How far did Islām spread?

civilisation flowed. But of course for the Muslim the work was divine and the achievement that of Allah."

Muḥammad's Death Leads to Division

[17] The prophet's death provoked a crisis. He died without any male progeny and without a clearly designated successor. As Philip Hitti states: "The caliphate [office of caliph] is therefore the oldest problem Islam had to face. It is still a living issue. . . . In the words of Muslim historian al-Shahrastāni [1086-1153]: 'Never was there an Islamic issue which brought about more bloodshed than the caliphate (*imāmah*).'" How was the problem solved back there in 632 C.E.? "Abu-Bakr . . . was designated (June 8, 632) Muḥammad's successor by some form of election in which those leaders present at the capital, al-Madīnah, took part."—*History of the Arabs.*

[18] The successor to the prophet would be a ruler, a *khalīfah,* or caliph. However, the question of the true successors to Muḥammad became a cause for divisions in the ranks of Islām. The Sunnī Muslims accept the principle of elective office rather than blood descent from the prophet. Therefore they believe that the first three caliphs, Abū Bakr (Muḥammad's father-in-law), 'Umar (the prophet's adviser), and 'Uthmān (the prophet's son-in-law), were the legitimate successors to Muḥammad.

[19] That claim is contested by the Shī'ite Muslims, who say that the true leadership comes through the prophet's blood line and through his cousin and son-in-law, 'Alī ibn Abī Ṭālib, the first *imām* (leader and successor), who married Muḥammad's favorite daughter, Fāṭimah. Their

---

17. What great problem faced Islām on the death of Muḥammad?
18, 19. What claims divide the Sunnī from the Shī'ite Muslims?

marriage produced Muḥammad's grandsons Ḥasan and Ḥusayn. The Shī'ites also claim "that from the beginning Allah and His Prophet had clearly designated 'Ali as the only legitimate successor but that the first three caliphs had cheated him out of his rightful office." (*History of the Arabs*) Of course, the Sunnī Muslims view that differently.

[20] What happened to 'Ali? During his rule as the fourth caliph (656-661 C.E.), a struggle over leadership arose between him and the governor of Syria, Mu'āwiyah. They joined battle, and then to spare further Muslim bloodshed, they threw their dispute open to arbitration. 'Ali's acceptance of arbitration weakened his case and alienated many of his followers, including the Khawārij (Seceders), who became his deadly foes. In the year 661 C.E., 'Ali was murdered with a poisoned sabre by a Khārijī zealot. The two groups (the Sunnī and the Shī'ah) were at loggerheads. The Sunnī branch of Islām then chose a leader from the Umayyads, wealthy Meccan chiefs, who were outside of the prophet's family.

[21] For the Shī'ah, 'Ali's firstborn, Ḥasan, the prophet's grandson, was the true successor. However, he resigned and was murdered. His brother Ḥusayn became the new imām, but he too was killed, by Umayyad troops on October 10, 680 C.E. His death or martyrdom, as the Shī'ah view it, has had a significant effect on the *Shī'at 'Ali*, the party of 'Ali, down to this day. They believe that 'Ali was the true successor to Muḥammad and the first "imām [leader] divinely protected against error and sin." 'Ali and his successors were considered by the Shī'ah to be infallible teachers with "the divine gift of impeccability."

---

20. What happened to Muḥammad's son-in-law 'Ali?
21. What are the Shī'ite viewpoints on Muḥammad's successors?

Mankind's Search for God

The largest segment of the Shī'ah believe that there have been only 12 true *imāms,* and the last of these, Muḥammad al-Muntaẓar, disappeared (878 C.E.) "in the cave of the great mosque at Sāmarra without leaving offspring." Thus "he became 'the hidden (*mustatir*)' or 'the expected (*muntaẓar*) imām.' . . . In due time he will appear as the Mahdi (divinely guided one) to restore true Islam, conquer the whole world and usher in a short millennium before the end of all things."—*History of the Arabs.*

[22] Every year, the Shī'ah commemorate the martyrdom of Imam Ḥusayn. They have processions in which some cut themselves with knives and swords and otherwise inflict suffering on themselves. In more modern times, Shī'ite Muslims have received much publicity because of their zeal for Islāmic causes. However, they represent only about 20 percent of the world's Muslims, the majority being Sunnī Muslims. But now, let us turn to some of the teachings of Islām and note how the Islāmic faith affects the daily conduct of Muslims.

God Is Supreme, Not Jesus

[23] The three major monotheistic religions of the world are Judaism, Christianity, and Islām. But by the time Muḥammad appeared toward the beginning of the seventh century C.E., the first two religions, as far as he was concerned, had wandered from the path of truth. In fact, according to some Islāmic commentators, the Qur'ān implies rejection of Jews and of Christians in stating: "Not (the path) of those who earn Thine anger nor of those who go astray." (Surah 1:7, *MMP*) Why is that?

---

22. How do the Shī'ah commemorate Ḥusayn's martyrdom?
23, 24. How did Muḥammad and the Muslims view Judaism and Christianity?

[24] A Qur'ānic commentary states: "The People of the Book went wrong: The Jews in breaking their Covenant, and slandering Mary and Jesus . . . and the Christians in raising Jesus the Apostle to equality with God" by means of the Trinity doctrine.—Surah 4:153-176, *AYA*.

[25] The principal teaching of Islām, for utter simplicity, is what is known as the *shahādah,* or confession of faith, which every Muslim knows by heart: *"La ilāh illa Allāh; Muḥammad rasūl Allāh"* (No god but Allah; Muḥammad is the messenger of Allah). This agrees with the Qur'ānic expression, "Your God is One God; there is no God save Him, the Beneficent, the Merciful." (Surah 2:163, *MMP*) This thought was stated 2,000 years earlier with the ancient call to Israel: "Listen, O Israel: Jehovah our God is one Jehovah." (Deuteronomy 6:4) Jesus repeated this foremost command, which is recorded at Mark 12:29, about 600 years before Muḥammad, and nowhere did Jesus claim to be God or to be equal to Him.—Mark 13:32; John 14:28; 1 Corinthians 15:28.

25. What parallel expressions do we find in the Qur'ān and the Bible?

The Five Pillars of Belief

1. **Belief in one God, Allāh (Surah 23:116, 117)**
2. **Belief in angels (Surah 2:177)**
3. **Belief in many prophets but one message. Adam was the first prophet. Others have included Abraham, Moses, Jesus, and "the Seal of the Prophets," Muḥammad (Surah 4:136; 33:40)**
4. **Belief in a judgment day (Surah 15:35, 36)**
5. **Belief in God's omniscience, prior knowledge, and determination of all events. Yet, man has freedom of choice in his actions. [Islāmic sects are divided on the issue of free will] (Surah 9:51)**

[26] Regarding God's uniqueness, the Qur'ān states: "So believe in God and His apostles. Say not 'Trinity': desist: it will be better for you: for God is One God." (Surah 4:171, *AYA*) However, we should note that true Christianity does not teach a Trinity. That is a doctrine of pagan origin introduced by apostates of Christendom after the death of Christ and the apostles.—See Chapter 11.*

Soul, Resurrection, Paradise, and Hellfire

[27] Islām teaches that man has a soul that goes on to a hereafter. The Qur'ān states: "Allah receiveth (men's) souls at the time of their death, and that (soul) which dieth not (yet) in its sleep. He keepeth that (soul) for which He hath ordained death." (Surah 39:42, *MMP*) At the same time, surah 75 is entirely devoted to "*Qiyāmat,* or the Resurrection" (*AYA*), or "The Rising of the Dead" (*MMP*). In part it says: "I do call to witness the Resurrection Day . . . Does man think that We cannot assemble his bones? . . . He questions: 'When is the Day of Resurrection?' . . . Has not He [Allāh] the power to give life to the dead?"—Surah 75: 1, 3, 6, 40, *AYA*.

[28] According to the Qur'ān, the soul can have different destinies, which can be either a heavenly garden of paradise or the punishment of a burning hell. As the Qur'ān states: "They ask: When is the Day of Judgement? (It is) the

---

* For further information on the Trinity and the Bible, see the brochure *Should You Believe in the Trinity?* published by the Watchtower Bible and Tract Society of New York, Inc., 1989.

---

26. (a) How do Muslims view the Trinity? (b) Is the Trinity Biblical?
27. What does the Qur'ān say about the soul and about the resurrection? (Contrast Leviticus 24:17, 18; Ecclesiastes 9:5, 10; John 5:28, 29.)
28. What does the Qur'ān say about hell? (Contrast Job 14:13; Jeremiah 19:5; 32:35; Acts 2:25-27; Romans 6:7, 23.)

Clockwise from top left:
Dome of the Rock, Jerusalem; mosques
in Iran, South Africa, and Turkey

day when they will be tormented at the Fire, (and it will be said unto them): Taste your torment (which ye inflicted)." (Surah 51:12-14, *MMP*) "For them [the sinners] is torment in the life of the world, and verily the doom of the Hereafter is more painful, and they have no defender from Allah." (Surah 13:34, *MMP*) The question is asked: "And what will explain to thee what this is? (It is) a Fire blazing fiercely!" (Surah 101:10, 11, *AYA*) This dire fate is described in detail: "Lo! Those who disbelieve Our revelations, We shall expose them to the Fire. As often as their skins are consumed We shall exchange them for fresh skins that they may taste the torment. Lo! Allah is ever Mighty, Wise." (Surah 4:56, *MMP*) A further description states: "Lo! hell lurketh in ambush . . . They will abide therein for ages. Therein taste they neither coolness nor (any) drink save boiling water and a paralysing cold."—Surah 78:21, 23-25, *MMP*.

[29] Muslims believe that a dead person's soul goes to the *Barzakh*, or "Partition," "the place or state in which people will be after death and before Judgment." (Surah 23:99, 100, *AYA*, footnote) The soul is conscious there experiencing what is termed the "Chastisement of the Tomb" if the person had been wicked, or enjoying happiness if he had been faithful. But the faithful ones must also experience some torment because of their few sins while alive. On the judgment day, each faces his eternal destiny, which ends that intermediate state.*

---

* On the subject of the soul and hellfire, compare these Bible texts: Genesis 2:7; Ezekiel 18:4; Acts 3:23. See *Reasoning From the Scriptures,* pages 168-75; 375-80, published by the Watchtower Bible and Tract Society of New York, Inc., 1985.

---

29. What is the Bible's teaching on the soul, hell, and hellfire?

³⁰ In contrast, the righteous are promised heavenly gardens of paradise: "And as for those who believe and do good works, We shall make them enter Gardens underneath which rivers flow to dwell therein for ever." (Surah 4:57, *MMP*) "On that day the dwellers of Paradise shall think of nothing but their bliss. Together with their wives, they shall recline in shady groves upon soft couches." (Surah 36:55, 56, *NJD*) "Before this We wrote in the Psalms, after the Message (given to Moses): 'My servants, the righteous, shall inherit the earth.'" The footnote to this surah refers the reader to Psalm 25:13 and 37:11, 29, as well as to the words of Jesus at Matthew 5:5. (Surah 21:105, *AYA*) The reference to wives now makes us turn to another question.

Monogamy or Polygamy?

³¹ Is polygamy the rule among Muslims? While the Qur'ān permits polygamy, many Muslims have only one wife. Because of the numerous widows that were left after costly battles, the Qur'ān made room for polygamy: "And if ye fear that ye will not deal fairly by the orphans, marry of the women, who seem good to you, two or three or four; and if ye fear that ye cannot do justice (to so many) then one (only) or (the captives) that your right hands possess." (Surah 4:3, *MMP*) A biography of Muḥammad by Ibn-Hishām mentions that Muḥammad married a wealthy widow, Khadījah, 15 years his senior. After her death he married many women. When he died he left nine widows.

³² Another form of marriage in Islām is called *mut'ah*. It

---

30. What are the righteous promised according to the Qur'ān? (Contrast Isaiah 65:17, 21-25; Luke 23:43; Revelation 21:1-5.)
31. What does the Qur'ān say about polygamy? (Contrast 1 Corinthians 7:2; 1 Timothy 3:2, 12.)
32. What is *mut'ah?*

Mankind's Search for God

is defined as "a special contract concluded between a man and a woman through offer and acceptance of marriage for a limited period and with a specified dowry like the contract for permanent marriage." (*Islamuna,* by Muṣṭafā al-Rāfiʿī) The Sunnīs call it a marriage for pleasure, and the Shīʿah, a marriage to be terminated in a specific period. States the same source: "The children [of such marriages] are legitimate and have the same rights as the children of a permanent marriage." Apparently this form of temporary marriage was practiced in Muḥammad's day, and he allowed it to continue. Sunnīs insist that it was prohibited later, while the Imāmīs, the largest Shīʿite group, believe that it is still in effect. In fact, many practice it, especially when a man is absent from his wife for a long period of time.

Islām and Daily Life

[33] Islām involves five principal obligations and five basic beliefs. (See boxes, pages 296, 303.) One of the obligations is that the devout Muslim turn to Mecca five times a day in prayer (*ṣalāt*). On the Muslim sabbath (Friday), the men flock to the mosque for prayer when they hear the haunting call of the muezzin from the minaret of the mosque. Nowadays many mosques play a recording rather than have a live voice give the call.

[34] The mosque (Arabic, *masjid*) is the Muslim place of worship, described by King Fahd Bin Abdul Aziz of Saudi Arabia as "the cornerstone for the call to God." He defined the mosque as "a place of prayer, study, legal and judicial activities, consultation, preaching, guidance,

33. What are the Five Pillars of Observance and of Belief?
34. What is a mosque, and how is it used?

education and preparation. . . . The mosque is the heart of Muslim society." These places of worship are now found all over the world. One of the most famous in history is the *Mezquita* (Mosque) of Córdoba, Spain, which for centuries was the largest in the world. Its central portion is now occupied by a Catholic cathedral.

Conflict With and Within Christendom

[35] Beginning in the seventh century, Islām spread westward into North Africa, eastward to Pakistan, India, and Bangladesh, and down to Indonesia. (See map, front endsheet.) As it did so, it entered into conflict with a militant Catholic Church, which organized Crusades to recover the Holy Land from the Muslims. In 1492 Queen Isabella and King Ferdinand of Spain completed the Catholic reconquest of Spain. Muslims and Jews had to convert or be expelled from Spain. The mutual tolerance that had existed under Muslim rule in Spain later evaporated under the influence of the Catholic Inquisition. However, Islām survived and in the 20th century has experienced resurgence and great growth.

[36] While Islām was expanding, the Catholic Church was going through its own turmoil, trying to keep unity in its ranks. But two powerful influences were about to burst on the scene, and they would shatter even further the monolithic image of that church. They were the printing press and the Bible in the language of the people. Our next chapter will discuss Christendom's further fragmentation under those and other influences.

---

35. In times past, what situation existed between Islām and Catholicism?
36. What developments were taking place in the Catholic Church while Islām was expanding?

The *Mezquita* of
Córdoba was at one time
the largest mosque in
the world (a Catholic
cathedral now
occupies the center)

The Five Pillars of Observance

1. Repeat the creed (*shahādah*): "No god but Allah;
   Muḥammad is the messenger of Allah" (Surah 33:40)
2. Prayer (*ṣalāt*) toward Mecca five times a day (Surah 2:144)
3. Charity (*zakāh*), the obligation to give a percentage of one's
   income and of the value of some property (Surah 24:56)
4. Fasting (*ṣawm*), especially during the month-long
   celebration of Ramaḍān (Surah 2:183-185)
5. Pilgrimage (*ḥajj*). Once in his lifetime, every male Muslim
   must make the journey to Mecca. Only illness and poverty
   are licit excuses (Surah 3:97)

The Bahā'ī Faith—Seeking World Unity

¹ The Bahā'ī faith is not a sect of Islām but is an offshoot of the Bābī religion, a group in Persia (today Iran) that broke away from the Shī'ite branch of Islām in 1844. The leader of the Bābīs was Mīrzā 'Alī Moḥammad of Shīrāz, who proclaimed himself the Bāb ("the Gate") and the *imām-mahdī* ("rightly guided leader") from the line of Muḥammad. He was executed by the Persian authorities in 1850. In 1863 Mīrzā Ḥoseyn Alī Nūrī, a prominent member of the Bābī group, "declared himself to be 'He whom God will make manifest,' whom the Bāb had foretold." He also took the name Bahā' Ullāh ("Glory of God") and formed a new religion, the Bahā'ī faith.

² Bahā' Ullāh was banished from Persia and was eventually imprisoned in Acco (today Acre, Israel). There he wrote his main work, *al-Kitāb al-Aqdas* (The Most Holy Book), and developed the doctrine of the Bahā'ī faith into a comprehensive teaching. At Bahā' Ullāh's death, the leadership of the fledgling religion passed to his son 'Abd ol-Bahā', then to his great-grandson, Shoghi Effendi Rabbānī, and in 1963 to an elected administrative body known as the Universal House of Justice.

³ Bahā'īs believe that God has revealed himself to man by means of "Divine Manifestations," including Abraham, Moses, Krishna, Zoroaster, the Buddha, Jesus, Muḥammad, the Bāb, and Bahā' Ullāh. They believe that these messengers were provided to guide mankind through an evolutionary process in which the appearance of the Bāb initiated a new age for mankind. The Bahā'īs say that to date his message is the fullest revelation of God's will and that it is the primary God-given instrument that will make world unity possible.—1 Timothy 2:5, 6.

⁴ One of the basic precepts of Bahā'ī is "that all the great religions of the world are divine in origin, that their basic principles are in complete harmony." They "differ only in the nonessential aspects of their doctrines."—2 Corinthians 6:14-18; 1 John 5:19, 20.

1, 2. How did the Bahā'ī faith get started?

3-7. (a) What are some Bahā'ī beliefs? (b) How do Bahā'ī beliefs differ from Bible teachings?

The Bahá'í shrine
at the world headquarters
in Haifa, Israel

5 Bahá'í beliefs include the oneness of God, the soul's immortality, and the evolution (biological, spiritual, and social) of mankind. On the other hand, they reject the common concept of angels. They also reject the Trinity, the reincarnation teaching of Hinduism, and man's fall from perfection and subsequent ransom through the blood of Jesus Christ.—Romans 5:12; Matthew 20:28.

6 The brotherhood of man and the equality of women are major features of Bahá'í belief. Bahá'ís practice monogamy. At least once a day, they pray any one of three prayers revealed by Bahá' Ulláh. They practice fasting from sunup to sundown during the 19 days of the Bahá'í month of 'Alá, which falls in March. (The Bahá'í calendar consists of 19 months, each having 19 days, with certain intercalary days.)

7 The Bahá'í faith does not have many set rituals, nor does it have clergy. Any who profess faith in Bahá' Ulláh and accept his teachings may be enrolled as members. They meet for worship on the first day of every Bahá'í month.

8 The Bahá'ís see themselves as having the mission of the spiritual conquest of the planet. They try to spread their faith through conversation, example, participation in community projects, and information campaigns. They believe in absolute obedience to the laws of the country in which they reside, and though they vote, they abstain from participation in politics. They prefer noncombatant duty in the armed forces when possible but are not conscientious objectors.

9 As a missionary religion, Bahá'í has experienced rapid growth in the last few years. The Bahá'ís estimate that there are nearly 5,000,000 believers worldwide, though actual adult enrollment in the faith is presently a little over 2,300,000.

8, 9. What is the Bahá'í mission?

CHAPTER 13

The Reformation—The Search Took a New Turn

"THE real tragedy of the medieval church is that it failed to move with the times. . . . Far from being progressive, far from giving a spiritual lead, it was retrograde and decadent, corrupt in all its members." So says the book *The Story of the Reformation* about the powerful Roman Catholic Church, which had dominated most of Europe from the 5th century to the 15th century C.E.

[2] How did the Church of Rome fall from its all-powerful position to become 'decadent and corrupt'? How did the papacy, which claimed apostolic succession, fail even to provide "a spiritual lead"? And what was the outcome of this failure? To find the answers, we need to examine briefly just what kind of church it had become and what role it played in mankind's search for the true God.

The Church at a Low Ebb

[3] By the end of the 15th century, the Church of Rome, with parishes, monasteries, and convents throughout its domain, had become the largest landholder in all Europe. It was reported that it owned as much as half the land in

---

1, 2. (a) How does one book on the Reformation describe the medieval Roman Catholic Church? (b) What questions are raised concerning the condition of the Church of Rome?

3. (a) What was the material condition of the Roman Church by the end of the 15th century? (b) How did the church try to maintain its grandeur?

These 16th-century woodcuts contrast Christ's rejection of money changers and the pope's sale of indulgences

France and Germany and two fifths or more in Sweden and England. The result? The "splendor of Rome grew immeasurably during the late 1400's and early 1500's, and its political importance prospered temporarily," says the book *A History of Civilization*. All the grandeur, however, came at a price, and to maintain it, the papacy had to find new sources of revenue. Describing the various means employed, historian Will Durant wrote:

"Every ecclesiastical appointee was required to remit to the papal Curia—the administrative bureaus of the papacy—half the income of his office for the first year ("annates"), and thereafter annually a tenth or tithe. A new archbishop had to pay to the pope a substantial sum for the pallium—a band of white wool that served as the confirmation and insignia of his authority. On the death of any cardinal, archbishop, bishop, or abbot, his personal possessions reverted to the papacy.... Every judgment or favor obtained from the Curia expected a gift in acknowledgment, and the judgment was sometimes dictated by the gift."

[4] The large sums of money that flowed into the papal coffers year after year eventually led to much abuse and corruption. It has been said that 'even a pope cannot touch pitch without soiling his fingers,' and church history of this period saw what one historian called "a succession of very worldly popes." These included Sixtus IV (pope, 1471-84), who spent large sums to build the Sistine Chapel, named after himself, and to enrich his many nephews and nieces; Alexander VI (pope, 1492-1503), the notorious Rodrigo Borgia, who openly acknowledged and promoted his illegitimate children; and Julius II (pope, 1503-13), a nephew of Sixtus IV, who was more devoted to wars, politics, and art than to his ecclesiastical duties. It was with full justification that the Dutch Catholic scholar Erasmus wrote in 1518: "The shamelessness of the Roman Curia has reached its climax."

[5] Corruption and immorality were not limited to the papacy. A common saying of the time was: "If you want to ruin your son, make him a priest." This is backed up by records of that time. According to Durant, in England, among "accusations of [sexual] incontinence filed in 1499, . . . clerical offenders numbered some 23 per cent of the total, though the clergy were probably less than 2 per cent of the population. Some confessors solicited sexual favors from female penitents. Thousands of priests had concubines; in Germany nearly all." (Contrast 1 Corinthians 6: 9-11; Ephesians 5:5.) Moral lapses also reached into other areas. A Spaniard of the time is said to have complained: "I see that we can scarcely get anything from Christ's ministers but for money; at baptism money . . . at marriage

---

4. How did the riches coming into the church affect the papacy?
5. What did contemporary records show regarding the moral conduct of the clergy?

money, for confession money—no, not extreme unction [last rites] without money! They will ring no bells without money, no burial in the church without money; so that it seemeth that Paradise is shut up from them that have no money."—Contrast 1 Timothy 6:10.

⁶ To summarize the state of the Roman Church at the beginning of the 16th century, we quote the words of Machiavelli, a famous Italian philosopher of that period:

"Had the religion of Christianity been preserved according to the ordinances of the Founder, the state and commonwealth of Christendom would have been far more united and happy than they are. Nor can there be a greater proof of its decadence than the fact that the nearer people are to the Roman Church, the head of their religion, the less religious are they."

Early Efforts at Reform

⁷ The crisis in the church was noted not only by men like Erasmus and Machiavelli but also by the church itself. Church councils were convened to address some of the complaints and abuses, but with no lasting results. The popes, basking in personal power and glory, discouraged any real efforts at reform.

⁸ Had the church been more serious at housecleaning, there would possibly have been no Reformation. But, as it was, cries for reform began to be heard from inside and outside the church. In Chapter 11 we have already mentioned the Waldenses and the Albigenses. Though they were condemned as heretics and ruthlessly crushed, they

---

6. How did Machiavelli describe the Roman Church? (Romans 2: 21-24)
7. What feeble efforts were made by the church to address some of the abuses?
8. What was the result of the church's continual negligence?

had awakened in the people a dissatisfaction with the abuses of the Catholic clergy and had kindled a desire to return to the Bible. Such sentiments found their expression in a number of early Reformers.

Protests From Within the Church

[9] Often referred to as "the morning star of the Reformation," **John Wycliffe** (1330?-84) was a Catholic priest and a professor of theology at Oxford, England. Well aware of the abuses in the church, he wrote and preached against such matters as corruption in the monastic orders, papal taxation, the doctrine of transubstantiation (the claim that the bread and wine used in the Mass literally change into the body and blood of Jesus Christ), the confession, and church involvement in temporal affairs.

[10] Wycliffe was particularly outspoken when it came to the church's neglect in teaching the Bible. Once he declared: "Would to God that every parish church in this land had a good Bible and good expositions on the gospel, and that the priests studied them well, and taught truly the gospel and God's commands to the people!" To this end, Wycliffe, in the last years of his life, undertook the task of translating the Latin Vulgate Bible into English. With the help of his associates, particularly Nicholas of Hereford, he produced the first complete Bible in the English language. It was undoubtedly Wycliffe's greatest contribution to mankind's search for God.

[11] Wycliffe's writings and portions of the Bible were

---

9. Who was John Wycliffe, and against what did he preach?
10. How did Wycliffe show his devotion to the Bible?
11. (a) What were Wycliffe's followers able to accomplish? (b) What happened to the Lollards?

Jan Hus at
the stake

The English
Reformer
and Bible
translator
John Wycliffe

distributed throughout England by a body of preachers
often referred to as "Poor Priests" because they went about
in simple clothing, barefoot, and without material possessions. They were also derisively called Lollards, from
the Middle Dutch word *Lollaerd,* or "one who mumbles
prayers or hymns." (*Brewer's Dictionary of Phrase and
Fable*) "In a few years, their numbers were very considerable," says the book *The Lollards.* "It was calculated that at
least one fourth of the nation were really or nominally
inclined to these sentiments." All of this, of course, did not
go unnoticed by the church. Because of his prominence
among the ruling and scholarly classes, Wycliffe was allowed to die in peace on the last day of 1384. His followers
were less fortunate. During the reign of Henry IV of
England, they were branded as heretics, and many of them
were imprisoned, tortured, or burned to death.

[12] Strongly influenced by John Wycliffe was the Bohe-
mian (Czech) **Jan Hus** (1369?-1415), also a Catholic priest
and rector of the University of Prague. Like Wycliffe, Hus
preached against the corruption of the Roman Church and
stressed the importance of reading the Bible. This quickly
brought the wrath of the hierarchy upon him. In 1403 the

12. Who was Jan Hus, and against what did he preach?

The Reformation—The Search Took a New Turn

authorities ordered him to stop preaching the antipapal ideas of Wycliffe, whose books they also publicly burned. Hus, however, went on to write some of the most stinging indictments against the practices of the church, including the sale of indulgences.* He was condemned and excommunicated in 1410.

[13] Hus was uncompromising in his support for the Bible. "To rebel against an erring pope is to obey Christ," he wrote. He also taught that the true church, far from being the pope and the Roman establishment, "is the number of all the elect and the mystical body of Christ, whose head Christ is; and the bride of Christ, whom of his great love he redeemed with his own blood." (Compare Ephesians 1:22, 23; 5:25-27.) For all of this, he was tried at the Council of Constance and was condemned as a heretic. Declaring that "it is better to die well than to live ill," he refused to recant and was burned to death at the stake in 1415. The same council also ordered that the bones of Wycliffe be dug up and burned even though he had been dead and buried for over 30 years!

[14] Another early Reformer was the Dominican monk **Girolamo Savonarola** (1452-98) of the San Marcos monastery in Florence, Italy. Swept along by the spirit of the Italian Renaissance, Savonarola spoke out against the corruption in both Church and State. Claiming as a basis Scripture, as well as visions and revelations that he said he

---

* Letters of pardon issued by the pope for sins.

---

13. (a) What did Hus teach was the true church? (b) What was the outcome of Hus' steadfastness?
14. (a) Who was Girolamo Savonarola? (b) What did Savonarola attempt to do, and what was the outcome?

had received, he sought to establish a Christian state, or theocratic order. In 1497 the pope excommunicated him. The following year, he was arrested, tortured, and hanged. His last words were: "My Lord died for my sins; shall not I gladly give this poor life for him?" His body was burned and the ashes thrown into the river Arno. Fittingly, Savonarola called himself "a forerunner and a sacrifice." Just a few years later, the Reformation burst forth in full force all over Europe.

A House Divided

[15] When the storm of the Reformation finally broke, it shattered the religious house of Christendom in Western Europe. Having been under the almost total domination of the Roman Catholic Church, it now became a house divided. Southern Europe—Italy, Spain, Austria, and parts of France—remained mostly Catholic. The rest fell into three main divisions: Lutheran in Germany and Scandinavia; Calvinist (or Reformed) in Switzerland, the Netherlands, Scotland, and parts of France; and Anglican in England. Scattered among these were smaller but more radical groups, first the Anabaptists and later the Mennonites, Hutterites, and Puritans, who in time took their beliefs to North America.

[16] Through the years, these main divisions further fragmented into the hundreds of denominations of today —Presbyterian, Episcopal, Methodist, Baptist, Congregational, to name just a few. Christendom truly became a house divided. How did these divisions come about?

---

15. How was Christendom in Western Europe divided by the Reformation movement?
16. Ultimately, what happened to Christendom's house? (Mark 3:25)

Luther and His Theses

¹⁷ If a decisive starting point of the Protestant Reformation has to be given, it would be October 31, 1517, when the Augustinian monk **Martin Luther** (1483-1546) nailed his 95 theses to the door of the castle church at Wittenberg in the German state of Saxony. However, what provoked this dramatic event? Who was Martin Luther? And against what did he protest?

¹⁸ Like Wycliffe and Hus before him, Martin Luther was a monk-scholar. He was also a doctor of theology and a professor of Biblical studies at the University of Wittenberg. Luther made quite a name for himself for his insight into the Bible. Though he had strong opinions on the subject of salvation, or justification, by faith rather than by works or by penance, he had no thought of breaking with

---

17. What could be given as the official starting point of the Protestant Reformation?
18. (a) Who was Martin Luther? (b) What prompted Luther to issue his theses?

Martin Luther, right, protested the sale of indulgences by the friar John Tetzel

the Church of Rome. In fact, the issuing of his theses was his reaction to a specific incident and was not a planned revolt. He was protesting the sale of indulgences.

[19] In Luther's time, papal indulgences were publicly sold not only for the living but also for the dead. "As soon as the coin in the coffer rings, the soul from Purgatory springs" was a common saying. To ordinary folk, an indulgence became almost an insurance policy against punishment for any sin, and repentance fell by the wayside. "Everywhere," wrote Erasmus, "the remission of purgatorial torment is sold; nor is it sold only, but forced upon those who refuse it."

[20] In 1517 John Tetzel, a Dominican friar, went to Jüterbog, near Wittenberg, to sell indulgences. The money thus obtained was partly to finance the rebuilding of St. Peter's Basilica in Rome. It was also to help Albert of Hohenzollern repay the money he had borrowed to pay the Roman Curia for the post of archbishop of Mainz. Tetzel mustered all his skills of salesmanship, and the people flocked to him. Luther was indignant, and he made use of the quickest means available to express publicly his opinion of the whole circuslike affair—by nailing 95 points of debate on the church door.

[21] Luther called his 95 theses *Disputation for Clarification of the Power of Indulgences.* His purpose was not so much to challenge the authority of the church as to point out the excesses and abuses regarding the sale of papal indulgences. This can be seen from the following theses:

19. In Luther's time, how were indulgences being exploited?
20. (a) Why did John Tetzel go to Jüterbog? (b) What was Luther's reaction to Tetzel's sale of indulgences?
21. What arguments did Luther use against the sale of indulgences?

"5. The pope has neither the will nor the power to remit any penalties, except those which he has imposed by his own authority....

20. Therefore the pope, when he speaks of the plenary remission of all penalties, does not mean really of all, but only of those imposed by himself....

36. Every Christian who feels true compunction has of right plenary remission of punishment and guilt even without letters of pardon."

[22] Aided by the recently invented printing press, these explosive ideas did not take long to reach other parts of Germany—and Rome. What started out as an academic debate on the sale of indulgences soon became a controversy over matters of faith and papal authority. At first, the Church of Rome engaged Luther in debate and ordered him to recant. When Luther refused, both the ecclesiastical and the political powers were brought to bear upon him. In 1520 the pope issued a bull, or edict, that forbade Luther to preach and ordered that his books be burned. In defiance Luther burned the papal bull in public. The pope excommunicated him in 1521.

[23] Later that year, Luther was summoned to the diet, or assembly, at Worms. He was tried by the emperor of the Holy Roman Empire, Charles V, a staunch Catholic, as well as by the six electors of the German states, and other leaders and dignitaries, religious and secular. When pressed once again to recant, Luther made his famous statement: "Unless I am convicted by Scripture and plain reason . . . , I cannot and I will not recant anything, for to

22. (a) What developed as Luther's message spread? (b) What happened in 1520 involving Luther, and what was the outcome? 23. (a) What was the Diet of Worms? (b) How did Luther state his position at Worms, and what was the result?

go against conscience is neither right nor safe. God help me. Amen." Consequently, he was declared an outlaw by the emperor. However, the ruler of his own German state, Elector Frederick of Saxony, came to his aid and offered him shelter in Wartburg castle.

[24] These measures, however, failed to curb the spread of Luther's ideas. For ten months, in the security of Wartburg, Luther devoted himself to writing and to Bible translation. He translated the Greek Scriptures into German from Erasmus' Greek text. The Hebrew Scriptures followed later. Luther's Bible turned out to be just what the common people needed. It was reported that "five thousand copies were sold in two months, two hundred thousand in twelve years." Its influence on the German language and culture is often compared to that of the *King James Version* on the English.

[25] In the years following the Diet of Worms, the Reformation movement gained so much popular support that in 1526 the emperor granted each German state the right to choose its own form of religion, Lutheran or Roman Catholic. However, in 1529, when the emperor reversed the decision, some of the German princes protested; hence the name Protestant was coined for the Reformation movement. The next year, 1530, at the Diet of Augsburg, an effort was made by the emperor to mend the differences between the two parties. The Lutherans presented their beliefs in a document, the Augsburg Confession, composed by Philipp Melanchthon but based on Luther's teachings. Although the document was most conciliatory in tone, the Roman Church rejected it, and the rift between

24. What did Luther accomplish while in Wartburg castle?
25. (a) How was the name Protestant coined? (b) What was the Augsburg Confession?

Protestantism and Catholicism became irreconcilable. Many German states sided with Luther, and the Scandinavian states soon followed suit.

Reform or Revolt?

[26] What were the fundamental points that divided the Protestants from the Roman Catholics? According to Luther, there were three. First, Luther believed that salvation results from "justification by faith alone" (Latin, *sola fide*)* and not from priestly absolution or works of penance. Second, he taught that forgiveness is granted solely because of God's grace (*sola gratia*) and not by the authority of priests or popes. Finally, Luther contended that all doctrinal matters are to be confirmed by Scripture only (*sola scriptura*) and not by popes or church councils.

[27] In spite of this, Luther, says *The Catholic Encyclopedia*, "retained as much of the ancient beliefs and liturgy as could be made to fit into his peculiar views on sin and justification." The Augsburg Confession states regarding the Lutheran faith that "there is nothing that is discrepant with the Scriptures, or with the Church Catholic, or even with the Roman Church, so far as that Church is known from writers." In fact, the Lutheran faith, as outlined in the Augsburg Confession, included such unscriptural doc-

---

* Luther was so insistent on the concept of "justification by faith alone" that in his translation of the Bible, he added the word "alone" to Romans 3:28. He was also suspicious of the book of James for its statement that "faith without works is dead." (James 2:17, 26) He failed to recognize that in Romans, Paul was speaking of works of the Jewish Law.—Romans 3:19, 20, 28.

---

26. According to Luther, what were the fundamental points dividing Protestantism and Catholicism?
27. (a) What unscriptural Catholic teachings and practices were retained by the Protestants? (b) What changes did the Protestants demand?

trines as the Trinity, immortal soul, and eternal torment, as well as such practices as infant baptism and church holidays and feasts. On the other hand, the Lutherans demanded certain changes, such as that the people be allowed to receive both wine and bread at Communion and that celibacy, monastic vows, and compulsory confession be abolished.*

[28] As a whole, the Reformation, as advocated by Luther and his followers, succeeded in breaking from the papal yoke. Yet, as Jesus stated at John 4:24, "God is a Spirit, and those worshiping him must worship with spirit and truth." It can be said that with Martin Luther, mankind's search for the true God only took a new turn; the narrow path of truth was still far off.—Matthew 7:13, 14; John 8:31, 32.

Zwingli's Reform in Switzerland

[29] While Luther was busy battling the papal emissaries and civil authorities in Germany, Catholic priest Ulrich Zwingli (1484-1531) started his reform movement in Zurich, Switzerland. That area being German-speaking, the people were already affected by the tide of reform from the north. Around 1519, Zwingli began to preach against indulgences, Mariolatry, clerical celibacy, and other doctrines of the Catholic Church. Though Zwingli claimed independence from Luther, he agreed with Luther in many areas and distributed Luther's tracts throughout the

---

* Martin Luther was married in 1525 to Katharina von Bora, a former nun who had escaped from a Cistercian cloister. They had six children. He stated that he married for three reasons: to please his father, to spite the pope and the Devil, and to seal his witness before martyrdom.

---

28. In what did the Reformation succeed, and in what did it fail?
29. (a) Who was Ulrich Zwingli, and against what did he preach? (b) How was Zwingli's reform different from Luther's?

country. In contrast with the more conservative Luther, however, Zwingli advocated the removal of all vestiges of the Roman Church—images, crucifixes, clerical garb, even liturgical music.

[30] A more serious controversy between the two Reformers, however, was on the issue of the Eucharist, or Mass (Communion). Luther, insisting on a literal interpretation of Jesus' words, 'This is my body,' believed that the body and blood of Christ were miraculously present in the bread and wine served at Communion. Zwingli, on the other hand, argued, in his treatise *On the Lord's Supper,* that Jesus' statement "must be taken figuratively or metaphorically; 'This is my body,' means, 'The bread signifies my body,' or 'is a figure of my body.'" Because of this difference, the two Reformers parted ways.

[31] Zwingli continued to preach his reform doctrines in Zurich and effected many changes there. Other cities soon followed his lead, but most people in the rural areas, being more conservative, clung to Catholicism. The conflict between the two factions became so great that civil war broke out between Swiss Protestants and Roman Catholics. Zwingli, serving as an army chaplain, was killed in the battle of Kappel, near the Lake of Zug, in 1531. When peace finally came, each district was given the right to decide its own form of religion, Protestant or Catholic.

Anabaptists, Mennonites, and Hutterites

[32] Some Protestants, however, felt that the Reformers did not go far enough in renouncing the shortcomings of the Catholic papist church. They believed that the Chris-

---

30. What was a key issue dividing Zwingli and Luther?
31. What was the outcome of Zwingli's work in Switzerland?
32. Who were the Anabaptists, and how did they acquire that name?

tian church should consist only of the practicing faithful who become baptized, rather than of all the people in a community or nation. Therefore, they rejected infant baptism and insisted on separation of Church and State. They secretly rebaptized their fellow believers and thus acquired the name Anabaptists (*ana* meaning "again" in Greek). Since they refused to bear arms, take oaths, or accept public office, they were viewed as a threat to society and were persecuted by Catholics and Protestants alike.

[33] At first the Anabaptists lived in small groups scattered through parts of Switzerland, Germany, and the Netherlands. As they preached what they believed everywhere they went, their numbers grew rapidly. A band of Anabaptists, swept along by their religious fervor, abandoned their pacifism and captured the city of Münster in 1534 and attempted to set it up as a communal, polygamous New Jerusalem. The movement was quickly put down with great violence. It gave Anabaptists a bad name, and they were practically stamped out. In reality, most Anabaptists were simple religious folk trying to live a separate and quiet life. Among the better organized descendants of the Anabaptists were the Mennonites, followers of the Dutch Reformer Menno Simons, and the Hutterites, under the Tyrolean Jacob Hutter. To escape persecution, some of them migrated to Eastern Europe—Poland, Hungary, even Russia—others to North America, where they eventually emerged as Hutterite and Amish communities.

Emergence of Calvinism

[34] The reform work in Switzerland moved ahead under

---

33. (a) What aroused violent action against the Anabaptists? (b) How did Anabaptist influence spread?
34. (a) Who was John Calvin? (b) What important book did he write?

John Calvin, left, had Michael Servetus, right, burned to death as a heretic

"Errors of the Trinity"

At age 20, Michael Servetus (1511-53), a Spaniard trained in law and medicine, published *De Trinitatis erroribus* (Errors of the Trinity), in which he stated that he "will not make use of the word Trinity, which is not to be found in Scripture, and only seems to perpetuate philosophical error." He denounced the Trinity as a doctrine "that cannot be understood, that is impossible in the nature of things, and that may even be looked on as blasphemous!"

For his outspokenness, Servetus was condemned by the Catholic Church. But it was the Calvinists who had him arrested, tried, and executed by slow burning. Calvin justified his actions in these words: "When the papists are so harsh and violent in defense of their superstitions that they rage cruelly to shed innocent blood, are not Christian magistrates shamed to show themselves less ardent in defense of the sure truth?" Calvin's religious fanaticism and personal hatred blinded his judgment and smothered Christian principles.
—Compare Matthew 5:44.

the leadership of a Frenchman named Jean Cauvin, or **John Calvin** (1509-64), who came in contact with Protestant teachings during his student days in France. In 1534 Calvin left Paris because of religious persecution and settled in Basel, Switzerland. In defense of the Protestants, he published *Institutes of the Christian Religion,* in which he summarized the ideas of the early church fathers and medieval theologians, as well as those of Luther and Zwingli. The work came to be regarded as the doctrinal foundation for all the Reformed churches established later in Europe and America.

[35] In *Institutes,* he set forth his theology. To Calvin, God is the absolute sovereign, whose will determines and rules over everything. In contrast, fallen man is sinful and totally undeserving. Salvation, therefore, is not dependent on man's good works but on God—hence, Calvin's doctrine of predestination, on which he wrote:

> "We assert, that by an eternal and immutable counsel, God has once for all determined, both whom He would admit to salvation, and whom He would condemn to destruction. We affirm that this counsel, as far as concerns the elect, is founded on His gratuitous mercy, totally irrespective of human merit; but that to those whom He devotes to condemnation, the gate of life is closed by a just and irreprehensible, but incomprehensible, judgment."

The austerity of such a teaching is also reflected in other areas. Calvin insisted that Christians must live holy and virtuous lives, abstaining not only from sin but also from pleasure and frivolity. Further, he argued that the church,

---

35. (a) What was Calvin's explanation for his doctrine of predestination? (b) How was the austerity of this doctrine reflected in other aspects of Calvin's teaching?

which is made up of the elect, must be freed of all civil restrictions and that only through the church can a truly godly society be established.

[36] Shortly after publishing *Institutes,* Calvin was persuaded by William Farel, another Reformer from France, to settle in Geneva. Together they worked to put Calvinism into practice. Their aim was to turn Geneva into a city of God, a theocracy of God-rule combining the functions of Church and State. They instituted strict regulations, with sanctions, covering everything from religious instruction and church services to public morals and even such matters as sanitation and fire prevention. A history text reports that "a hair-dresser, for example, for arranging a bride's hair in what was deemed an unseemly manner, was imprisoned for two days; and the mother, with two female friends, who had aided in the process, suffered the same penalty. Dancing and card-playing were also punished by the magistrate." Harsh treatment was meted out to those who differed from Calvin on theology, the most notorious case being the burning of Spaniard Miguel Serveto, or Michael Servetus.—See box, page 322.

[37] Calvin continued to apply his brand of reform in Geneva until his death in 1564, and the Reformed church became firmly established. Protestant reformers, fleeing persecution in other lands, flocked to Geneva, took in Calvinist ideas, and became instrumental in starting reform movements in their respective homelands. Calvinism

36. (a) What did Calvin and Farel attempt to do in Geneva? (b) What strict regulations were instituted? (c) What was one notorious result of Calvin's extreme measures, and how did he justify his actions?
37. How was Calvin's influence extended far beyond the boundaries of Switzerland?

Mankind's Search for God

soon spread to France, where the Huguenots (as the French Calvinist Protestants were called) suffered severe persecution at the hands of the Catholics. In the Netherlands, Calvinists helped establish the Dutch Reformed Church. In Scotland, under the zealous leadership of the former Catholic priest John Knox, the Presbyterian Church of Scotland was established along Calvinist lines. Calvinism also played a role in the Reformation in England, and from there it went with the Puritans to North America. In this sense, although Luther set the Protestant Reformation in motion, Calvin had by far the greater influence in its development.

Reformation in England

[38] Quite apart from the reform movements in Germany and Switzerland, the English Reformation can trace its roots back to the days of John Wycliffe, whose anticlerical preaching and emphasis on the Bible engendered the Protestant spirit in England. His effort in translating the Bible into English was followed by others. William Tyndale, who had to flee from England, produced his New Testament in 1526. He was later betrayed in Antwerp and strangled at the stake, and his body was burned. Miles Coverdale completed Tyndale's work of translation, and the entire Bible appeared in 1535. The publication of the Bible in the language of the people was no doubt the single most powerful factor that contributed to the Reformation in England.

[39] The formal break from Roman Catholicism took place when Henry VIII (1491-1547), named Defender of

---

38. How was the Protestant spirit in England engendered by the work of John Wycliffe?
39. What role did Henry VIII play in the Reformation in England?

the Faith by the pope, declared the Act of Supremacy in 1534, setting himself up as the head of the Church of England. Henry also closed the monasteries and divided their property among the gentry. In addition, he ordered that a copy of the Bible in English be placed in every church. However, Henry's action was more political than religious. What he wanted was independence from papal authority, especially over his marital affairs.* Religiously he remained Catholic in every way but name.

⁴⁰ It was during the long reign (1558-1603) of Elizabeth I that the Church of England became Protestant in practice though remaining largely Catholic in structure. It abolished allegiance to the pope, clerical celibacy, confession, and other Catholic practices, yet it retained an episcopal form of church structure in its hierarchy of archbishops and bishops as well as orders of monks and nuns.# This conservatism caused considerable dissatisfaction, and various dissenting groups appeared. The Puritans demanded a more thorough reform to purify the church of all Roman Catholic practices; the Separatists and Independents insisted that church affairs should be run by local elders (presbyters). Many of the dissidents fled to the Netherlands or to North America, where they further developed their Congregational and Baptist churches. There also sprung up in England the Society of Friends

---

* Henry VIII had six wives. In opposition to the pope's wishes, his first marriage was annulled, and another ended in divorce. He had two wives beheaded, and two died natural deaths.

The Greek word *e·pi′sko·pos* is translated "bishop" in English Bibles such as the *King James Version*.

---

40. (a) What changes took place in the Church of England during the reign of Elizabeth I? (b) What dissenting groups eventually developed in England, the Netherlands, and North America?

(Quakers) under George Fox (1624-91) and the Methodists under John Wesley (1703-91).—See chart below.

What Were the Effects?

⁴¹ Having considered the three major streams of the Reformation—Lutheran, Calvinist, and Anglican—we must stop to assess what the Reformation accomplished. Undeniably, it changed the course of history of the Western world. "The effect of the Reformation was to elevate the people to a thirst for liberty and a higher and purer citizenship. Wherever the Protestant cause extended, it made the masses more self-asserting," wrote John F. Hurst in his book *Short History of the Reformation*. Many scholars believe that Western civilization as we know it today would have been impossible without the Reformation. Be that as it may, we must ask: What did the Reformation

41. (a) In the opinion of some scholars, what effect did the Reformation have on human history? (b) What questions are of serious concern?

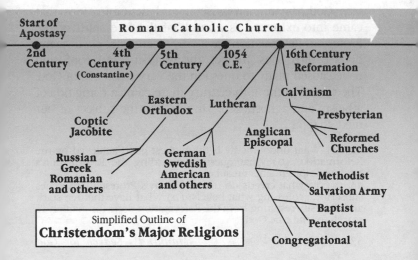

Simplified Outline of
Christendom's Major Religions

accomplish *religiously?* What did it do in behalf of mankind's search for the true God?

⁴² The highest good the Reformation achieved, no doubt, was that it made the Bible available to the common people in their own language. For the first time, people had before them the whole of God's Word to read, so that they could be nourished spiritually. But, of course, more is needed than just reading the Bible. Did the Reformation bring people freedom not only from papal authority but also from the erroneous doctrines and dogmas that they had been subjected to for centuries?—John 8:32.

⁴³ Nearly all the Protestant churches subscribe to the same creeds—the Nicene, Athanasian, and Apostles' creeds—and these profess some of the very doctrines that Catholicism has been teaching for centuries, such as the Trinity, immortal soul, and hellfire. Such unscriptural teachings gave the people a distorted picture of God and his purpose. Rather than aid them in their search for the true God, the numerous sects and denominations that came into existence as a result of the free spirit of the Protestant Reformation have only steered people in many diverse directions. In fact, the diversity and confusion have caused many to question the very existence of God. The result? In the 19th century there came a rising tide of atheism and agnosticism. That will be the subject of our next chapter.

---

42. (a) What undoubtedly is the highest good achieved by the Reformation? (b) What question regarding the Reformation's true accomplishments must be asked?
43. (a) To what creeds do most of today's Protestant churches subscribe, professing what beliefs? (b) What have the free spirit and diversity resulting from the Reformation done for mankind's search for the true God?

CHAPTER 14

Modern Disbelief
Should the Search Continue?

"God is no longer a habitual concern for human beings. Less and less do they call him to mind as they go through their days or make their decisions. . . . God has been replaced by other values: income and productivity. He may once have been regarded as the source of meaning for all human activities, but today he has been relegated to the secret dungeons of history. . . . God has disappeared from the consciousness of human beings."—*The Sources of Modern Atheism.*

I T WAS not many years ago that God was very much a part of the lives of people of the Western world. To be socially acceptable, one had to give evidence of faith in God, even if not everyone earnestly practiced what he professed to believe. Any doubts and uncertainties were discreetly kept to oneself. To express them in public would be shocking and perhaps even lay one open to censure.

² Today, however, the tables are turned. To have any strong religious conviction is considered by many to be narrow-minded, dogmatic, even fanatic. In many lands, we

---

1. (Include introduction.) (a) How does the book *The Sources of Modern Atheism* describe belief in God among people today? (b) How is modern disbelief in sharp contrast with conditions not many years ago?
2. (a) Why have many people stopped searching for God? (b) What questions must be asked?

see a prevailing indifference toward, or lack of interest in, God and religion. Most people no longer search for God because they either do not believe he exists or are unsure about it. In fact, some have used the term "post-Christian" to describe our era. Some questions, therefore, must be asked: How did the idea of God become so far removed from people's life? What were the forces that gave rise to this change? Are there sound reasons for continuing the search for God?

Backlash of the Reformation

[3] As we saw in Chapter 13, the Protestant Reformation of the 16th century brought about a marked change in the way people viewed authority, religious or otherwise. Self-assertion and freedom of expression took the place of conformity and submission. While most people remained within the framework of traditional religion, some moved along more radical lines, calling into question the dogmas and fundamental teachings of the established churches. Still others, noting the role religion had played in the wars, sufferings, and injustices throughout history, became skeptical of religion altogether.

[4] As early as 1572, a report entitled *Discourse on the Present State of England* noted: "The realm is divided into three parties, the Papists, the Atheists, and the Protestants. All three are alike favoured: the first and second because, being many, we dare not displease them." Another estimate gave the figure of 50,000 as the number of atheists in Paris in 1623, although the term was used rather loosely. In any

---

3. What was one outcome of the Protestant Reformation?
4. (a) How did contemporary records describe the extent of atheism in England and France in the 16th and 17th centuries? (b) Who came out into the open as a result of the efforts made during the Reformation to throw off the papal yoke?

case, it is clear that the Reformation, in its effort to throw off the domination of papal authority, had also brought into the open those who challenged the position of the established religions. As Will and Ariel Durant put it in *The Story of Civilization: Part VII—The Age of Reason Begins:* "The thinkers of Europe—the vanguard of the European mind—were no longer discussing the authority of the pope; they were debating the existence of God."

The Assault by Science and Philosophy

⁵ In addition to the fragmenting of Christendom itself, there were other forces at work that further weakened its position. Science, philosophy, secularism, and materialism played their roles in raising doubts and fostering skepticism about God and religion.

⁶ The expansion of scientific knowledge called into question many of the church's teachings that were based on erroneous interpretation of Bible passages. For example, astronomical discoveries by men like Copernicus and Galileo posed a direct challenge to the church's geocentric doctrine, that the earth is the center of the universe. Furthermore, understanding of the natural laws that govern the operations of the physical world made it no longer necessary to attribute hitherto mysterious phenomena, such as thunder and lightning or even the appearance of certain stars and comets, to the hand of God or Providence. "Miracles" and "divine intervention" in human affairs also came under suspicion. All of a sudden, God and religion seemed outdated to many, and some of those who considered themselves up-to-date quickly turned their back on

5. What forces hastened the rise of disbelief in God?
6. (a) How did the expansion of scientific knowledge affect many of the church's teachings? (b) What did some do who considered themselves up-to-date?

God and flocked to the worship of the sacred cow of science.

⁷ The severest blow to religion, no doubt, was the theory of evolution. In 1859 the English naturalist Charles Darwin (1809-82) published his *Origin of Species* and presented a direct challenge to the Bible's teaching of creation by God. What was the response of the churches? At first the clergy in England and elsewhere denounced the theory. But opposition soon faded. It seemed that Darwin's speculations were just the excuse sought by many clergymen who were entertaining doubts in secret. Thus, within Darwin's lifetime, "most thoughtful and articulate clergy had worked their way to the conclusion that evolution was wholly compatible with an enlightened understanding of scripture," says *The Encyclopedia of Religion*. Rather than come to the defense of the Bible, Christendom yielded to the pressure of scientific opinion and played along with what was popular. In so doing, it undermined faith in God.—2 Timothy 4:3, 4.

⁸ As the 19th century wore on, critics of religion became bolder in their attack. Not content with just pointing out the failings of the churches, they began to question the very foundation of religion. They raised questions such as: What is God? Why is there a need for God? How has belief in God affected human society? Men like Ludwig Feuerbach, Karl Marx, Sigmund Freud, and Friedrich Nietzsche offered their arguments in philosophical, psychological, and sociological terms. Theories such as 'God is nothing more than the

7. (a) What was no doubt the severest blow to religion? (b) What was the response of the churches to Darwinism?
8. (a) What did 19th-century critics of religion call into question? (b) What were some popular theories proposed by critics of religion? (c) Why did many people quickly embrace the antireligious ideas?

Darwin, Marx, Freud, Nietzsche, and others proposed theories that undermined faith in God

projection of man's imagination,' 'Religion is the opium of the people,' and 'God is dead' all sounded so new and exciting compared with the dull and unintelligible dogmas and traditions of the churches. It seemed that finally many people had found an articulate way of expressing the doubts and suspicions that had been lurking in the back of their minds. They quickly and willingly embraced these ideas as the new gospel truth.

The Great Compromise

⁹ Under assault and scrutiny by science and philosophy, what did the churches do? Instead of taking a stand for what the Bible teaches, they gave in to the pressures and compromised even on such fundamental articles of faith as creation by God and the authenticity of the Bible. The result? Christendom's churches began to lose credibility, and many people began to lose faith. The failure of the

9. (a) What did the churches do when under assault by science and philosophy? (b) What were the results of the churches' compromise?

churches to come to their own defense left the door wide open for the masses to march out. To many people, religion became no more than a sociological relic, something to mark the high points in one's life—birth, marriage, death. Many all but gave up the search for the true God.

[10] In the face of all of this, it is logical to ask: Have science and philosophy really signed the death warrant of belief in God? Does the failure of the churches mean the failure of what they claim to teach, namely, the Bible? Indeed, should the search for God continue? Let us examine these issues briefly.

Basis for Belief in God

[11] It has been said that there are two books that tell us about the existence of God—the "book" of creation, or nature around us, and the Bible. They have been the basis for belief for millions of people past and present. For example, a king of the 11th century B.C.E., impressed by what he observed in the starry heavens, exclaimed poetically: "The heavens are declaring the glory of God; and of the work of his hands the expanse is telling." (Psalm 19:1) In the 20th century, an astronaut, looking at the spectacular view of the earth from his spacecraft as it circled the moon, was moved to recite: "In the beginning God created the heaven and the earth."—Genesis 1:1, *KJ.*

[12] These two books, however, are under attack by those who claim no belief in God. They say that scientific investigation of the world around us has proved that life came into existence not by intelligent creation but by blind

---

10. What urgent questions must be considered?
11. (a) What two books have long been the basis for belief in God? (b) How have these books affected people?
12. How have the book of creation and the Bible been under attack?

chance and the haphazard process of evolution. They argue, therefore, that there was no Creator and that it follows that the question of God is superfluous. Furthermore, many of them believe that the Bible is simply out-of-date and illogical, hence, not worthy of belief. Consequently, for them, there is no longer any basis for belief in the existence of God. Is all of this true? What do the facts show?

By Chance or by Design?

[13] If there was no Creator, then life must have started spontaneously by chance. For life to have come about, somehow the right chemicals would have had to come together in the right quantities, under the right temperature and pressure and other controlling factors, and all would have had to be maintained for the correct length of time. Furthermore, for life to have begun and been sustained on earth, these chance events would have had to be repeated thousands of times. But how likely is it for even one such event to take place?

[14] Evolutionists admit that the probability of the right

13. What would have had to take place for life to have come about by chance?
14. (a) How remote is the probability that one simple protein molecule will be formed by chance? (b) How do mathematical calculations affect the idea of life's originating spontaneously?

The "book" of creation and the Bible give the basis for belief in God

atoms and molecules falling into place to form just one simple protein molecule is 1 in 10^{113}, or 1 followed by 113 zeros. That number is larger than the estimated total number of atoms in the universe! Mathematicians dismiss as never taking place anything that has a probability of occurring of less than 1 in 10^{50}. But far more than one simple protein molecule is needed for life. Some 2,000 different proteins are needed just for a cell to maintain its activity, and the chance that all of them will occur at random is 1 in $10^{40,000}$! "If one is not prejudiced either by social beliefs or by a scientific training into the conviction that life originated [spontaneously] on the Earth, this simple calculation wipes the idea entirely out of court," says astronomer Fred Hoyle.

[15] On the other hand, by studying the physical world, from the minute subatomic particles to the vast galaxies, scientists have discovered that all known natural phenomena appear to follow certain basic laws. In other words, they have discovered logic and order in everything that is taking place in the universe, and they have been able to express this logic and order in simple mathematical terms. "Few scientists can fail to be impressed by the almost unreasonable simplicity and elegance of these laws," writes a professor of physics, Paul Davies, in the magazine *New Scientist*.

[16] A most intriguing fact about these laws, however, is that in them there are certain factors whose values must be

---

15. (a) What have scientists discovered in their study of the physical world? (b) What did a professor of physics say about the laws in nature?
16. (a) What are some fundamental constants in the laws of nature? (b) What would happen if the values of these constants were changed even slightly? (c) What did a professor of physics conclude about the universe and our existence?

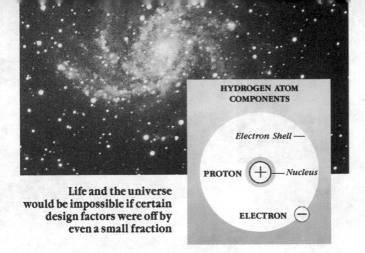

HYDROGEN ATOM COMPONENTS

Electron Shell —

PROTON $\left(+\right)$ —*Nucleus*

ELECTRON $\left(-\right)$

Life and the universe would be impossible if certain design factors were off by even a small fraction

fixed precisely for the universe, as we know it, to exist. Among these fundamental constants are the unit of electric charge on the proton, the masses of certain fundamental particles, and Newton's universal constant of gravitation, commonly denoted by the letter G. On this, Professor Davies continues: "Even minute variations in the values of some of them would drastically alter the appearance of the Universe. For example, Freeman Dyson has pointed out that if the force between nucleons (protons and neutrons) were only a few per cent stronger, the Universe would be devoid of hydrogen. Stars like the Sun, not to mention water, could not exist. Life, at least as we know it, would be impossible. Brandon Carter has shown that very much smaller changes in G would turn all stars into blue giants or red dwarfs, with equally dire consequences for life." Thus, Davies concludes: "In this case it is conceivable that there might be only one possible Universe. If that is so, it is a remarkable thought that *our own existence as conscious beings is an inescapable consequence of logic.*"—Italics ours.

The more we know
about the world around us,
the more evidence we have
of an intelligent Creator

¹⁷ What can we deduce from all of this? First of all, if the universe is governed by laws, then there must be an intelligent lawmaker who formulated or established the laws. Furthermore, since the laws governing the operation of the universe appear to be made in anticipation of life and conditions favorable to its sustenance, purpose is clearly involved. *Design* and *purpose*—these are not characteristics of blind chance; they are precisely what an intelligent Creator would manifest. And that is just what the Bible indicates when it declares: "What may be known about God

17. (a) What do the design and purpose in the universe clearly indicate? (b) How is this confirmed in the Bible?

is manifest among them, for God made it manifest to them. For his invisible qualities are clearly seen from the world's creation onward, because they are perceived by the things made, even his eternal power and Godship."—Romans 1: 19, 20; Isaiah 45:18; Jeremiah 10:12.

Abundant Evidence Around Us

[18] Of course, design and purpose are seen not only in the orderly workings of the universe but also in the way living creatures, simple and complex, carry on their daily activities, as well as in the way they interact with one another and with the environment. For example, almost every part of our human body—the brain, the eye, the ear, the hand—shows design so intricate that modern science cannot fully explain it. Then there are the animal and plant worlds. The annual migration of certain birds over thousands of miles of land and sea, the process of photosynthesis in plants, the development of one fertilized egg into a complex organism with millions of differentiated cells with specialized functions—just to give a few examples—are all outstanding evidence of intelligent design.*

[19] Some argue, however, that increased knowledge of science has provided explanations for many of these feats. True, science has explained, to a certain extent, many things that were once a mystery. But a child's discovery of how a

---

* For a detailed explanation of these proofs of God's existence, see the book *Life—How Did It Get Here? By Evolution or by Creation?* published by the Watchtower Bible and Tract Society of New York, Inc., 1985, pages 142-78.

---

18. (a) In what else can design and purpose be seen? (b) What familiar examples of intelligent design can you give?
19. (a) Does a scientific explanation of how some things work prove that there is no intelligent design or designer? (b) What can we learn by studying the world around us?

Evidence of the Bible's Authenticity

Unique Authorship: From its first book, Genesis, to its last, Revelation, the Bible is composed of 66 books written by some 40 writers of vastly different social, educational, and professional backgrounds. The writing was done over a period of 16 centuries, from 1513 B.C.E. to 98 C.E. Yet, the end result is a book harmonious and coherent, outlining the logical development of a prominent theme—the vindication of God and his purpose through the Messianic Kingdom.—See box, page 241.

Historical Accuracy: Events recorded in the Bible are in full harmony with proved historical facts. The book *A Lawyer Examines the Bible* remarks:

"While romances, legends and false testimony are careful to place the events related in some distant place and some indefinite time, . . . the Bible narratives give us the date and place of the things related with the utmost precision." (Ezekiel 1: 1-3) And *The New Bible Dictionary* states: "[The writer of Acts] sets his narrative in the framework of contemporary history; his pages are full of references to city magistrates, provincial governors, client kings, and the like, and these references time after time prove to be just right for the place and time in question."—Acts 4:5, 6; 18:12; 23:26.

Scientific Accuracy: Laws on quarantine and hygiene were

watch works does not prove that the watch was not designed and made by someone. Likewise, our understanding the marvelous ways in which many of the things in the physical world function does not prove that there is no intelligent designer behind them. On the contrary, the more we know about the world around us, the more evidence we have for the existence of an intelligent Creator, God. Thus, with an open mind, we can agree with the psalmist as he acknowledged: "How many your works are, O Jehovah! All

given to the Israelites in the book of Leviticus when the surrounding nations knew nothing about such practices. The cycle of rain and evaporation from the ocean, unknown in ancient times, is described at Ecclesiastes 1:7. That the earth is spherical and suspended in space, not confirmed by science until the 16th century, is stated at Isaiah 40:22 and Job 26:7. More than 2,200 years before William Harvey published his findings about the circulation of the blood, Proverbs 4:23 pointed out the role of the human heart. Thus, while the Bible is not a science textbook, where it touches on matters relating to science, it displays a depth of understanding far in advance of its time.

Unerring Prophecies: The destruction of ancient Tyre, the fall of Babylon, the rebuilding of Jerusalem, and the rise and fall of the kings of Medo-Persia and Greece were foretold in such detail that critics charged, in vain, that they were written after the fact. (Isaiah 13:17-19; 44:27–45:1; Ezekiel 26:3-7; Daniel 8:1-7, 20-22) Prophecies about Jesus that were made centuries before his birth were fulfilled in detail. (See box, page 245.) Jesus' own prophecies about the destruction of Jerusalem were accurately fulfilled. (Luke 19: 41-44; 21:20, 21) Prophecies about the last days given by Jesus and the apostle Paul are being fulfilled in our own time. (Matthew 24; Mark 13; Luke 21; 2 Timothy 3:1-5) Yet, the Bible attributes all the prophecies to one Source, Jehovah God.—2 Peter 1:20, 21.

of them in wisdom you have made. The earth is full of your productions."—Psalm 104:24.

The Bible—Can You Believe It?

[20] Belief in the existence of God, however, is not enough to move people to search for him. Today there are millions of people who have not totally rejected belief in God, but

---

20. What shows that belief in God is not enough to move one to search for him?

that has not moved them to search for God. American pollster George Gallup, Jr., observes that "you really don't find much difference between the churched and unchurched in terms of cheating, tax evasion, and pilferage, largely because there is a lot of social religion." He adds that "many are just putting a religion together that is comfortable for them and titillates them and is not necessarily challenging. Somebody called it religion à la carte. That's the central weakness of Christianity in this country [U.S.A.] today: There is not a sturdiness of belief."

[21] That "central weakness" is largely the result of lack of knowledge and faith in the Bible. But what basis is there for believing the Bible? First of all, it should be noted that down through the ages, probably no other book has been more unjustly criticized, abused, hated, and attacked than the Bible. Yet, it has survived all of that and turned out to be the most widely translated and circulated book on record. That in itself makes the Bible an outstanding book. But there is abundant proof, convincing evidence, that the Bible is a book inspired of God and worthy of our belief. —See box, pages 340-1.

[22] Even though many people have more or less assumed that the Bible is unscientific, contradictory, and out-of-date, the facts show otherwise. Its unique authorship, its historical and scientific accuracy, and its unerring prophecies all point to one inevitable conclusion: The Bible is the inspired Word of God. As the apostle Paul put it: "All Scripture is inspired of God and beneficial."—2 Timothy 3:16.

21, 22. (a) What makes the Bible an outstanding book? (b) What is the basic evidence of the Bible's authenticity? Explain.

Meeting the Challenge of Disbelief

²³ Having considered the evidence from the book of creation and the Bible, what can we conclude? Simply, that these books are as valid today as they have always been. When we are willing to look at the matter objectively rather than be swayed by preconceived ideas, we find that any objections can be overcome in a reasonable manner. The answers are there, if only we are willing to search for them. Jesus said, "Keep on seeking, and you will find."—Matthew 7:7; Acts 17:11.

²⁴ In the final analysis, most people who have given up in the search for God have not done so because they have carefully examined the evidence for themselves and found the Bible to be untrue. Rather, many of them have been turned away by Christendom's failure to present the true God of the Bible. As the French writer P. Valadier stated: "It was the Christian tradition that produced atheism as its fruit; it led to the murder of God in the consciences of men because it presented them with an unbelievable God." Be that as it may, we can take comfort in the words of the apostle Paul: "What, then, is the case? If some did not express faith, will their lack of faith perhaps make the faithfulness of God without effect? Never may that happen! But let God be found true, though every man be found a liar." (Romans 3:3, 4) Yes, there is every reason to continue the search for the true God. In the remaining chapters of this book, we will see how the search has been taken to a successful completion and what the future holds for mankind.

---

23. What can we conclude regarding the Bible when we look at the facts?
24. (a) Why have many given up in their search for God? (b) In what can we take comfort? (c) What will be considered in the remainder of this book?

CHAPTER 15

A Return to the True God

"I am giving you a new commandment, that you love one another; just as I have loved you, that you also love one another. By this all will know that you are my disciples, if you have love among yourselves."—John 13:34, 35.

WITH those words, Jesus established a criterion for those claiming to be his true followers. Christian love would have to transcend all racial, tribal, and national divisions. It would require that true Christians should be "no part of the world," just as Jesus was, and is, "no part of the world."—John 17:14, 16; Romans 12:17-21.

[2] How does the Christian show himself to be "no part of the world"? For example, how should he act with regard to the turbulent politics, revolutions, and wars of our times? The Christian apostle John wrote, in harmony with Jesus' words above: "Everyone who does not carry on righteousness does not originate with God, neither does he who does not love his brother. For this is the message which you have heard from the beginning, that we should have love for one another." And Jesus himself explained why his disciples did not fight to deliver him, saying: "My kingdom is no part of this world. If my kingdom were part of this world, my attendants would have fought . . . But, as it is, my kingdom is not from this source." Even with Jesus' life at stake, those attendants did not get involved in settling the controversy

1, 2. What should be the effects of love among true Christians?

according to the warring ways of the world.—1 John 3:10-12; John 18:36.

³ Over 700 years before Christ, Isaiah prophesied that people of all nations would gather to Jehovah's true worship and would learn war no more. He said: "And it must occur in the final part of the days that the mountain of the house of Jehovah will become firmly established above the top of the mountains,... and to it all the nations must stream. And many peoples will certainly go and say: 'Come, you people, and let us go up to the mountain of Jehovah, to the house of the God of Jacob; and he will instruct us about his ways, and we will walk in his paths.' For out of Zion law will go forth, and the word of Jehovah out of Jerusalem. And he will certainly render judgment among the nations and set matters straight respecting many peoples. And they will have to beat their swords into plowshares and their spears into pruning shears. Nation will not lift up sword against nation, neither will they learn war anymore."*—Isaiah 2:2-4.

⁴ Which of all the religions in the world has been out-standing in meeting these requirements? Who have refused to learn war in spite of prisons, concentration camps, and death sentences?

Christian Love and Neutrality

⁵ Jehovah's Witnesses are known worldwide for their individual conscientious stand of Christian neutrality. They have endured prisons, concentration camps, torture,

---

* These last two sentences are found on the "Isaiah Wall" in front of the UN buildings as well as on a statue in the UN gardens, and in effect, their fulfillment is one of the aims of the UN.

3, 4. (a) What did Isaiah prophesy regarding "the final part of the days"? (b) What questions require an answer?
5. What record of Christian neutrality have Jehovah's Witnesses established as individuals, and why?

UN peace statue states: "We shall beat our swords into plowshares"; the "Isaiah Wall" gives the Biblical text

deportations, and persecution throughout the 20th century because they have refused to sacrifice their love and unity as a worldwide congregation of Christians drawn to God. In Nazi Germany during the years 1933-45, about a thousand Witnesses died and thousands were imprisoned, on account of their refusal to cooperate with Hitler's war effort. Likewise, under Franco in formerly Fascist Spain, hundreds of young Witnesses went to prison and many spent an average of ten years each in military prisons rather than learn war. To this day in several countries, many young Witnesses of Jehovah languish in prisons because of their stand on Christian neutrality. However, Jehovah's Witnesses do not interfere with the governments in their military programs. The Witnesses' unwavering Christian neutrality in political matters has been one of the constants of their beliefs throughout all the conflicts and wars of the 20th century. It stamps them as true followers of Christ and separates them from Christendom's religions.—John 17:16; 2 Corinthians 10:3-5.

Mankind's Search for God

Christian Neutrality in Pagan Rome

In accordance with the principles of love and peace that Jesus taught, and based on their personal study of God's Word, early Christians would not participate in wars or in training for them. Jesus had said: "My kingdom is no part of this world. If my kingdom were part of this world, my attendants would have fought that I should not be delivered up to the Jews. But, as it is, my kingdom is not from this source."—John 18:36.

At as late a date as 295 C.E., Maximilianus of Theveste, son of a Roman army veteran, was conscripted for military service. When the proconsul asked him his name, he answered: "Now, why do you want to know my name? I have a conscientious objection to military service: I am a Christian. . . . I can't serve; I can't sin against my conscience." The proconsul warned him that he would lose his life if he did not obey. "I won't serve. You may behead me, but I won't serve the powers of This World; I *will* serve my God."—*An Historian's Approach to Religion,* by Arnold Toynbee.

In modern times, personal study of the Bible has led individual Witnesses of Jehovah worldwide to follow the dictates of conscience in taking a similar stand. In some countries many paid the supreme price, especially in Nazi Germany, where they were shot, hanged, and beheaded during World War II. But their worldwide unity, based on Christian love, has never been broken. No one has ever died in war at the hands of one of the Christian Witnesses of Jehovah. How different world history might have been if every professing Christian had also lived by Christ's rule of love!—Romans 13:8-10; 1 Peter 5:8, 9.

⁶ By holding to the Bible and to the example of Christ, Jehovah's Witnesses demonstrate they are practicing the worship of the true God, Jehovah. They recognize God's love

6, 7. What have Jehovah's Witnesses come to understand regarding Christianity?

as reflected in the life and sacrifice of Jesus. They understand that true Christian love results in an indivisible worldwide brotherhood—above political, racial, and national divisions. In other words, Christianity is more than international; it is *supranational,* transcending national boundaries, authority, or interests. It views the human race as one family with a common progenitor and with a common Creator, Jehovah God.—Acts 17:24-28; Colossians 3:9-11.

⁷ While nearly all other religions have been involved in wars—fratricidal and homicidal—Jehovah's Witnesses have shown that they take to heart the prophecy of Isaiah 2:4, quoted previously. 'But,' you might ask, 'where did Jehovah's Witnesses come from? How do they function?'

God's Long Line of Witnesses

⁸ Over 2,700 years ago, the prophet Isaiah also uttered the following invitation: "Search for Jehovah, you people, while he may be found. Call to him while he proves to be near. Let the wicked man leave his way, and the harmful man his thoughts; and let him return to Jehovah, who will have mercy upon him, and to our God, for he will forgive in a large way."—Isaiah 55:6, 7.

⁹ Centuries later, the Christian apostle Paul explained to those Greeks in Athens who were "given to the fear of the [mythological] deities": "[God] made out of one man every nation of men, to dwell upon the entire surface of the earth, and he decreed the appointed times and the set limits of the dwelling of men, for them to seek God, if they might grope for him and really find him, although, in fact, he is not far off from each one of us."—Acts 17:22-28.

¹⁰ Certainly God was not far off from his human creations

8, 9. What invitation has God extended to mankind?
10. How do we know that God was not far off from Adam and Eve and their children?

Adam and Eve. He spoke to them, communicating his commandments and wishes. Furthermore, God did not conceal himself from their sons Cain and Abel. He counseled hateful Cain when he showed envy regarding his brother's sacrifice to God. However, rather than change his form of worship, Cain showed jealous, religious intolerance and murdered his brother Abel.—Genesis 2:15-17; 3:8-24; 4:1-16.

¹¹ Abel, by his faithfulness to God even to death, became the first martyr.* He was also the first witness of Jehovah and the forerunner of a long line of integrity-keeping witnesses all down through history. Thus Paul could state: "By faith Abel offered God a sacrifice of greater worth than Cain, through which faith he had witness borne to him that he was righteous, God bearing witness respecting his gifts; and through it he, although he died, yet speaks."—Hebrews 11:4.

¹² In that same letter to the Hebrews, Paul lists a whole series of faithful men and women, such as Noah, Abraham, Sarah, and Moses, who, by their record of integrity, came to form a 'great cloud of witnesses [Greek, *mar·ty'ron*]' who have served as examples and encouragement for others wanting to know and serve the true God. They were men and women who had a relationship with Jehovah God. They had sought and found him.—Hebrews 11:1–12:1.

¹³ Outstanding among such witnesses was the one

---

* The Greek word *mar'tyr,* from which the English word "martyr" is derived ("one who bears witness by his death," *An Expository Dictionary of New Testament Words,* by W. E. Vine), actually means "witness" ("one who avers, or can aver, what he himself has seen or heard or knows by any other means," *A Greek-English Lexicon of the New Testament,* by J. H. Thayer).

---

11. (a) What does the word "martyr" mean? (b) How did Abel become the first martyr?
12. Who are further examples of Jehovah's faithful witnesses?
13. (a) Why is Jesus an outstanding manifestation of God's love? (b) In what special way is Jesus an example to his followers?

described in the book of Revelation, "Jesus Christ, 'the Faithful Witness.'" Jesus is yet another clear evidence of God's love, for as John wrote: "We ourselves have beheld and are bearing witness that the Father has sent forth his Son as Savior of the world. Whoever makes the confession that Jesus Christ is the Son of God, God remains in union with such one and he in union with God. And we ourselves have come to know and have believed the love that God has in our case." Born a Jew, Jesus was a true witness and died a martyr in faithfulness to his Father, Jehovah. Christ's authentic followers down through the ages would likewise be witnesses of him and of the true God, Jehovah.—Revelation 1:5; 3:14; 1 John 4:14-16; Isaiah 43:10-12; Matthew 28:19, 20; Acts 1:8.

[14] Isaiah's prophecy indicated that a return to the true God, Jehovah, would be a feature of "the final part of the days," or what other parts of the Bible term "the last days."* In view of the religious diversity and confusion that we have described in this book, the question arises: Who in these last days in which we live have really searched for the true God, to serve him "with spirit and truth"? To answer that question, we must first turn our attention to events of the 19th century. —Isaiah 2:2-4; 2 Timothy 3:1-5; John 4:23, 24.

A Young Man in Search of God

[15] In 1870 a zealous young man, Charles Taze Russell (1852-1916), began to ask many questions about Christen-

---

* For a detailed consideration of "the last days," see *You Can Live Forever in Paradise on Earth,* published by the Watchtower Bible and Tract Society of New York, Inc., 1982, chapter 18.

---

14. What question now requires an answer?
15. (a) Who was Charles Taze Russell? (b) What were some of his religious doubts?

dom's traditional teachings. As a youth, he worked in his father's haberdashery in the bustling industrial city of Allegheny (now part of Pittsburgh), Pennsylvania, U.S.A. His religious background was Presbyterian and Congregational. However, he was perturbed by such teachings as predestination and eternal torment in hellfire. What were his reasons for doubting these basic doctrines of some of Christendom's religions? He wrote: "A God that would use his power to create human beings whom he foreknew and predestinated should be eternally tormented, could be neither wise, just nor loving. His standard would be lower than that of many men."—Jeremiah 7:31; 19:5; 32:35; 1 John 4:8, 9.

Jehovah's Witnesses believe in Christ's ransom sacrifice for mankind's sins

¹⁶ While still in his late teens, Russell started a weekly Bible study group with other young men. They began to analyze the Bible's teachings on other subjects, such as immortality of the soul as well as Christ's ransom sacrifice and his second coming. In 1877, at the age of 25, Russell sold his share in his father's prospering business and began a full-time preaching career.

¹⁷ In 1878 Russell had a major disagreement with one of his collaborators, who had rejected the teaching that Christ's death could be an atonement for sinners. In his rebuttal Russell wrote: "Christ accomplished various good things for us in his death and resurrection. He was our substitute in death; he died the just *for* the unjust—*all* were unjust. Jesus Christ by the grace of God tasted death for *every man*. . . . He became the author of eternal salvation unto all them that obey him." He continued: "To redeem is to buy back. What did Christ buy back for all men? Life. We lost it by the disobedience of the first Adam. The second Adam [Christ] bought it back with his own life."—Mark 10:45; Romans 5: 7, 8; 1 John 2:2; 4:9, 10.

¹⁸ Always a staunch advocate of the ransom doctrine, Russell severed all ties with this former collaborator. In July 1879, Russell started to publish *Zion's Watch Tower and Herald of Christ's Presence,* known worldwide today as *The Watchtower—Announcing Jehovah's Kingdom.* In 1881 he, in association with other dedicated Christians, established a nonprofit Bible society. It was called Zion's Watch Tower Tract Society, known today as the Watch Tower Bible and

16, 17. (a) What teachings deeply interested Russell's Bible study group? (b) What major disagreement arose, and how did Russell answer?
18. (a) What followed the disagreement over the ransom? (b) What pattern did the Bible Students follow regarding donations?

Tract Society of Pennsylvania, the legal agency that acts in behalf of Jehovah's Witnesses. From the very beginning, Russell insisted that there would be no collections taken at congregation meetings nor contributions solicited through the Watch Tower publications. The people who joined Russell in deep Bible study became known simply as the Bible Students.

A Return to Bible Truth

[19] As a result of their Bible study, Russell and his associates came to reject Christendom's teachings of a mysterious "Most Holy Trinity," an inherently immortal human soul, and eternal torment in hellfire. They also rejected the need for a separate seminary-trained clergy class. They wanted to return to the humble origins of Christianity, with spiritually qualified elders to lead the congregations without thought of a salary or remuneration.—1 Timothy 3:1-7; Titus 1:5-9.

[20] In their investigation of God's Word, those Bible Students were keenly interested in the prophecies of the Christian Greek Scriptures related to "the end of the world" and to Christ's "coming." (Matthew 24:3, *KJ*) By turning to the Greek text, they discovered that Christ's "coming" was, in fact, a *"pa·rou·si'a,"* or *invisible presence.* Therefore, Christ had given his disciples information about the evidence of his invisible presence in the time of the end, not a future visible coming. Along with this study, those Bible students had a keen desire to understand the Bible's chronology in relation to Christ's presence. Without understanding all the details, Russell and his associates realized that 1914 would be a crucial date in human history.—Matthew 24:3-22; Luke 21:7-33, *Int.*

----

19. What teachings of Christendom did the Bible Students reject?
20. What did those Bible Students discover regarding Christ's *pa·rou·si'a* and 1914?

[21] Russell knew that a great preaching work had to be done. He was conscious of the words of Jesus recorded by Matthew: "And this good news of the kingdom will be preached in all the inhabited earth for a witness to all the nations; and then the end will come." (Matthew 24:14; Mark 13:10) There was a sense of urgency to the activity of those Bible Students prior to 1914. They believed that their preaching activity would culminate in that year, and therefore they felt they should expend every effort to help others to know "this good news of the kingdom." Eventually, C. T. Russell's Bible sermons were being published in thousands of newspapers around the world.

Tests and Changes

[22] In 1916, at the age of 64, Charles Taze Russell died suddenly in the course of a preaching tour across the United States. Now what would happen to the Bible Students? Would they fold up as if they were followers of a mere man? How would they face the tests of World War I (1914-18), in which slaughter the United States would soon be involved?

[23] The reaction of most of the Bible Students was typified by the words of W. E. Van Amburgh, an official of the Watch Tower Society: "This great worldwide work is not the work of one person. It is far too great for that. It is God's work and it changes not. God has used many servants in the past and He will doubtless use many in the future. Our consecration is not to a man, or to a man's work, but *to do the will of God,* as He shall reveal it unto us through His Word and providential leadings. God is still at the helm."—1 Corinthians 3:3-9.

[24] In January 1917, Joseph F. Rutherford, a lawyer and

---

21. What responsibility did Russell and his fellow believers feel?
22-24. (a) What was the reaction of most of the Bible Students when C. T. Russell died? (b) Who succeeded Russell as president of the Watch Tower Society?

keen student of the Bible, was elected as the second president of the Watch Tower Society. He had a dynamic personality and could not be intimidated. He knew that God's Kingdom had to be preached.—Mark 13:10.

Renewed Zeal and a New Name

²⁵ The Watch Tower Society organized conventions in the United States in 1919 and in 1922. After the persecution of World War I in the United States, it was almost like another Pentecost for the few thousand Bible Students at that time. (Acts 2:1-4) Instead of yielding to fear of man, they took up with even more vigor the Bible call to go out and preach to the nations. In 1919 the Watch Tower Society produced a companion magazine to the *Watch Tower* called *The Golden Age,* known worldwide today as *Awake!* This has served as a powerful instrument to awaken people to the significance of the times in which we live and to build confidence in the Creator's promise of a peaceful new world

²⁶ During the 1920's and 1930's, the Bible Students gave more and more emphasis to the early Christian method of preaching—from house to house. (Acts 20:20) Each believer had the responsibility to witness to as many people as possible regarding Christ's Kingdom rule. They came to see clearly from the Bible that the great issue before mankind was that of universal sovereignty and that this would be settled by Jehovah God's crushing Satan and all his ruinous works on earth. (Romans 16:20; Revelation 11:17, 18) In the context of this issue, it was appreciated that the salvation of man was secondary to the vindication of God as the rightful Sovereign. Therefore, there would have to be on earth

---

25. How did the Bible Students respond to the challenge in the years following the first world war?
26. (a) To what responsibility did the Bible Students give more and more emphasis? (b) What clearer understanding of the Bible did the Bible Students receive?

What Jehovah's Witnesses Believe

Question: What is a soul?

Answer: In the Bible the soul (Hebrew, *ne′phesh;* Greek, *psy-khe′*) is a person or an animal or the life that a person or an animal enjoys.

"And God went on to say: 'Let the earth put forth living souls according to their kinds, domestic animal and moving animal and wild beast of the earth according to its kind.' And Jehovah God proceeded to form the man out of dust from the ground and to blow into his nostrils the breath of life, and the man came to be a living soul."—Genesis 1:24; 2:7.

Animals and man ARE living souls. The soul is not something with a separate existence. It can and does die. "Look! All the souls —to me they belong. As the soul of the father so likewise the soul of the son—to me they belong. The soul that is sinning—it itself will die."—Ezekiel 18:4.

Question: Is God a Trinity?

Answer: Jehovah's Witnesses believe that Jehovah is the un-equaled Sovereign Lord of the universe. "Listen, O Israel: Jehovah our God is one Jehovah." (Deuteronomy 6:4) Christ Jesus as the Word was a spirit creation and came to earth in obedience to his Father's will. He is in subjection to Jehovah. "But when all things will have been subjected to him [Christ], then the Son himself will also subject himself to the One who subjected all things to him, that God may be all things to everyone."—1 Corinthians 15:28; see also Matthew 24:36; Mark 12:29; John 1:1-3, 14-18; Colossians 1:15-20.

Jehovah's Witnesses meet regularly in Kingdom Halls for Bible study

The holy spirit is God's active force, or energy in action, not a person.—Acts 2:1-4, 17, 18.

Question: Do Jehovah's Witnesses worship or venerate idols?

Answer: Jehovah's Witnesses do not practice any form of idolatry, whether it involves idols, persons, or organizations.

"We know that an idol is nothing in the world, and that there is no God but one. For even though there are those who are called 'gods,' whether in heaven or on earth, just as there are many 'gods' and many 'lords,' there is actually to us one God the Father, out of whom all things are, and we for him; and there is one Lord, Jesus Christ, through whom all things are, and we through him."—1 Corinthians 8:4-6; see also Psalm 135:15-18.

Question: Do Jehovah's Witnesses celebrate Mass or Communion?

Answer: Jehovah's Witnesses do not believe in transubstantiation, a Roman Catholic teaching. They do celebrate the Lord's Evening Meal on the date corresponding to the Jewish Nisan 14 (usually in March or April) as an annual memorial of Christ's death. At this meeting they pass around the congregation unleavened bread and red wine in symbol of Christ's sinless body and sacrificial blood. Only those with the hope of reigning with Christ in his heavenly Kingdom partake of the emblems.—Mark 14:22-26; Luke 22:29; 1 Corinthians 11: 23-26; Revelation 14:1-5.*

* For a further consideration of this subject, see *Reasoning From the Scriptures*, published by the Watchtower Bible and Tract Society of New York, Inc., 1985, pages 261-9.

Kingdom Halls: Ichihara City, Japan (previous page), and Boituva, Brazil

faithful witnesses willing to testify to God's purposes and supremacy. How was this need satisfied?—Job 1:6-12; John 8:44; 1 John 5:19, 20.

²⁷ In July 1931, the Bible Students held a convention in Columbus, Ohio, during which the thousands present adopted a resolution. In it they joyfully embraced "the name which the mouth of the Lord God has named," and they declared: "We desire to be known as and called by the name, to wit, 'Jehovah's witnesses.'" Ever since that date, Jehovah's Witnesses have become known worldwide not only for their distinctive beliefs but also for their zealous house-to-house and street ministry. (See pages 356-7.)—Isaiah 43:10-12; Matthew 28:19, 20; Acts 1:8.

²⁸ In 1935 the Witnesses came to a clearer understanding regarding the heavenly Kingdom class, who will reign with Christ, and their subjects on the earth. They already knew that the number of anointed Christians called to rule with Christ from the heavens would be only 144,000. So, what would be the hope for the rest of mankind? A government needs subjects to justify its existence. This heavenly government, the Kingdom, would also have millions of obedient subjects here on earth. These would be the "great crowd, which no man was able to number, out of all nations and tribes and peoples and tongues," who cry out: "Salvation we owe to our God [Jehovah], who is seated on the throne, and to the Lamb [Christ Jesus]."—Revelation 7:4, 9, 10; 14:1-3; Romans 8:16, 17.

²⁹ This understanding about the great crowd helped Jehovah's Witnesses to see that they had before them a tremen-

---

27. (a) What momentous event took place in 1931? (b) What are some of the Witnesses' distinctive beliefs?
28. In 1935 what clearer understanding did the Witnesses receive regarding Kingdom rulership?
29. What challenge did the Witnesses perceive and accept?

dous challenge—to find and teach all those millions who were searching for the true God and who would form the "great crowd." It would involve an international educational campaign. It would require trained speakers and ministers. Schools would be needed. All of this was envisioned by the next president of the Watch Tower Society.

Worldwide Search for Seekers of God

[30] In 1931 there were under 50,000 Witnesses in fewer than 50 lands. The events of the 1930's and 1940's did not make their preaching any easier. This period saw the rise of Fascism and Nazism and the outbreak of World War II. In 1942 J. F. Rutherford died. The Watch Tower Society would need vigorous leadership in order to give further impetus to the preaching of Jehovah's Witnesses.

[31] In 1942, at the age of 36, Nathan H. Knorr was chosen to be the third president of the Watch Tower Society. He was an energetic organizer with clear insight into the need to promote the preaching of the good news in all the world as fast as possible, even though the nations were still embroiled in World War II. As a result, he immediately put into effect a plan for a school to train missionaries, called the Watchtower Bible School of Gilead.* The first hundred students, all full-time ministers, were enrolled in January 1943. They studied the Bible and related ministerial subjects intensively for nearly six months before being sent out to their assignments, mainly in foreign countries. Up to 1990,

---

* Gilead, derived from *Gal·'edh'* in Hebrew, means "Witness Heap." See also *Insight on the Scriptures,* Volume 1, pages 882, 942. —Genesis 31:47-49.

---

30. What events of the 1930's and 1940's affected the Witnesses?
31. What began functioning in 1943 to expand the preaching of the good news?

89 classes have graduated, and thousands of ministers have gone out from Gilead to serve around the world.

[32] In 1943 there were only 126,329 Witnesses preaching in 54 countries. In spite of atrocious opposition from Nazism, Fascism, Communism, and Catholic Action as well as from the so-called democracies during World War II, by 1946 Jehovah's Witnesses had reached a peak of over 176,000 Kingdom preachers. Forty-four years later, there were nearly four million active in over 200 lands, islands, and territories. Without a doubt, their clear identification by name and action has served to make them known worldwide. But other factors have been involved that have greatly influenced their effectiveness.—Zechariah 4:6.

A Bible Education Organization

[33] Jehovah's Witnesses hold weekly Bible study meetings in their Kingdom Halls that serve over 60,000 congregations throughout the earth. These meetings are not based on ritual or on emotion but on the gaining of accurate knowledge of God, his Word, and his purposes. Therefore, Jehovah's Witnesses come together three times a week to increase their understanding of the Bible and to learn how to preach and teach its message to others.—Romans 12:1, 2; Philippians 1:9-11; Hebrews 10:24, 25.

[34] For example, a midweek meeting includes the Theocratic Ministry School, in which members of the congregation may be enrolled. This school, presided over by a qualified Christian elder, serves to train men, women, and children in the art of teaching and self-expression in accordance with Bible principles. The apostle Paul stated: "Let

---

32. What progress has been made by Jehovah's Witnesses since 1943?
33. Why do Jehovah's Witnesses have Kingdom Halls?
34. What is the purpose of the Theocratic Ministry School?

Some Countries Where Witnesses Preach

Country	Active Witnesses	Country	Active Witnesses
Argentina	79,000	Japan	138,000
Australia	51,000	Korea	57,000
Brazil	267,000	Lebanon	2,500
Britain	117,000	Mexico	277,000
Canada	98,000	Nigeria	137,000
Colombia	42,000	Philippines	102,000
El Salvador	18,000	Poland	91,000
Finland	17,000	Portugal	36,000
France	109,000	Puerto Rico	24,000
Germany, F. R.	129,000	South Africa	46,000
Greece	24,000	Spain	78,000
Hungary	10,000	U.S.A.	818,000
India	9,000	Venezuela	47,000
Italy	172,000	Zambia	72,000
		36 under ban	220,000

1989 World Figures   60,192 Congregations   3,787,000 Witnesses

your utterance be always with graciousness, seasoned with salt, so as to know how you ought to give an answer to each one." In their Christian meetings, the Witnesses also learn how to express the Kingdom message "with a mild temper and deep respect."—Colossians 4:6; 1 Peter 3:15.

[35] On a different day, the Witnesses also meet for a 45-minute Bible discourse followed by a one-hour congregation consideration (by means of questions and answers) of a

35. What are some other meetings the Witnesses hold, and what are their benefits?

Bible theme related to Christian teaching or conduct. Members of the congregation are free to participate. Every year the Witnesses also attend three larger meetings, assemblies and conventions of one to four days, where thousands usually gather to listen to Bible discourses. As a result of these and other free meetings, each Witness deepens his or her knowledge of God's promises for this earth and for mankind in addition to acquiring an excellent education in Christian morals. Each one is drawn closer to the true God, Jehovah, by following the teachings and example of Christ Jesus. —John 6:44, 65; 17:3; 1 Peter 1:15, 16.

How Are the Witnesses Organized?

[36] Logically, if Jehovah's Witnesses hold meetings and are organized to preach, they must have someone to take the lead. However, they do not have a paid clergy class nor do they have any charismatic leader on a pedestal. (Matthew 23:10) Jesus said: "You received free, give free." (Matthew 10:8; Acts 8:18-21) In each congregation, there are spiritually qualified elders and ministerial servants, many of whom have secular employment and care for a family, who voluntarily take the lead in teaching and directing the congregation. This is precisely the model set by first-century Christians.—Acts 20:17; Philippians 1:1; 1 Timothy 3:1-10, 12, 13.

[37] How are these elders and ministerial servants appointed? Their appointments are made under the supervision of a governing body of anointed elders from various lands whose function is parallel to that of the body of apostles and elders in Jerusalem who took the lead in the early Christian congre-

36. (a) Do the Witnesses have a paid clergy class? (b) Who, then, take the lead in the congregation?
37. How are elders and ministerial servants appointed?

gation. As we saw in Chapter 11, no one apostle had the primacy over the others. They came to their decisions as a body, and these were respected by the congregations scattered throughout the ancient Roman world.—Acts 15:4-6, 22, 23, 30, 31.

³⁸ The same arrangement functions for the Governing Body of Jehovah's Witnesses today. They hold weekly meetings at their world headquarters in Brooklyn, New York, and instructions are then sent from there to the Branch Committees around the world that superintend the ministerial activity in each country. By following the example of the earliest Christians, Jehovah's Witnesses have been able to cover vast portions of the earth with the preaching of the good news of

---

38. How does the Governing Body function?

Assembly Halls of Jehovah's Witnesses: Aerial view of hall in East Pennines, England

Assembly Hall, Fort Lauderdale, Florida, U.S.A., used for English, Spanish, and French programs

Watch Tower Society World Headquarters, Brooklyn, New York; (from top left) offices, factories, and residences (highlighted)

God's Kingdom. That work continues on a global scale. —Matthew 10:23; 1 Corinthians 15:58.

Flocking to the True God

[39] During the 20th century, Jehovah's Witnesses have prospered throughout the earth. This has even been true in lands where they have been under ban or proscription. These bans were imposed mainly by regimes that failed to understand the neutral position of Jehovah's Witnesses regarding the political and nationalistic allegiances of this world. (See box, page 347.) Yet, in such lands, tens of thousands of people have turned to God's Kingdom as the only true hope for peace and security for mankind. In most nations a tremendous witness has been given, and now there

---

39. (a) Why do the Witnesses take a neutral stand on political issues? (b) How have the Witnesses prospered under ban?

Mankind's Search for God

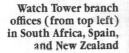

Watch Tower branch offices (from top left) in South Africa, Spain, and New Zealand

are millions of active Witnesses everywhere.—See chart, page 361.

⁴⁰ With their Christian love and their hope of "a new heaven and a new earth," Jehovah's Witnesses are looking to the near future for world-stirring events that must soon put an end to all injustice, corruption, and unrighteousness on this earth. For that reason they will continue to visit their neighbors in a sincere effort to bring honesthearted ones nearer to the true God, Jehovah.—Revelation 21:1-4; Mark 13:10; Romans 10:11-15.

⁴¹ Meanwhile, according to Bible prophecy, what does the future hold for mankind, for religion, and for this polluted earth? Our final chapter will answer that vital question. —Isaiah 65:17-25; 2 Peter 3:11-14.

40, 41. (a) What do Jehovah's Witnesses now await? (b) What question still must be answered?

CHAPTER 16

The True God and Your Future

"In this mysterious universe, there is one thing of which Man can feel certain. Man himself is certainly not the greatest spiritual presence in the Universe. . . . There is a presence in the Universe that is spiritually greater than Man himself. . . . Man's goal is to seek communion with the presence behind the phenomena, and to seek it with the aim of bringing his self into harmony with this absolute spiritual reality."—*An Historian's Approach to Religion,* by Arnold Toynbee.

D URING most of the last six thousand years, mankind has searched, with greater or lesser zeal, to find that "absolute spiritual reality." Each major religion has given that reality a different name. Depending on what your religion may be—Hindu, Muslim, Buddhist, Shinto, Confucian, Taoist, Jewish, Christian, or any other—you have a name for the "absolute spiritual reality." But the Bible gives this reality name, gender, and personality—Jehovah, the living God. That unique God said to Cyrus the Great of Persia: "I am Jehovah, and there is no one else. With the exception of me there is no God. . . . I myself have made the earth and have created even man upon it."—Isaiah 45: 5, 12, 18; Psalm 68:19, 20.

---

1. (Include introduction.) (a) What did historian Toynbee recognize about man and the universe? (b) How does the Bible identify the "absolute spiritual reality"?

² Jehovah is the true end of mankind's search for God. Jehovah has revealed himself as the God of prophecy who can tell the end from the beginning. He said through Isaiah the prophet: "Remember the first things of a long time ago, that I am the Divine One and there is no other God, nor anyone like me; the One telling from the beginning the finale, and from long ago the things that have not been done; the One saying, 'My own counsel will stand, and everything that is my delight I shall do'; . . . I have even spoken it; I shall also bring it in. I have formed it, I shall also do it."—Isaiah 46:9-11; 55:10, 11.

³ With such a reliable God of prophecy, we can know what is going to happen to the world system of divisive religions. We can also predict what will befall the powerful political organizations that seem to control the world's destiny. Even more, we can foretell what end awaits "the god of this system of things," Satan, who "has blinded the minds of the unbelievers" by a multitude of religions that have led mankind away from the true God, Jehovah. And why has Satan done this blinding work? In order "that the illumination of the glorious good news about the Christ, who is the image of God, might not shine through."
—2 Corinthians 4:3, 4; 1 John 5:19.

⁴ We can also know what lies beyond these foretold events. In what condition will the earth finally be found? Polluted? Ruined? Deforested? Or will there be a regeneration of the earth and the human race? As we shall see, the

---

2. If we want to have reliable information on the future, to whom should we turn, and why?
3. (a) What events can we foresee through Bible prophecy? (b) What has Satan done to the unbelievers, and why?
4. What questions about the earth and man's future need to be answered?

Bible answers all these questions. But first let us turn our attention to events of the immediate future.

"Babylon the Great" Identified

⁵ The Bible book of Revelation was revealed to the apostle John on the island of Patmos in the year 96 C.E. It paints vivid pictures of major events to take place in the time of the end, the time in which, according to Biblical evidence, mankind has been living since 1914.* Of those symbolic pictures that John saw in vision, one is of a gaudy, brash harlot, called "Babylon the Great, the mother of the harlots and of the disgusting things of the earth." In what condition was she? "I saw that the woman was drunk with the blood of the holy ones and with the blood of the witnesses of Jesus."—Revelation 17:5, 6.

⁶ Whom does this woman represent? We are not left to guess her identity. By a process of elimination, she can be unmasked. In that same vision, John hears an angel say: "Come, I will show you the judgment upon the great harlot who sits on many waters, with whom the kings of the earth committed fornication, whereas those who inhabit the earth were made drunk with the wine of her fornication." If the kings, or rulers, of the earth fornicate with her, then it means that the harlot cannot represent the ruling political elements of the world.—Revelation 17:1, 2, 18.

⁷ The same account tells us that "the traveling mer-

------

* For a detailed coverage of the last days, see *You Can Live Forever in Paradise on Earth,* published by the Watchtower Bible and Tract Society of New York, Inc., 1982, pages 148-54.

------

5. What did John see in vision?
6. Why does Babylon the Great not represent the ruling political elements of the world?
7. (a) Why does Babylon the Great not represent the commercial elements? (b) What does Babylon the Great represent?

chants of the earth became rich due to the power of her shameless luxury." Therefore Babylon the Great cannot represent the business, or "merchant," elements of the world. Yet, the inspired text says: "The waters that you saw, where the harlot is sitting, mean peoples and crowds and nations and tongues." What other principal element of this world system is left that fits the description of a symbolic harlot fornicating with the political rulers, trading with business interests, and sitting in glory over the peoples, crowds, nations, and tongues? It is false religion in all its different guises!—Revelation 17:15; 18:2, 3.

⁸ This identification of Babylon the Great is confirmed by an angel's condemnation of her for her "spiritistic practice [by which] all the nations were misled." (Revelation 18:23) All forms of spiritism are religious and demon inspired. (Deuteronomy 18:10-12) Thus, Babylon the Great must symbolize a religious entity. Biblical evidence shows that she is Satan's entire world empire of false religion, promoted by him in the minds of men in order to divert attention from the true God, Jehovah.—John 8:44-47; 2 Corinthians 11:13-15; Revelation 21:8; 22:15.

⁹ As we have seen throughout this book, there are common threads going right through the confused tapestry of the world's religions. Many religions have their roots in mythology. Nearly all are tied together by some form of belief in a supposed immortal human soul that survives death and goes to a hereafter or transmigrates to another creature. Many have the common denominator of belief in a dreadful place of torment and torture called hell. Others are connected by ancient pagan beliefs in triads, trinities, and mother goddesses. Therefore, it is only appropriate

---

8. What further facts confirm Babylon the Great's identification?
9. What common threads are found in many religions?

that they should all be grouped together under the one composite symbol of the harlot "Babylon the Great."—Revelation 17:5.

Time to Flee From False Religion

[10] What does the Bible foretell will be the final destiny of this globe-encircling harlot? In symbolic language, the book of Revelation describes her destruction at the hands of political elements. These are symbolized by "ten horns" that support the United Nations, "a scarlet-colored wild beast" that is the image of Satan's bloodstained political system.—Revelation 16:2; 17:3-16.*

[11] This destruction of Satan's world empire of false religion will be the result of God's adverse judgment of these religions. They will have been found guilty of spiritual fornication because of complicity with their oppressive political paramours and their support of them. False religion has stained its skirts with innocent blood as it has patriotically played along with the elite ruling class of each nation in its wars. Therefore, Jehovah puts it into the hearts of the political elements to perform his will against Babylon the Great and devastate her.—Revelation 17:16-18.

[12] With such a future staring world religions in the face, what should you do? The answer is in what John heard a voice out of heaven saying: "Get out of her, my people, if you do not want to share with her in her sins, and if you

---

* For a detailed consideration of these prophecies in Revelation, see the book *Revelation—Its Grand Climax At Hand!*, published by the Watchtower Bible and Tract Society of New York, Inc., 1988, chapters 33-37.

10. What end is prophesied for the religious harlot?
11. (a) Why is false religion condemned by God? (b) What will happen to Babylon the Great?
12. (a) What must you do now to be spared when Babylon is destroyed? (b) What teachings distinguish the true religion?

do not want to receive part of her plagues. For her sins have massed together clear up to heaven, and God has called her acts of injustice to mind." Therefore, now is the time to obey the angel's injunction to get out of Satan's empire of false religion and join in Jehovah's true worship. (See box, page 377.)—Revelation 17:17; 18:4, 5; compare Jeremiah 2:34; 51:12, 13.

Armageddon Near

[13] Revelation states that "in one day her plagues will come, death and mourning and famine, and she will be completely burned with fire." By all the Bible's prophetic indications, that "one day," or short time of swift execution, is now near. In fact, the destruction of Babylon the Great will usher in a period of "great tribulation" that culminates in "the war of the great day of God the Almighty . . . Har–Magedon." That war, or battle, of Armageddon will lead to defeat for Satan's political system and to his being abyssed. A righteous new world will dawn! —Revelation 16: 14-16; 18:7, 8; 21:1-4; Matthew 24:20-22.

[14] Already, another outstanding Bible prophecy is approaching fulfillment before our eyes. The apostle Paul prophesied and warned: "Now as for the times and the seasons, brothers, you need nothing to be written to you. For you yourselves know quite well that Jehovah's day is coming exactly as a thief in the night. Whenever it is that they are saying: 'Peace and security!' then sudden destruction is to be instantly upon them just as the pang of distress upon a pregnant woman; and they will by no means escape."—1 Thessalonians 5:1-3.

[15] It would appear that the nations that were formerly

---

13. What events must soon take place?
14, 15. What Bible prophecy is apparently approaching fulfillment?

belligerent and suspicious of one another are now moving cautiously toward a situation in which they will be able to declare world peace and security. Therefore, from still another angle, we know that the day of Jehovah's judgment upon false religion, the nations, and their ruler, Satan, is near.—Zephaniah 2:3; 3:8, 9; Revelation 20:1-3.

[16] Millions today are living their lives as if only material values were lasting and worth while. Yet, what this corrupt world offers is shallow and transient. That is why John's counsel is so pertinent: "Do not be loving either the world or the things in the world. If anyone loves the world, the love of the Father is not in him; because everything in the world—the desire of the flesh and the desire of the eyes and the showy display of one's means of life—does not originate with the Father, but originates with the world. Furthermore, the world is passing away and so is its desire, but he that does the will of God remains forever." Would you not prefer to remain forever?—1 John 2:15-17.

A Promised New World

[17] Since God is going to judge the world through Christ Jesus, what will follow? Long ago, in the Hebrew Scriptures, God prophesied that he would carry out his original purpose toward mankind on this earth, namely, to have an obedient human family enjoy perfect life on a paradise earth. Satan's attempted subversion of that purpose has not annulled God's promise. Thus, King David could write: "For evildoers themselves will be cut off, but those hoping in Jehovah are the ones that will possess the earth. And just a little while longer, and the wicked one will be no more . . . The righteous themselves will possess the earth, and

---

16. Why is John's counsel so pertinent today?
17. What does the future hold for those who seek the true God?

The earth has the potential to be a paradise—for this a permanent, righteous world government is needed, and it is promised by God

they will reside forever upon it."—Psalm 37:9-11, 29; John 5:21-30.

¹⁸ In what condition will the earth be thereafter? Totally polluted? Burned out? Deforested? Not at all! Jehovah originally intended that the earth should be a clean, balanced, paradise park. The potential for that exists in spite of man's abuses of the earth. But Jehovah has promised that he will "bring to ruin those ruining the earth." A situation approaching global ruin has existed only in the 20th century. All the more reason, then, to believe that soon Jehovah will take action to protect his property, his creation.—Revelation 11:18; Genesis 1:27, 28.

18-20. What changes will take place on this earth?

[19] This change is to take place shortly under God's arrangement of "a new heaven and a new earth." It will not mean a new sky and a new planet but, rather, a new spiritual rulership over a renewed earth inhabited by a society of regenerated humankind. In that new world, there will be no room for exploitation of fellow humans or of animals. There will be no violence or bloodshed. There will be no homelessness, no starvation, no oppression.—Revelation 21:1; 2 Peter 3:13.

[20] God's Word states: "'And they will certainly build houses and have occupancy; and they will certainly plant vineyards and eat their fruitage. They will not build and someone else have occupancy; they will not plant and

Before returning to heaven, Jesus commanded his disciples to preach and teach the good news in all the earth

someone else do the eating. For like the days of a tree will the days of my people be; and the work of their own hands my chosen ones will use to the full. . . . The wolf and the lamb themselves will feed as one, and the lion will eat straw just like the bull; and as for the serpent, his food will be dust. They will do no harm nor cause any ruin in all my holy mountain,' Jehovah has said."—Isaiah 65:17-25.

The Foundation of the New World

[21] 'How will all of this be possible?' you might ask. Because "God, who cannot lie, promised before times long lasting" that mankind would be restored and have everlasting life in perfection. And the basis of this hope is that which the apostle Peter expressed in his first letter to fellow anointed Christians: "Blessed be the God and Father of our Lord Jesus Christ, for according to his great mercy he gave us a new birth to a living hope *through the resurrection of Jesus Christ from the dead,* to an incorruptible and undefiled and unfading inheritance."—Titus 1:1, 2; 1 Peter 1:3, 4.

[22] The resurrection of Jesus Christ is fundamental to the hope of a righteous new world because he has been appointed by God to rule from the heavens over a cleansed earth. Paul also emphasized how vital Christ's resurrection is when he wrote: "However, now Christ has been raised up from the dead, the firstfruits of those who have fallen asleep in death. For since death is through a man, resurrection of the dead is also through a man. For just as in Adam all are dying, so also in the Christ all will be made alive."—1 Corinthians 15:20-22.

[23] Christ's sacrificial death as a corresponding ransom

21. Why is the new world a certainty?
22. What is fundamental to the new world hope, and why?
23. (a) Why is Christ's resurrection vital? (b) What command did the resurrected Jesus give to his followers?

and his resurrection laid the basis for the hope of "a new heaven," Kingdom rulership, and a transformed, regenerated human race, "a new earth" society. His resurrection also gave impetus to the preaching and teaching done by his faithful apostles. The account tells us: "However, the eleven disciples went into Galilee to the mountain where [the resurrected] Jesus had arranged for them, and when they saw him they did obeisance, but some doubted. And Jesus approached and spoke to them, saying: 'All authority has been given me in heaven and on the earth. Go therefore and make disciples of people of all the nations, baptizing them in the name of the Father and of the Son and of the holy spirit, teaching them to observe all the things I have commanded you. And, look! I am with you all the days until the conclusion of the system of things.'"—Matthew 19:28, 29; 28:16-20; 1 Timothy 2:6.

[24] The resurrection of Jesus also guarantees another blessing for mankind—the resurrection of the dead. Jesus' raising of Lazarus from the dead was a token of a more all-embracing resurrection in the future. (See pages 249-50.) Jesus had said: "Do not marvel at this, because the hour is coming in which all those in the memorial tombs will hear his voice and come out, those who did good things to a resurrection of life, those who practiced vile things to a resurrection of judgment."—John 5:28, 29; 11:39-44; Acts 17:30, 31.

[25] What joy to be able to welcome back our loved ones, each generation likely doing that successively! There in the new world, each person will then be able to decide under perfect conditions whether he or she will worship the true

---

24. What further blessing does Jesus' resurrection guarantee?
25. (a) What choice will be available to all in the new world? (b) What form of religion will prevail in the new world?

*H*ow to Identify the True Religion

1. The true religion worships the only true God, Jehovah. —Deuteronomy 6:4, 5; Psalm 146:5-10; Matthew 22:37, 38.

2. The true religion offers access to God by means of Christ Jesus. —John 17:3, 6-8; 1 Timothy 2:5, 6; 1 John 4:15.

3. The true religion teaches and practices unselfish love. —John 13:34, 35; 1 Corinthians 13: 1-8; 1 John 3:10-12.

4. The true religion remains untainted by worldly politics and conflicts. It is neutral in time of war. —John 18:36; James 1:27.

Witnesses preaching in
the Netherlands

5. The true religion lets God be true by accepting the Bible as God's Word. Romans 3:3, 4; 2 Timothy 3:16, 17; 1 Thessalonians 2:13.

6. The true religion does not condone war or personal violence. —Micah 4:2-4; Romans 12: 17-21; Colossians 3:12-14.

7. The true religion successfully unites people of every race, language, and tribe. It does not preach nationalism or hatred, but love. —Isaiah 2:2-4; Colossians 3:10, 11; Revelation 7: 9, 10.

8. The true religion advocates serving God, not for selfish gain or a salary, but out of love. It does not glorify men. It glorifies God. —1 Peter 5:1-4; 1 Corinthians 9:18; Matthew 23: 5-12.

9. The true religion proclaims the Kingdom of God as man's sure hope, not some political or social philosophy. —Mark 13:10; Acts 8:12; 28:23, 30, 31.

10. The true religion teaches the truth regarding God's purpose for man and the earth. It does not teach the religious lies of immortal soul and eternal torment in hell. It teaches that God is love. —Judges 16:30; Isaiah 45:12, 18; Matthew 5:5; 1 John 4:7-11; Revelation 20:13, 14.

God, Jehovah, or lose life as an opposer. Yes, in the new world, there will be only one religion, one form of worship. All praise will go to the loving Creator, and every obedient human will echo the words of the psalmist: "I will exalt you, O my God the King, and I will bless your name to time indefinite, even forever. . . . Jehovah is great and very much to be praised, and his greatness is unsearchable."—Psalm 145:1-3; Revelation 20:7-10.

[26] Now that you have made a comparison of the major religions of the world, we invite you to investigate further God's Word, the Bible, on which the beliefs of Jehovah's Witnesses are based. Prove for yourself that the true God can be found. Whether you are Hindu, Muslim, Buddhist, Shinto, Confucian, Taoist, Jewish, Christian, or of any other faith, now is the time to examine your relationship to the true and living God. Probably your religion was decided for you by your place of birth, over which you had no control. Surely, nothing is lost by examining what the Bible says about God. This could be your opportunity of a lifetime really to know the Sovereign Lord God's purpose for this earth and mankind upon it. Yes, your sincere search for the true God can be satisfied by studying the Bible with Jehovah's messengers, his Witnesses, who brought you this book.

[27] Not in vain did Jesus say: "Keep on asking, and it will be given you; keep on seeking, and you will find; keep on knocking, and it will be opened to you." You can be among those who have found the true God if you heed the prophet Isaiah's message: "Search for Jehovah, you people, while he

---

26. Why should you examine God's Word, the Bible?
27. (a) What invitation does Jesus extend to you? (b) In harmony with the theme of this book, what does Isaiah invite everyone to do?

**The resurrection of the dead will bring joy
to the human family earth wide**

may be found. Call to him while he proves to be near. Let the wicked man leave his way, and the harmful man his thoughts; and let him return to Jehovah, who will have mercy upon him, and to our God, for he will forgive in a large way."—Matthew 7:7; Isaiah 55:6, 7.

²⁸ If you are searching for the true God, feel free to contact Jehovah's Witnesses.* Without cost they will be happy to help you to know intimately the Father and his will while there is yet time.—Zephaniah 2:3.

---

* For list of addresses, see page 384.

---

28. Who can help you to find the true God?

Picture Credits _____ Pictures are listed below by page number and, where necessary, are numbered in parentheses in order of appearance on page (clockwise from top left). ■ Page 4, (1) Ladislav Janicek, Transglobe Agency, Hamburg; (3) Camerapix; (4) G. Deichmann, Transglobe Agency, Hamburg. ■ Page 21, (1) Photo: Andy Bernhaut Archive; (2) Sung Kyun Kwan University, Seoul, Korea. ■ Page 25, Reproduced from *Medicine and the Artist (Ars Medica)* by permission of the Philadelphia Museum of Art (Hermann Struck). ■ Page 27, By permission of the British Library. ■ Page 33, (1) Musée Guimet, Paris; (4) Ernst Haas, Transglobe Agency, Hamburg. ■ Page 36, By courtesy of the University of Hong Kong. ■ Page 39, Based on a map copyrighted by Pictorial Archive (Near Eastern History) Est. and Survey of Israel. ■ Page 47, The University Museum, University of Pennsylvania (neg. #22065). ■ Page 50, Courtesy of the Trustees of The British Museum. ■ Page 55, (1, 2) Courtesy of The British Museum. ■ Page 57, Musée du Louvre, Paris. ■ Page 61, (1, 3) Courtesy of English Heritage; (2) Courtesy of Colchester and Essex Museum. ■ Page 63, (1) Pictorial Archive (Near Eastern History) Est.; (2, 3) Courtesy of The British Museum; (4) Musée du Louvre, Paris. ■ Page 64,

Would you welcome more information or a free home Bible study?

Write Watch Tower at appropriate address below.

ALASKA 99507: 2552 East 48th Ave., Anchorage. **AUSTRALIA:** Box 280, Ingleburn, N.S.W. 2565. **BAHAMAS:** Box N-1247, Nassau, N.P. **BARBADOS:** Fontabelle Rd., Bridgetown. **BELIZE:** Box 257, Belize City. **CANADA L7G 4Y4:** Box 4100, Halton Hills (Georgetown), Ontario. **ENGLAND NW7 1RN:** The Ridgeway, London. **FIJI:** Box 23, Suva. **GERMANY:** Postfach 20, W-6251 Selters/Taunus 1. **GHANA:** Box 760, Accra. **GUAM 96913:** 143 Jehovah St., Barrigada. **GUYANA:** 50 Brickdam, Georgetown 16. **HAWAII 96819:** 2055 Kam IV Rd., Honolulu. **HONG KONG:** 4 Kent Road, Kowloon Tong. **INDIA:** Post Bag 10, Lonavla, Pune Dis., Mah. 410 401. **IRELAND:** 29A Jamestown Road, Finglas, Dublin 11. **JAMAICA:** Box 180, Kingston 10. **JAPAN:** 1271 Nakashinden, Ebina City, Kanagawa Pref., 243-04. **KENYA:** Box 47788, Nairobi. **LEEWARD ISLANDS:** Box 119, St. Johns, Antigua. **LIBERIA:** P.O. Box 10-0380, 1000 Monrovia 10. **MALAYSIA:** 28 Jalan Kampar, Off Jalan Landasan, 41300 Klang, Sel. **NEW ZEALAND:** P.O. Box 142, Manurewa. **NIGERIA:** P.M.B. 1090, Benin City, Bendel State. **PAKISTAN:** 197-A Ahmad Block, New Garden Town, Lahore 54600. **PANAMA:** Apartado 6-2671, Zona 6A, El Dorado. **PAPUA NEW GUINEA:** Box 636, Boroko, N.C.D. **PHILIPPINES, REPUBLIC OF:** P. O. Box 2044, 1099 Manila [186 Roosevelt Ave., San Francisco del Monte, 1105 Quezon City]. **SIERRA LEONE:** P. O. Box 136, Freetown. **SOUTH AFRICA:** Private Bag 2067, Krugersdorp, 1740. **SWITZERLAND:** Ulmenweg 45, P.O. Box 225, CH-3602 Thun. **TRINIDAD AND TOBAGO, REP. OF:** Lower Rapsey Street & Laxmi Lane, Curepe. **UNITED STATES OF AMERICA:** 25 Columbia Heights, Brooklyn, N.Y. 11201. **WESTERN SAMOA:** P. O. Box 673, Apia. **ZAMBIA, REP. OF:** Box 21598, Kitwe. **ZIMBABWE:** 35 Fife Avenue, Harare.